Looking for Transwonderland

Looking for Transwonderland

Travels in Nigeria

NOO SARO-WIWA

GRANTA

Granta Publications, 12 Addison Avenue, London W11 4QR

First published in Great Britain by Granta Books 2012

A CIP catalogue record for this book
is available from the British Library.

3 5 7 9 10 8 6 4 2

ISBN 978 1 84708 030 1

Typeset by M Rules
Printed and bound by CPI Group (UK) Ltd, Croydon, CR0 4YY

In loving memory of Sara Al-Bader (1976–2010),
my dear friend and inspiration.
You'll never be forgotten.

Contents

Prologue

The deep voices boomed loudly enough to jolt me from my mid-morning snooze. My eyes opened up to a predominantly male crowd of Nigerians clustered near the information desk in the centre of Gatwick Airport's departure lounge, gesticulating angrily.

'You are treating us like animals!' one man barked at the blond airport official, who absorbed the verbal barrage with a passive, slightly bemused smirk. 'Are we not human beings, like you?' A mechanical fault had delayed our flight to Lagos indefinitely, and some of the Nigerian passengers – always alive to the whiff of conspiracy – smelt something fishy. They gathered in a circle around a fellow passenger who had appointed himself as spokesman for their suspicions. Angling his head towards the mezzanine, this *oga* sermonised at maximum volume about Gatwick's strategy to humiliate us, and Virgin's stinginess in not providing a replacement aircraft.

Others waved their compensatory food vouchers at the information desk staff, shouting at point-blank range about Gatwick's deliberate withholding of information. They huffed and pontificated, everyone offering a theory on why the plane was grounded, gradually transforming the tranquillity of the departure lounge into the tumult of an angry football terrace.

But whoever decided to send in armed police to monitor the situation was taking an unnecessary precaution. I wanted to tell them not to panic: Nigerians like to shout at the tops of our voices, whether we're telling a joke, praying in church or rocking a baby to sleep. I also wanted to tell them that we're not crazy – decades of political corruption have made us deeply suspicious of authority – but there was no one to discuss this with, so I had no choice but to sit and watch our national image sink further in the eyes of the world.

When two Italian men walked past, one of them giggled to his friend, tapped his forehead and said the word '*mentale*' before swinging round to take one last derisive glance at the spectacle. The English travellers, more understated in their feelings, shrugged their shoulders at one another and smiled with their eyes, while two spiky-haired employees at a nearby electronics shop chatted amongst themselves and gestured their condemnation of the crowd's behaviour.

An hour later, the airport information officer switched on the tannoy to inform the Nigerian passengers of a 50 per cent discount on our next return flight.

'We apologise for the delay,' the woman began, but her words were drowned out by the disgruntled crowd, which was now clamouring for extra food vouchers. She tried again, this time half bellowing down the microphone. 'Can you *please* be quiet, I'm trying to *help* you!' The entire departure lounge flinched in surprise.

'We lack discipline,' an older Nigerian lady murmured to me as she shook her head in shame. She and I, along with the silent majority of Lagos-bound passengers, watched from one side, not sure whether to laugh or cry.

Being Nigerian can be the most embarrassing of burdens. We're constantly wincing at the sight of some of our compatriots, who have committed themselves to presenting us as a nation of ruffians. Their efforts are richly rewarded at airports, where the very nature of such venues ensures that our rowdy reputation enjoys an extensive, global reach. I've always dreaded airports for that reason. They are also places where, as a Nigerian raised in England, I'm forced to watch the European and African mindsets collide in a way that equally splits my loyalty and disdain towards both: I wanted to spank that Italian for misunderstanding our behaviour and revelling in his sense of superiority; I also cringed at the noisy Nigerian passengers for their paranoia, ill discipline and obliviousness to British cultural norms.

But the embarrassment and sense of cultural dislocation were nothing new. These airport fiascos began for me back in 1983, when a similar scenario saw my family and 300 irate Nigeria Airways passengers bussed like low-grade cattle to a faraway hotel in Brighton until our delayed flight was ready. I was too young to understand the circumstances surrounding the delay, yet I remember the shouting, chaos and feelings of national shame with visceral clarity. From that day onwards, travelling from England to Nigeria became a source of anxiety for me, a journey I repeated only under duress.

As a teenager, I virtually had to be escorted by the ankles onto a Nigeria Airways flight at the start of the summer holidays, not only because I wanted to avoid all that airport angst, but also because I didn't want to reach the ultimate destination. Having to spend those two months in my unglamorous, godforsaken motherland with its penchant for noise and disorder felt like a punishment. I wanted a *real* holiday, riding banana boats in Barbados or eating pizzas by the Spanish Steps, like my school friends. But my parents didn't have the money or the inclination for that sort of thing.

'We're going *home*,' they insisted with the firmness of people who knew better than to waste exotic travel on the very young. Come July each year, I would pack my bags and prepare to serve my annual sentence in a country where the only 'development' I witnessed was the advance of new wall cracks and cobwebs, and where 'growth' simply meant larger damp stains on the ceiling. Nothing ever seemed to change for the better politically or economically in 1980s Nigeria.

I would arrive at an airport that hadn't been refurbished in twenty years. The humid viscous air, pointlessly stirred by sleepy ceiling fans, would smother me like a pillow and gave a foretaste of the decrepitude and discomfort that lay ahead. Back then, when international flying was considered the height of sophistication, many of the child passengers were dressed as if attending a black-tie event. Parents tarted up their little girls in frilly party dresses; the boys sweated it out in bow ties and dinner jackets; while armed thieves (otherwise known as government soldiers) rummaged through everyone's luggage at customs. Only in Nigeria could you see machine guns, tuxedos, army fatigues and evening frocks together at an airport. The insane aesthetic summarised my country's vanities and bathos more clearly than anything else, and it depressed me. I wanted out.

I wanted to go back to the place I called home: leafy Surrey, a bountiful paradise of Twix bars and TV cartoons and leylandii trees, far removed from the heat and chaos of Nigeria. I was a toddler when the family moved here in 1978. It was during the oil boom, when the Nigerian currency, the naira (₦), enjoyed near-parity with the British pound, and a middle-class Nigerian life could easily be transferred to England. With plans to give us English schooling, my father settled the family in the UK while he continued to work in Nigeria as a property developer, writer and businessman. For months at a time, our family was headed by our homesick mother. She cooked plantain and grappled with central heating and the other novelties of English life. We watched *Sesame Street* and scribbled naughtily on the walls when not scanning the fridge for snacks.

But the luxuries of English life were not what my father had brought his children to England for. We were here to get an *education*, and he was terrified we'd all gone soft, which is why our summer returns to Nigeria sometimes included a brutal acculturation fortnight in our village. The experience was a 'character-building' one in which we were forced to live without electricity, running water and – the most egregious of deprivations – television. It was a tropical gulag. Nameless aunts and uncles would claw lovingly at our faces and mock us for not speaking our native language fluently. 'O bee kruawa?' they would deliberately ask us, cackling at our non-response. For dinner they fed us intensely savoury dishes such as ground rice and okra soup, eaten by the light of a kerosene lamp and washed down with body-temperature Coca-Cola. Then at bedtime we provided the meals for an invisible but frighteningly audible army of mosquitoes and sandflies. By dawn, our arms were covered in itchy lumps that looked like strawberries, only bigger, and our fingernails had turned black from the nocturnal scratching of sweaty flesh.

Having a cooling shower was the only incentive to get up and face the new day, yet even achieving that was a chore in itself. You had to fetch the water first. We didn't have to trek all the way to the river, but the jerrycans still needed to be dragged from my grandmother's house 20 metres away from ours, which wasn't easy when the water weighed more than we did.

Concerned that all this suffering wasn't sufficiently authentic, my father later instructed my grandmother to take us everywhere she went. We were to shadow her every move to get a true taste of village life. But she interpreted this diktat more literally than my father intended, and tried waking us for pre-dawn prayers. Faking sleep, my siblings and I cowered against the hot, sticky bed sheets as her lamplit silhouette banged against the window and called out our names: 'Zina! Noo! Tedum! Aakeh! Wake up!' I had never suffered such cold sweats in such a hot place.

By contrast, my parents believed that without their country they were nothing. My mother habitually referred to our Surrey residence as the 'house'. Nigeria was 'home', the place where her parents and siblings lived, where her wilted energies blossomed and her pale skin toasted to its original brown. At 'home', she sparkled in Nigerian traditional clothing, rather than battling the British winter air in woollens and thick overcoats. At 'home' she was no longer the alienated housewife but the Madam, handing over laundry and shopping lists to the servant while she caught up with old friends.

My father's patriotism was even more fervent. He carpeted our hallway in green to match the colour of the national flag, and once interrupted a crucial TV episode of *Little House on the Prairie* to teach me verses of the national anthem – a pointed stand against our Americanisation. Even our passports remained resolutely Nigerian, a snub to gold-dusted British citizenship.

One year, when I was twelve, my father tried to instil a love of country in his children by taking us on a road trip to see the beautiful side of Nigeria. From our home town of Port Harcourt in the south we travelled north into the interior. My sister, younger brother and I sat in the back of our Peugeot 504 while our father puffed on his pipe in the front passenger seat and hummed with us to Richard Clayderman, a deeply uncool classical pianist who performed covers of 1970s pop songs. Our driver, Sonny (who hated those tinkling Bee Gees and Barbra Streisand covers), drove in agonised silence through the central highlands.

Throughout the trip we were repeatedly reminded of how lucky we were to travel in this way. 'Very few Nigerians have seen as much of the country as you,' my father would say on the way to the Yankari National Park Game Reserve, to the new capital city Abuja, to Jos and to Kano. But I was too young to grasp this privilege. Fun as the trip was in parts, I still wasn't sold on the country.

The following year, on our last holiday in the motherland, my opinion was finally cemented. While my mother stayed behind in England, my siblings and I were unexpectedly introduced to two half-sisters we'd never met nor known about, the product of my father's polygamous 'other life' in Nigeria. He called it tradition. I took it as a betrayal. It clarified the fuzz of parental tension that my childhood antennae had picked up on but never quite understood: the arguments, the clothes my father regularly bought for our 'cousins'; my mother fuming tearfully about 'that woman'. Luckily, being children, we had the emotional elasticity to adjust to the situation. By holiday's end, the two halves of the family had warmed to each other, but Nigerian family life now seemed to me as treacherous and unpredictable as the military dictatorship that destabilised Nigeria during those years. Had someone told me then that the holiday of 1990 was to be our last in Nigeria, I would have performed cartwheels down the street. Little did I know that the reason for our future absence would be so grim.

Our ethnic group, the Ogoni, have relied on the Delta for fishing and farming for centuries, but ever since oil was discovered in 1956 and extracted primarily by Shell Oil, this fertile agricultural region has suffered oil spills and pollution from gas flares, which are used for eliminating waste gas, a by-product of oil extraction. A succession of corrupt governments squandered profits that should have developed the region economically, leaving the Ogoni and other Delta peoples in a bind: we are unable to develop industrially, yet we struggle to cultivate our polluted land and we're fishing gradually emptying rivers.

In the early 1990s, my father, Ken Saro-Wiwa, had started a campaign against government corruption and environmental degradation by Shell. His battle led to his being arrested and imprisoned several times. The optimist in me believed the situation would resolve itself relatively uneventfully, a perception he himself fuelled. Solitary confinement did not stop him occupying himself with the relative minutiae of our everyday lives, demanding by letter that I tell him about my exam results and the universities I had applied to. His focus on such matters made it easy for me to underestimate the implications of his arrest. But a phone call from my mother on the evening of 10 November 1995 destroyed that illusion.

My father's murder severed my personal links with Nigeria. Though safe to travel, I was not obliged by my mother to go there any more, nor did I have the desire. Nigeria was an unpiloted juggernaut of pain, and it became the repository for all my fears and disappointments; a place where nightmares did come true. As a word and as a brand, it connoted negativity. The green of the national flag reminded me not of life and vegetation but of murky quagmires. Nigeria sapped my self-esteem; it was the hostile epicentre of a life in which we languished at the margins in England, playing second fiddle in my father's life. I wanted nothing to do with the country. In the ten years after my father's death, I returned only twice for very brief visits, to attend his official funeral in 2000 and his actual burial in 2005.

In the meantime, I concentrated on other parts of the world, scratching the travel itch that had tormented me in my childhood: Europe, South America, North America, the Middle East, West and Southern Africa – I made up for my misspent youth. But as the world grew smaller and less mysterious, Nigeria began to take on a certain mystique, especially as I was no longer forced to spend time there. Writing travel guidebooks in other West African countries made me question my juvenile notions of West Africa as an unappealing destination. I saw alpine valleys in Guinea, Ghanaian Ashanti sculptures that were fit for the Queen's living room, and in Côte d'Ivoire I ate braised fish that makes me salivate even now. Didn't such things exist in Nigeria too? How could a country of 140 million people, stretching from the tropical rainforest of the Atlantic coast to the fringes of the Sahara, *not* be interesting? There had to be more besides the media reports of kidnappings and the scam e-mails from 'Sani Abacha's wife' wanting to split her millions with me. Suddenly I found myself in the unfamiliar position of wanting to visit Nigeria independently, exploring its breadth, and voyaging to this final frontier that has perhaps received fewer voluntary visitors than outer space.

There was another reason why I felt ready to return. Obligations of the First Born had forced my eldest brother, Ken Jr, to go back to Nigeria. Reluctantly, he had taken over the family business and reacquainted himself with Ogoniland, while I hunkered down in England. I pitied him. But he adapted and, over the years, nestled into Nigerian life without losing his sanity. Things weren't so bad, he assured me. In time, his successful plunge proved to be an inspiration, more powerful than any of our father's stern reminders that we should go back to the country at some point and use our good education to help people.

But re-engaging with Nigeria meant disassociating it from the painful memories lurking in my mind's dark matter. I needed to travel freely around the country, as part-returnee and part-tourist with the innocence of the outsider, untarnished by personal associations. Then, hopefully, I could learn to be less scared of it, perhaps even like it, and consider it a potential 'home'. My trip would begin in Lagos, the biggest city, in the south-west. I would travel to the arid Muslim north, then down to the central highland plateau and north-east, before moving on to the tropical lowlands in the south and south-east, including my home town of Port Harcourt. Along the way, I would revisit some of the places my father showed me; see them with adult eyes.

It was almost midnight when the passengers finally boarded the plane at Gatwick in haphazard style. They talked loudly and clogged the aisles, wedging bulky hand luggage in the overhead carriages.

'We will be landing in Lagos at 6.20 a.m. local time,' the captain announced. Those words triggered old spasms of apprehension. The plane took off and I ascended, moving away from England's lights and into the black canvas of night, trying not to write my unease all over it.

I

Centre of Excellence

Lagos

The plane broke through the clouds and swung low over a sea of palm trees that abruptly became endless tracts of metal rooftops. That vista still choked my heart with dread. I made my way through the airport's mustiness and out through the exit, where I was ambushed by the clammy aroma of gasoline, so familiar and potent.

When describing the character of our biggest city, Nigerians always like to tell a wry anecdote about the man who steps off a plane and is greeted with a sign that reads: THIS IS LAGOS. The message offers him nothing in the way of a cheerful welcome, nor can he even take it as a warning (since such a gesture would imply that the authorities actually care for his safety). What the sign provides is an indifferent announcement of his arrival in a city that he is visiting at his own risk; a blunt disclaimer. If he can't handle the squalid, uncompromising callousness then he should tuck his tail between his legs and go somewhere else, because This Is Lagos – *take it or leave it.*

Lagosians will be the first to tell you that their city is a disaster of urban non-planning characterised by overcrowding, aggressive driving, traffic 'go-slows', impatience, armed robberies and overflowing sewage, all of it existing alongside pockets of dubiously begotten wealth and splendour. If Lagos were a person, she would wear a Gucci jacket and a cheap hair weave, with a mobile phone in one hand, a second set in her back pocket, and the mother of all scowls on her face. She would usher you impatiently through her front door at an extortionate price before smacking you to the floor for taking too long about it. 'This,' she would growl while searching your pockets for more cash, 'is Lagos.'

With this image in mind I rolled into town on paranoid alert, my Visa card stuffed down my bra and some emergency banknotes folded inside my shoe. I'd been warned several times to expect danger at any given moment and to treat everyone as a potential predator. But in reality, the roadside signage that confronted me was a sedate WELCOME TO LAGOS, a message of warmth and optimism which, when I first saw it, seemed almost chilling in its apparent sarcasm, like some kind of sick joke. The same went for the car number plates, which were all printed with the motto 'Centre of Excellence', a ridiculous conceit if ever there was one.

As my taxi driver made his way towards Satellite Town, I struggled to discern which part of the city we were driving through. In Lagos, place names exist largely in people's minds. There were barely any signs or distinguishing landmarks, just a monotonous sequence of characterless, blocky, oil-boom 1970s architecture, fruit sellers, corrugated iron rooftops, iconic yellow buses, beggars and motorcycles that repeated itself mile after mind-boggling mile under a carpet of litter scattered in all directions, like confetti.

Every square metre of the city was scribbled with informal advertising. The buildings and lamp posts, even the sloping undersides of the numerous pedestrian bridges, beseeched me to buy this product or call that number. Presiding over everything were a variety of uniformed authoritarians: black-clad traffic wardens orchestrating the symphony of horns, and police swaggering about in black shirts and green army trousers. A man wearing a deep red outfit ushered the vehicles along with sticks, whacking cars as if they were donkeys, before casually swiping the back of a boy's leg as he crossed the road.

I watched one uniformed man try to prise open a car door, then sheepishly concede defeat when the driver hastily punched down the door lock. These officers were predators and guardians all at once, and everyone knew it.

Young gang members, known as Area Boys, also stake out their territory along the roads and collect cash from drivers. Employed by politicians to intimidate voters during the gubernatorial elections, they've been rewarded with uniforms and a licence to extort on the expressways. Now they clothe their scrawny bodies in green-and-white shirts and patrol the streets, waiting for bus conductors to lean out of the buses and slap money into their palms.

Once upon a time, Lagos was a placid cluster of islands and creeks separated from the Atlantic by lagoons, where local men caught fish, the cry of white ibis could be heard and snakes shimmied among the bushes. By the fifteenth century, the area had become a busy slave port. Under British colonial rule it became Nigeria's economic and political capital. The grasses, wild birds and trees were quickly devoured by urbanisation, its wild metastasis cluttering the cityscape so densely it seems to have made a crater that has sent the rest of the country tumbling into it. Nobody knows how many people live in Lagos; it could be 10 million, it could be 17 million – no one is counting the teams of street urchins and shanty dwellers, or the illegal buildings erected under the distracted eyes of previous governments.

Although peopled by every Nigerian ethnicity, Lagos is a city of the Yoruba, the dominant ethnic group in the south-west. Their melodic lingua franca sounded in the streets around me, as foreign to my ears as any language from Cameroon or Ghana. I had arrived in a country I had never lived in, and a city I'd visited only briefly twice before, among a thoroughly foreign-sounding people. It was the most alienating of homecomings. I might as well have arrived in the Congo.

*

My taxi driver turned off the Badagry Expressway and went through the narrow, sandy shop-lined streets of Satellite Town, a suburb several miles away from downtown Lagos. As our destination drew near, I shrank into my seat, wishing I could stay in the car forever, suspended in this comfortable no-man's-land between the airport and my aunt's house. I was scared of reaching her home and starting this trip in earnest, turning months of mental planning into live action.

We pulled up at the rusty gates of a small, one-storey house. It belonged to Aunty Janice, a friend of my mother's, with whom I was staying. The ravages of city life had made little impact on her beautiful face, still pixie-like and strong-jawed at sixty-three, with a steeliness, borne out of past disappointments, that could see her temperament quickly flip from gregariousness to anger. She smiled warmly and gave me a customarily loose hug before putting my bags in her daughter's small bedroom. My bed would be the living-room sofa. Aunty Janice paused to examine my face, which was momentarily infantilised under her warm gaze; we hadn't met since I was a small child. She had barely put on weight, nor lost any of her physical dexterity.

Her house, however, had aged far more quickly. We sat down and chatted in a living room with patchy linoleum floor tiles and unpainted walls. The wooden armchairs and a sofa had been spruced up with blue-and-white checked upholstery. In the absence of cupboard space, clutter lay exposed on the dining table and window sill; in the bathroom and kitchen, the taps and shower head were purely of ornamental value: there was no running water. And, while Aunty Janice's sons were saving up for a refurbishment and generator, she had to rely on NEPA, the feckless state electricity supplier.

Janice, embarrassed, had given me advance warning that her house was not what I was 'used to'. The house's decrepitude was certainly at odds with her glamorous past. Her husband had been a diplomat during the oil boom years of the 1970s and 1980s. His job took them to Geneva, Warsaw, Rome and London. While they were living in Lagos, Janice set up a fashion company selling clothes to Lagos's ascendant middle class. She showed me frail orange newspaper cuttings about her clothes shop, La Moda, which was inspired by her days in Italy. The newspaper's images were as faded as her ambitions, and accompanied by an unrecognisably coherent prose – a far cry from the ungrammatical gibberish that appears in some Nigerian newspapers today.

Janice and her husband were friends with my parents in Lagos during the Biafran civil war, when the glow of Nigerian independence had already faded. Pre-war Nigeria of those days was almost unrecognisable to me. My mother described a country filled with factories that produced cars, candles and other everyday necessities; hospitals were well-stocked with genuine medicines, and patients didn't have to supply their own bed linen. Bookshops and libraries abounded, and Latin was taught in schools; fewer cars roamed the roads, which the Public Works Department maintained with cohorts of labourers who constantly fixed the potholes and tamed the roadside grasses. It was when the military regimes began giving contracts to private contractors that the grasses began to encroach on the tarmac, and everything declined.

Aunty Janice's economic fortunes also declined after a dramatic divorce. She became homeless and stayed at women's hostels, friends' houses and various types of Church accommodation before eventually reclaiming her marital home in Satellite Town. Her old sewing machine now lay idle in the storage room, a relic, like everything else in the house, of an irretrievable era.

Staying with Aunty Janice was to be a lesson in dignified living under basic conditions. There were rules. We were banned from combing our hair outside the bedroom in case the odd strand floated into the kitchen water drum. There was also a fastidious system for washing up the dishes and soaking them, using minimal amounts of water and soap. As far as Janice was concerned, nobody could do it as well as she could.

'You're not doing it correctly,' her reedy voice called out from behind me. Shaking her head at my efforts, she dismissed me from the task and finished it herself, as with all the other household chores. Watching her sprightly frame moving around the house, I found it strange to see her, once an employer of domestic help, doing such tasks herself.

'I cannot live outside Lagos,' she said. 'It's crazy, but I like it. There's always lots of events. If I had the funds I would be attending weddings every Saturday!' Janice told me this at one in the morning while ironing the dress she would wear for a friend's daughter's marriage ceremony later that day. The lights, still switched on from the last blackout, had lit up the house in a blaze of restored power. Janice rushed out of bed to finish the task as it was the only time the electricity had worked that day. 'If I don't iron tonight I will not be able to attend,' she explaianed.

Such inconveniences always threw me into an existentialist sulk, but Aunty Janice said she would rather 'die' than leave Lagos. 'This is where I belong,' she smiled. 'It's not beautiful, but there are things that happen here that don't happen anywhere else. This is where the *action* is.'

Aunty Janice was also one of the most devout Christians I had ever met. At two o'clock that morning, I was roused by footsteps and vituperative hisses. Shadows floated across the candlelit walls. Janice was pacing around the living room and praying for the 'evil spirits' and 'witches' to 'Die, die, die, die, die, die, die, die, die, die, die, die, die, die, die, die!' A verbal machine-gun attack. I watched from the sofa, groggy but compelled, as she squeezed shut her eyes and pummelled the air with an imploring fist. Twenty minutes passed before she ended her trance and retired to her bedroom.

Praying at that time of day was a strategic decision, Janice told me the next morning; it was designed to coincide with witches' scheduled activities.

'They are everywhere,' she warned. 'On this street, everywhere. You won't know who they are . . . this is reality, not fiction.'

Janice's daughter Mabel was a quiet, laid-back twenty-seven-year-old journalist with supermodel proportions. Like many Nigerians her age, she was too poor to get an apartment of her own.

'I just need my own space,' she sighed, after Janice ordered her to sweep the floor mid-way through our conversation the next morning. Some days, before going to work, Mabel would spend a good half-hour collecting back-breakingly heavy buckets of water from the well behind the house, and pouring them into big water drums in the kitchen and bathrooms. Life inside the home seemed as arduous as life on the streets, a seamless transition from one exertion to the next.

Yet Mabel rode the tumult of Lagos life calmly and imperviously, returning home each night from the rough commute looking as stylish and fresh in her heels and skirt as she did in the morning. She worked for a local lifestyle publication, yet she felt no urgency to show up for work before midday most of the time.

'Isn't your boss annoyed if you come into work late?' I asked.

'No, they don't care,' she said with a shrug of her lips. 'There won't be a spare computer, anyway. I have to wait until the others have finished using it. And I'm never paid on time. They haven't given me a pay cheque in five months. They don't pay you, so why should you go to the office in the morning?'

'How do you survive?'

'You have to look for money from other people. I asked a friend to lend me ₦5,000 until I get paid.'

'No wonder people don't do their jobs properly!'

In my previous visits to Nigeria, I had noticed a contrast between the sluggishness and ineptitude of city workers and the work ethic of traditional village society. City workers operated with a lethargy

I often mistook for attitude or laziness. My father made the same mistake. He chided restaurant waiters for their sloppiness. He would glare at them, pipe snatched from his mouth, as they belatedly laid down the cutlery on his orders. People were underpaid, I knew, but the extent of their arrears was a revelation. I promised myself I wouldn't get annoyed if ever I received poor service. This culture of late payments – rarely pursued through the slow legal system – bred financial mistrust too. Landlords often demand hefty two-year deposits when renting out property.

'In England, they sometimes pay people *before* they do their job,' I told Mabel. 'My publishers gave me money for this trip in advance.'

'Are you *serious*?' Mabel gasped.

'Yeah.'

'You see ... that's why you work hard.'

Her job wasn't well paid. Journalism and its pitiful remuneration carries no prestige in Nigeria – telecoms and banking are where the money is. But Mabel loved her job too much ever to do anything else; she was too laid-back to adopt the entrepreneurial spirit.

I myself couldn't get into the travelling spirit. The following day, I sat anchored to that same sofa, scared of facing Lagos, which, in my anxiety, seemed ever more dangerous, a volatile booby trap. I flicked through my guidebook for an attraction that might lure me out of the house.

'My car is not working, so you will have to take the buses,' Aunty Janice said when I told her I'd be venturing out. Her words came as a shock. I hadn't given serious thought to how I would get around town, and somewhere in the evasive fog of my mind I had envisaged someone driving me around; I'd never experienced Nigeria in any other way. The idea of hiring a car, especially in a city like Lagos, didn't appeal. My sense of direction is laughably bad, and I lacked that curious mix of patience and bloody-mindedness required to negotiate Nigerian traffic successfully. Anyone wanting to drive through the city's ungoverned crowds has to aggressively assume right of way at all times. Politeness and compromise will get you nowhere. Lagos drivers, governed not by the Highway Code but the 'My Way' Code, will routinely pull out of T-junctions without checking for oncoming traffic for fear of showing weakness to other drivers.

I refused to participate in that.

Anyway, even if Aunty Janice had owned a functioning car, she had better things to do than act as my chauffeur. She assured me that using public transport would be no problem so long as I was 'educated' about it. For forty-five minutes, she gave me a stern tutorial on how to identify rogue buses, pay for tickets and avoid thieves, before dispatching me onto the street in a baptism of fire.

A bullet shower of traffic whizzed by me on the expressway. I timidly flagged down a minibus taxi, known as a *danfo*. Danfos are condemned hand-me-downs from Europe, so decrepit that one can watch the tarmac moving beneath one's feet. The conductor, dressed in torn shorts and floppy slippers, clung casually to the side as he solicited more passengers from the roadside, hurriedly waving people into the vehicle without thought for their age or physical condition.

'*Wale, wale!*' he barked at me. 'Enter, enter!' I could see that transport men work faster and more furiously because they receive their salaries up front – a rare example in Nigeria of time equalling money. I scrambled on board and searched for somewhere to sit. The danfo's original seats had been replaced with metallic benches designed to cram five people into rows originally meant for three. It was a tight squeeze in any nation, but the Nigerian love affair with starchy foods made it even tougher for me to squash myself in among so much 'rice booty'.

'Please, shift yourself,' one chubby man complained as he tried to find space next to another.

'But you are too fat, now,' his neighbour replied in typically frank fashion. As both of them fought to get comfortable, they frowned at each other's thighs and angrily advised one another on how to manage their body weight. Nothing in Lagos comes without a struggle or a squabble, which was fine with me. Despite my embarrassment at Gatwick, the Nigerian propensity for arguing is, in my opinion, one of the finest attributes of our nation. It tallies perfectly with my argumentative nature, which sees no reason to let go of an injustice just because the matter at hand is 'trivial'. If my opponent has a personality flaw, which lies behind the injustice that has caused the argument, the dispute needs to be pursued until he or she understands the error of their ways. I don't care how long it takes. Lagosians – perhaps feeling the same way as me, or perhaps exercising their frustrations in an oppressive society – will participate in any argument on a bus. Rarely do you hear someone interrupting the proceedings with a withering plea to 'stop arguing'. *Everybody* takes sides, backing their man or woman, as if they each had a personal stake in the affair. But Lagosian fury dissipates as quickly as it erupts, and beneath the uninhibited displays of anger were ready smiles and a fundamental decency. The person who slipped and bumped his head while entering a minibus was greeted with a chorus of 'Sorry, o,' from fellow passengers.

Outside the window I looked out for Mile Two, a busy transport hub on the mainland. There, I needed to switch vehicles in order to continue to Lagos Island, the downtown area. I didn't want to ask anyone if we'd reached Mile Two. Aunty Janice had advised me to keep my mouth shut to prevent any British vowels from tumbling out. Thieves were everywhere, she warned, and if they heard that I was from London, they would take advantage of me.

'Mile Two!' the conductor announced. I jumped out and walked through rain puddles, crowds and dozens of parked danfos. After asking in my best Nigerian accent which bus was bound for Lagos Island, I was shown to a largely empty vehicle and took a seat.

Waiting for the bus to fill up and reach (beyond) maximum capacity was the hardest part of the journey, thanks to the lack of physical space, steaming humidity and the hawkers constantly swarming around the vehicles. These vendors attracted attention by using their lips to make a very loud and high-pitched squeaking noise that tingled down my spine. One after another they came, squeaking in my ear and waving dried plantain chips, socks or handkerchiefs so close to my face I wanted to slap them away. Some merchants offered me exactly the same product as the person I had turned down just seconds previously. Untroubled by the market saturation, they kept coming and coming, imploring and squeaking and slowly nibbling at my sanity.

Just as I savoured a lull in the noise, an old blind beggar woman, guided on the shoulder by her young relative, sang Islamic prayers and shook a tambourine by my window. This noise, combined with the heat and cacophony of shouting and horn tooting, almost sent me over the edge. I realised that if I were to protect my sanity I quickly needed to find some inner peace, since it couldn't be found externally. Blocking my ears didn't work, and any 'relaxing' deep breaths only drew in the stench of petrol fumes and rotting refuse. Achieving mental relaxation required a kind of strength I didn't have, yet the Lagosians around me maintained a stoic serenity.

A man boarded the minibus and stooped in front of the passengers to bellow the gospel at us. 'Brothers and sisters, before we complete this journey, let us *pray*!' Everyone lowered their heads and closed their eyes while the preacher called for the 'blood of Christ to cover this bus and protect us from thieves'. By the time the bus pulled out of the motor park and rattled along the expressway, we had received a full service of hymn, prayers, and a sermon steaming with ideological fervour.

The preacher railed against abortion, painting a scenario of an aborted foetus confronting its mother in heaven on Judgement Day.

'*You killed me*,' he intoned in a mock-baby voice. '*Wetin I do?*' I learnt from this point onwards that there was no need to attend church in Nigeria – the church *always* found me no matter where I hid. And if people weren't trying to sell God, they were selling something else, from motivational pamphlets to medicines. The city's population density offers endless opportunities for everyone to pitch their wares, and danfos are especially handy for securing a captive audience. Once the preacher sat down, he was immediately replaced by another passenger promoting a medicine he wanted us to buy. More shouting. Like many Lagosians of all professions, he was selling merchandise on the side in order to make ends meet.

This man was offering sachets of Chinese mistletoe tea as a cure-all for every illness under the sun. Among other things, he claimed it could reduce hair loss, boost your immune system and improve the fertility of women who 'suffer *wahala* for womb'. For thirty minutes he itemised the tea's magic powers with a surprisingly seductive eloquence and sincerity. In fact, all Lagos salesmen have an earthy and genuine sales pitch that is devoid of all that shady infomercial patter I'm accustomed to. Perhaps it's easier for them to relax when they know they can rely on their audience's gullibility and patience. After the mistletoe tea man finished his pitch, I watched in amazement at how many passengers reached into their pockets to buy some.

I stared out of the window and tried to make sense of the cityscape. A torrent of humanity poured out of buses and streamed along the streets and bridges as if heading towards a big event. To the novice eye, Lagos looks a chaotic jumble, but I could see that there was method in the madness, a tapestry of interweaving lives and agendas criss-crossing each other a million times over.

People cram themselves into any conceivable space. The spaces beneath the flyovers are used as car washes, bus stations and ad hoc mosques. I saw a pig farm by the expressway, and men getting shaves and haircuts on the grass of a busy roundabout; the Ita Toyin Food Canteen stood proudly on the edge of a vast rubbish dump near the National Theatre. Women sold oranges next to ditches filled with evil-looking sewage sludge so black and shiny it was almost beautiful. Hawkers were selling an eccentric jumble of items, convinced that they would eventually find a buyer who would want that random squash racket or set of weighing scales. A man even roamed through the rush-hour traffic carrying two large, framed oil paintings of waterfalls. It was hard to imagine anyone buying them spontaneously and wedging them inside their vehicle. But the vendor had no such doubts, and as he strode confidently from car to car, his die-hard salesmanship appeared to be driven by something greater than financial desperation, as if he genuinely *believed* in his product.

Belief, especially self-belief, seems a vital ingredient in helping people get through life in Lagos. There's no room for equivocation or weakness. People have to compete for what they want in an environment that punishes the unambitious, the sick and the incapacitated. Street vendors need sharp eyesight in order to catch the lingering stare of a potential customer. And they need fast legs to respond to that interest and sprint alongside the moving traffic to exchange their merchandise for cash. While legless beggars lean against the central reservations and moan for charity that rarely swings their way, their more proactive counterparts arrogantly weave through the traffic on makeshift skateboards and demand money far more successfully. The beggars' buff biceps and chests were a reminder that in this twenty-first-century urban jungle, the laws of natural selection still apply.

Hustling is the lifeblood of Nigeria's economy since our corrupt politicians have not diversified from the crude oil that has served their bank accounts so well. Around 60 per cent of people in urban areas earn unofficial wages in the informal economy as petty traders, construction workers, food sellers. Life for these Nigerians is an incalculable struggle. The arithmetic of their survival was totally lost on me: $2 (around ₦300) is the most they might earn in one day, with 90 per cent of the country somehow surviving on less than this. Only half the population meets the official breadline of 50 cents, says the UN. Water for bathing and washing clothes is a luxury these people must save up for. Their homes are desperate erections of corrugated iron, tarpaulin and slabs of old wood; some sleep outdoors.

At a glance, the insouciant muscularity of the beggars' bodies masks the ravages of regularly skipped meals, not to mention tooth decay, depression, dulled IQs and parasitic infections. Often illiterate, these people are deaf to the city's posters and billboards that speak endlessly of God's love for them. One in five of the barefoot toddlers defecating on the roadsides won't live long enough to start primary school. Their births and deaths are not registered in any formal sense. They enter and exit the world unnoticed by government, with few photographs to commemorate their brief existence. Forced to live like animals yet cursed with the fears of human consciousness, the plight of these Nigerians made me question not just the purpose of life, but the very point of it. Compared to these people, Aunty Janice belonged to a privileged stratum.

Naturally, corruption is the main cause. Politicians steal $140 billion a year from Africa – a quarter of the continent's GDP – mainly by controlling trade licences and skimming funds from government contracts. No facet of the economy goes unaffected: every road, school, oil drum, hospital or vaccine shipment is milked for cash. It diminishes the quality and quantity of everything in the country, including our self-esteem. For it doesn't matter what I might achieve in life, these street scenes represent me; in England, cheerful telephone queries about the provenance of my name are occasionally met with silence when I tell them I'm Nigerian. The world judges me according to this mess, and looking at it made me feel rather worthless.

*

The danfo finally arrived at the CMS bus stop on Lagos Island, a major transport hub, and I emerged from the vehicle, sweating and tottering like a newborn giraffe. Looming ahead of me was the rangy former headquarters of the state electricity company, NEPA, its neon sign appropriately non-functioning. Further away, the upper floors of a skyscraper had partially collapsed, a vision of post-apocalyptic neglect. Lagos Island was once the commercial centre of the city. But when Abuja became the country's new capital, the government neglected Lagos Island's infrastructure, and big companies abandoned it in favour of neighbouring Victoria Island and Ikoyi. But the Island still looks the part, with its corporate architecture and concreted canyons that create the urban echoey acoustics I love so much. In between the crumbling skyscrapers stands the occasional Brazilian building. They were built by freed slaves who had returned to Nigeria from Brazil in the mid-nineteenth century after slavery was abolished. By the 1880s, almost a tenth of Lagos's population was Brazilian. Some of them were successful merchants in Brazil, who continued their transatlantic trade when they returned to Nigeria. Others were trained carpenters, masons and bricklayers, who used their skills to replicate the baroque styles of eighteenth-century Brazilian houses: Portuguese-style pointed arched windows, wrought-iron balustrades, ornate ceiling cornicing and colourful facades. The buildings cling wearily to their beauty. Preservation is a distant priority for everyone – even the 1970s office blocks now dwarfing the Brazilian houses are subject to the same neglect, withering in the aftermath of the oil boom that funded their construction.

I walked past the former State House, once a residence of colonial governors. On its front, the statues of several white horses reared majestically towards the sky as if fleeing the hordes of yellow buses and fruit stalls below. Traders have taken over the island's streets with their piles of stereos, bananas, film DVDs, torches, body lotion, batteries, sunglasses and shoes, turning Lagos's defined street grid into a contiguous mass of confusion. Nigerians love to transform every place into a giant market, no matter how grand the location. We'll grab any opportunity to sell, discarding all sense of pomp and ceremony. If Nigeria conducted a space exploration programme, you *know* that women would be offering bananas to the astronauts as they climbed aboard the shuttle. Perhaps knowing this, the authorities fenced off the small grassy Tinubu Square where a bronze statue of a man in ragged clothing reads a book above the inscribed words: *Knowledge is power.* Without the protective fencing, the statue would undoubtedly be smothered by a throng of illiterate hawkers.

This part of Lagos felt feral and impenetrable. But I was here as a tourist, and I wanted to make a 'destination' out of this city. The National Museum down by the racecourse was an obvious and easy place to start, a buoy to cling to in this wild sea. I entered the museum's gate. Its large grounds were probably the only place in Lagos Island where I could walk freely, away from the maddening crowds. After I paid for my ticket at reception, the museum guide, a thin man with pointy sideburns and carefully plucked eyebrows, welcomed me with an unsmiling hello. He pointed at a map of Nigeria outside the entrance to the exhibit room. 'Nigeria is made up of three main tribes,' he began automatically.

'I know . . . I'm Nigerian,' I informed him, piqued at being mistaken for a foreigner in my own country, especially when speaking in my best Nigerian accent. The museum guide was thrown by my declaration. His speech had been well rehearsed for the foreigners and schoolchildren who make up the majority of visitors to the museum, but I sensed he wasn't sure how to tweak his spiel for the likes of me. And so he carried on regardless, and I listened regardless, both of us enacting this charade for the benefit of nobody.

We walked into the quiet, dimly lit exhibition room. A female employee sat slumped asleep on a chair in the corner. She surfaced briefly to look at me before nodding off again. I felt a strange obligation to tread lightly and not disturb her. There were no other visitors in the room. Around me were glass cabinets containing artefacts and clothing belonging to various ethnic groups: bronze sculptures from the old Benin empire; chain mail from the Islamic north, and a camel saddle made from leather, wood, brass and iron. The museum provided no other information. Each artefact was simply labelled 'camel saddle' or 'Yoruba drum' without any clue about its age, rarity, provenance or cultural significance. The museum guide had no extra information either, but he insisted on giving me a guided tour anyway.

Just as he showed me some divination symbols, the power cut out and threw the entire museum into semi-darkness. 'I'm coming,' he said to me, as he rushed out to switch on the power generator. I stood in the shadows and waited patiently. Eventually, I decided to view the rest of exhibition by myself. I squinted at some bows and arrows, Yoruba bracelets intricately carved from ivory, and the silhouettes of the splendidly clothed waxwork figures of a northern emir and a Calabar chief, towering scarily in the twilight gloom.

When the lights finally came back on, the museum guide re-emerged with a bearded German tourist who had just arrived at the museum. The sight of the European visitor woke the dozing female staffer like a splash of cold water; she immediately stood up to lavish him with attention, both she and her colleague hovering around the man as if money might ooze from his pores at any moment. All interest in me disappeared. I felt irked. Why focus all their attention on this German when they'd be better off getting a juicy tip from him and me both?

Across the courtyard, I stepped inside a room housing exquisite Benin empire elephant tusks carved with low-relief hieroglyphs. The female staffer followed me inside (museum rules) and resumed her snoozing in another corner chair. I left her there and went through to the gallery next door, which was filled with contemporary paintings, including Japanese manga-style drawings. My favourite was an oil on canvas depicting a woman sitting on the back

of a motorcycle taxi. A double victim of fashion and Nigeria's transport system, her low-cut hipster jeans rudely revealed the crack of
her backside. In a spirit of playfulness or sternness – I couldn't tell
which – the painting was titled *Watch Your Back*. The Nigeria I
knew as a child was never this interesting or humanised, never filled
with artwork. I was enjoying being a tourist, even if I hadn't been
happy with the museum guide for presuming I was one.

I moved on to another annex of the museum, which displayed
the car in which President Murtala Mohammed was assassinated in
1976. Mohammed was an army general who took power in a coup
in 1975 and presided over a fractious military regime, another
episode of the violence that had undermined Nigeria ever since it
gained independence. The sight of the car punctured my mood
and plunged me back into the mire of Nigerian history and
politics.

Until 1960, Nigeria was ruled by the British. They introduced
Western education to the south, and also developed it economically,
exploiting its ports and oil, but they preserved the north's pre-colonial emirate system. The north was divided into several mini-states,
each centred around a paramount ruler or emir. This structure made
it easy for the British to exercise colonial rule without having to
spend money on employing colonial administrators. They interfered
little with the emirate system, its sharia law or its traditional Islamic
education. Consequently, the north fell behind the south in terms
of modern education and economic development.

Because they outnumbered the rest of the country according to
the census, northerners were allocated more seats in the Federal
Legislature after Nigeria gained independence in 1960. The three
main parliamentary parties reflected the dominant ethnic make-up
of the country: Muslim Hausas in the north, the Igbos in the south-
east and the Yorubas in the south-west. Abubakar Tafawa Balewa,
a quiet northerner, was elected the country's first prime minister.

At the time, my mother was a ten-year-old living in our

Ogoniland village, where traditional life continued despite the discovery of oil in 1957. She fetched water from the stream and wore new uniforms on Empire Day and prayed at the small church. My father, in his late teens, was a student in the city of Ibadan, the first member of his family to attend university.

By the time Nigeria became a republic in 1963, the tensions caused by ethnic and economic inequalities were already surfacing. The less educated northerners feared being dominated in a new, westernised political system. In the central region, the Tiv people held violent protests over minority rights, and factional fighting broke out in the Yoruba West, leading to the imprisonment of the country's main opposition leader on spurious treason charges. By this stage, government corruption had already taken root.

General elections were held in 1965 but were sullied by boycotts and alleged fraud. Riots broke out. The following year, a group of mainly Igbo army officers overthrew the government and assassinated Balewa, the prime minister.

The replacement military government couldn't govern effectively or produce a new constitution that satisfied all Nigerians (we're still dissatisfied to this day). When the military tried to change the country's federal structure, a second coup was staged, led by a Ngas, General Yakubu Gowon. Igbos living in the north were massacred in attacks intended to avenge the killing of Balewa. The killings fuelled a growing desire among the Igbo people to separate from Nigeria and create a nation state of their own, and in 1967, they declared the eastern region an independent state called Biafra, which included the oil-rich Niger Delta – Nigeria's main source of wealth. A brutal civil war ensued.

At the start of the war, my parents were living in Nsukka, an Igbo town. The government had asked Nigerians to return to their broader regional homelands, so my father transferred his PhD from Ibadan University to Nsukka University in the south-east of the country. It was here that he met my mother, who was living with

her sister and brother-in-law in Nsukka town. Without TV and
objective newspapers, my mother, then seventeen, had little sense
of danger. But the placidity of normal life was gradually eroded by
rumours that 'Northerners' were out to kill everyone. My mother
only started to believe the rumours and fear the worst when she
heard the morale-boosting Igbo war songs on the radio, and the wail
of air raids accompanied by anti-aircraft gunfire. Nsukka's non-Igbo
residents began returning to their home towns in convoys of
lorries. My parents returned to Ogoniland and stayed with my
father's parents.

There, they realised that the war 'facts' they'd been hearing were
merely propaganda. Ogonis speculated heatedly on our place within
the struggle. The whole of south-eastern Nigeria − Ogoniland
included − had been bundled under the Biafra rubric without any
consultation. There was discomfort about that. The Igbo people
already dominated us economically and politically in the south-east.
If Biafra became a fully fledged country, would our language and
culture be eradicated?

My parents decided to flee Biafra and live in the federal part of
Nigeria. Early one morning, disguised as simple fishermen, they
boarded a canoe. Bombs and gunfire exploded from the war front
ahead. The sound of it compelled others to retreat, but my parents
were determined to leave and forged ahead counter-intuitively,
rowing through the mangrove creeks to Bonny, a federally controlled port. From there, they took a ship to Lagos, where they
started a temporary new life. My brother Ken Jr was born in the city
the following year, in 1968.

Two years and one million civilian deaths later, Biafra finally sur-
rendered. My father had returned to the war front to serve as an
administrator in Bonny, and when the war ended, he took a job as
the Commissioner for Works in our home town of Port Harcourt.
During the next six years, my second brother Gian was born, followed by Zina and me.

Throughout the 1970s, a reunited Nigeria rebuilt itself with the help of dizzy oil prices. Soon after the war, our president, General Gowon, declared that Nigeria would return to civilian rule in four years. Accused of dragging his feet, he was overthrown in a coup led by General Murtala Mohammed in 1975. Many of this new leader's policies went down well with the public. Mohammed sacked any army and government staff associated with Gowon, and he reverted to the former national census. It had recorded a lower Hausa population, with implications for the make-up of the Federal Assembly. But his Supreme Military Council boosted federal powers at the expense of state-level government, and it took over the media. As Mohammed made his way to the army barracks in Lagos a year later, his limousine was ambushed and he was killed by a round of bullets.

This black limousine now stood in the museum. Every bullet hole and every window crack painted a brutally exact image of his death. Despite the damage, the car looked in finer condition than many of the vehicles plying Lagos's streets today. The public display of Mohammed's violated car contrasted acutely for me with the secrecy that had surrounded my father's murder. He was hanged along with eight of his colleagues at a prison in Port Harcourt. Our families were informed after the executions, which had been carried out furtively and without warning, behind closed doors, the victims' remains kept from us for more than a decade. Not being an eye-witness to it all was a blessing, but it has left me with a displaced curiosity about the details of other murders.

The car was the only museum artefact that roused the imagination or gave any insight into Nigeria's modern history. The museum's current curator showed no such imagination when creating the photography exhibit near Mohammed's car. Black-and-white photos of every post-independence leader hung on the walls, but the museum offered no written information about how these men got into power, or what good (if any) they did for the country. The guide materialised from behind to inform me that I was looking at photographs of our former leaders.

'This is Nigeria's first prime minister, Tafawa Balewa, and this is—' He paused suddenly. 'Are you married?'

'No,' I replied, stunned by the timing and irrelevance of the question. We exchanged lingering, unsmiling stares before he turned to the photos and resumed his run-through of the faces on the wall.

There was a photo of Olusegun Obasanjo, a lieutenant general who succeeded Murtala Mohammed as president, with his characteristically small eyes and flared nostrils. In 1979 he became the first military man to restore Nigeria to civilian rule through elections that were widely known to have been rigged. Next to Obasanjo's picture was the photo of his successor, Shehu Shagari. His forehead bulged over a round face and gently protuberant eyes. Shagari, a northerner, presided over four years of highly corrupt rule and economic mismanagement. The national debt soared and so did unemployment, while the economy shrank by 8 per cent. Shagari was shunted aside in another military coup, led by Major-General Muhammadu Buhari, a slim, chisel-faced man whose moustache hung beneath prominent cheekbones. He lasted two years before being overthrown by the man in the museum's next photo, General Ibrahim Badamasi Babangida. His features – gap-toothed, with a square face and cuddly physique – looked deceptively honest. At first, Babangida made all the right noises: he restored press freedom and released political prisoners; but he took corruption to a new and unprecedented level.

A return to civilian rule was promised in 1990, but Babangida pushed it back to 1993. During that time, the military government gave the illusion of democracy by creating two puppet political parties, which it tightly controlled. After holding local-level elections, Babangida eventually allowed a general election in 1993. Although his good friend, a wealthy entrepreneur called Moshood Abiola, was declared the winner in this relatively fair election, General Babangida annulled the result. Deadly riots ensued, and the general handed over power to an interim government.

Within twelve months, Babangida's deputy, General Sani Abacha, pushed the new authorities aside and assumed power. His face in the photograph emanated ruthlessness: tribal marks stretched vertically between reptilian eyes and a sour pout; a brooding assassin. Abacha governed Nigeria with an iron fist. He disbanded all political parties and government institutions, including the Senate, and replaced them with army men.

In 1994 Abiola, the presumed winner of the 1993 elections, declared himself president before being arrested on treason charges and kept in solitary confinement. A growing opposition lobbied to reinstate the Senate, and workers went on strike to campaign for Abiola's release from prison. Abacha, intolerant of all dissent, jailed union leaders. The former president Obasanjo was imprisoned for plotting to overthrow the government. My father and eight of his colleagues were jailed and falsely charged with inciting the murder of four other Ogoni activists, even though all of them had been prevented from entering Ogoniland on the day of the murders. The tribunal set up to try them was declared rigged by human rights organisations. Witnesses who testified against them later admitted to receiving bribes. The Ogoni Nine's subsequent executions ignited international condemnation, and led to Nigeria's expulsion from the Commonwealth.

In 1998, Abacha died of a sudden heart attack. He was succeeded by General Abdulsalami Abubakar, a bespectacled, cleft-chinned man who allowed general elections to be held in 1999. Former head of state Obasanjo won the presidency and served two terms in office before being succeeded in the 2007 elections by Umaru Yar'Adua, a former chemistry professor whose thin lips and arched nose seem to originate north of the Sahara. It was the first time that Nigeria had had two successive democratic administrations.

The museum's apathetic display of these photographs placed murderous dictators next to the few democratically elected presidents. All judgement had been withheld, along with any information. A novice would have no idea that during its forty-seven years of independence Nigeria has lurched from one kleptocracy to the next. The leaders' photographs resembled a series of criminal mugshots, a line-up of chief suspects in the ruination of Nigeria. The sight of them soured my tourist's jaunt. For all their talk and intentions, most of these men pocketed billions of the country's wealth, ruined the infrastructure, devalued the education system and obliterated Nigerians' trust in one another, cultivating a dog-eat-dog attitude in all corners of life. A lack of professionalism characterises the top echelons of government, and extends down to the ordinary workers, including the managers of this museum. Nothing works, talent goes to waste, and nepotism is rife.

I stepped outside. It was already 4.30 p.m. Aunty Janice had instructed me to be back indoors by sunset at 6.30 p.m. for safety's sake. I was surprised that visiting the museum was the only thing I achieved that day. When people told me that heavy traffic allowed you to complete only 'one thing per day' in Lagos, I thought they were exaggerating. But my watch told me it was time to hurry back to the mainland and Satellite Town.

By the glittering blue lagoon, I stood next to the main ring road to flag down a motorcycle taxi, or *okada*. Okadas are the scourge of Nigeria's roads. These Chinese-made, 100cc motorcycles buzz around the streets in their thousands, like a plague of giant flies. They're popular because they're cheap and fast and can weave through the traffic go-slows that consume such a huge proportion of people's days. They barely existed as a form of transport in the 1980s, but when public transport fails, and the increasingly teeming roads aren't expanded, two wheels become the best option.

The okada drivers zip around at homicidal speeds, without any regard for who or what lies ahead of them. No one is safe. They will use every available space, even cutting off their wing mirrors to squeeze through the traffic more easily. While they're willing to avoid inanimate objects such as market stalls and fruit tables, pedestrians and anything else with limbs and reflexes are considered fair game. Walking down a street, I never knew quite when an okada would fly into me. They would surprise me from all angles, sometimes from the side, sometimes from behind and sometimes against the flow of traffic. When one is inevitably mown down by an okada at some point, the drivers can be startlingly unrepentant. Mabel had recently been hit by an okada, and lost a tiny chunk of her left leg. 'I *told* you,' the scowling driver had snorted. In his mind, Mabel had paid the right price for disrupting his precious momentum; her well-being hadn't been worth the slightest deceleration.

I had never intended to ride one of these things, but time was running out. Just one day in Lagos had taught me to blend into my surroundings by wearing a streetwise frown and barking my request. The okada man initially refused to take me to the bus stop I wanted ('It's too far'), but when I offered to double the fare he ordered me to 'Sit down.' The two of us sped off, and now that I was an okada passenger rather than a pedestrian, my disdain for these bikes disappeared.

As we rode away from the museum, I privately applauded my driver's aggression when he mounted the pavement and beeped two terrified pedestrians out of the way. Back on the main ring road, he swerved violently through traffic, cussing any car driver who tried to run us off the road. My mood changed slightly when he slid close enough past the cars to endanger my kneecaps, and the wind yanked my headscarf from my head, tossing it far behind me. When my driver suddenly applied the brakes, I slammed jaw-first into his back, then clawed his torso as he lurched forward. At that moment, I could see why Nigerians are so religious: an okada ride will have the staunchest atheist praying for Christ's protection.

Twenty minutes later, I boarded a danfo, which dropped me off near Aunty Janice's house. My life was threatened again when trying to cross the expressway to reach Satellite Town. Without traffic lights – of which Lagos has only a handful – my fellow pedestrians and I were at the mercy of the cars and lorries. As soon as a sizeable gap in the traffic appeared, the old, the young, the suited and the crippled sprinted across the expressway as if fleeing an apocalypse. We hurdled the central reservation and then stood on the other side of it, panting and scouring the second half of the expressway for another suitable gap. The wait seemed endless. In a moment of optimistic madness I leapt forward, only to be pinned back by the outstretched arm of the woman beside me.

'Please, I beg, o,' she warned. She kept her arm there until she could shepherd me to safety on the other side.

By the time I arrived back at Aunty Janice's, I had the ravaged appearance of a fugitive: sweaty, saddle-sore and flinching at any sudden movement in my visual periphery. The sunlight and fumes had furrowed my forehead, but everyone else around me seemed unflustered and collected. Men regally attired in white *agbada* robes sidestepped goat shit and puddles. Their clothes were clean, their foreheads uncreased, and they barely perspired. Without a composed temperament, Aunty Janice told me, life in the city can chop years off your life span. At this rate I think I'd be finished at fifty.

2

Oil and People on Water

Lagos

While I spent my childhood summers in a modest house on the periphery of a quiet neighbourhood in the humdrum town of Port Harcourt, some of my wealthy Nigerian schoolmates were living my dreams in Victoria Island, the most expensive part of Lagos, once a genuine island, but now joined by a land bridge to the mainland. Their lives were an inaccessible blur of nightclubs, boat clubs and neon-lit restaurants – far more exciting than England. VI, as it is known, might even have been an adequate proxy for all those Caribbean holidays I craved but, frustratingly, my father never took us to Lagos. Now I had come to Victoria Island independently, to reacquaint myself with proper pavements, supermarkets, familiar global brands and air conditioning.

In the absence of informal traders, the streets felt sedate and spacious. Residential mansions lay strategically inconspicuous behind guarded security gates, and the okadas wove at deferential speeds between the tinted-windowed 4 x 4s. Here, Nigeria dusts itself down and shakes hands with world commerce: Chinese, Thai and Italian restaurants, foreign banks, art galleries and sports bars lined the streets. By the water's edge stood several embassies, their dozen or so armed guards chatting under the shade of palm trees. Further east, a string of boat clubs lined the island edges, overlooking the lagoon where some people were jet-skiing. I was inspired. I hoped the two middle-aged British expats drinking by the boat club's bar might know more. There was wariness in their gaze, the dread I recognised in westerners' faces when an African approaches them for something. Swallowing my pride, I asked them where I could rent jet skis. They pointed me to the next boat club along. It had jet skis, the manager said, but their engines had broken down and couldn't be fixed in Nigeria; new engines would have to be imported. I stared longingly at the yellow jets skis bobbing in the water, sleek and useless.

I looked for something else to do. At the suggestion of the new Nigerian version of *Time Out* magazine, I visited Terra Kulture, a cultural centre-cum-restaurant. The walls were smothered in elegant black-and-white photographs of Victor Olaiya, Fela Kuti and other illustrious musicians. Sunlight flooded through the wall-to-ceiling windows, which looked out on to fresh, immaculate gardens. Rarely did Lagos architecture have such a therapeutic effect. When the staff told me that my plate of rice and plantain would cost me an eye-watering $18, I accepted that I was paying not just for food but the scant commodities of style and serenity.

Upstairs was the art gallery, manned by a young, alert assistant with high, Cameroonian cheekbones and an industrious smile. Thank goodness for the private sector. He encouraged me to look around. The paintings and modern portraiture and aerial photographs of the Lagos skyline were charming, though none of them matched the exquisiteness of the ancient abstract sculptures. At the back of the gallery, a theatre was staging one of its regular afternoon plays. I joined an audience of about two dozen people seated sporadically on wooden chairs. After an hour's delay, the lights dimmed, and the spotlights bore down onto the stage. In the opening scene, an actress pushed another actress in a wheelchair and tried to enter the stage living room, but the wheelchair got stuck in the doorway. For sixty toe-curling seconds, the lady pushed and heaved and tried to roll the wheels over the door threshold. The seated actress, feigning paraplegia, looked on with self-imposed helplessness while the audience took it all in without a snigger.

Eventually the play started. It was a family drama set in the aftermath of a politician's death as his three daughters discover some nasty truths about their father. The director was aiming to give insight into the complications of Nigerian family life, but the audience's behaviour interested me far more. During the play, people chatted amongst themselves or spoke on their cell phones at unapologetic volume. Even more distracting was the unsolicited audience participation in the stage action. As the plot unfolded, spectators vented their opinions. 'Story!' one lady shouted out when one of the characters lied about something ('story' is a word Nigerians use when accusing someone of lying).

Annoyed by these frequent disruptions, I kissed my teeth and harrumphed and sighed and stamped my feet, hoping that these raucous spectators would get the message. They were oblivious to my irritation, and I ended up losing the plot of the play entirely. Audience participation can be a beautiful thing, and call-and-response is one of my favourite aspects of African culture. Nothing is more powerful than watching an audience replying to a speaker's words, emoting between his or her phrases and amplifying the sentiment (the singer Erykah Badu's live version of 'Tyrone' is a form of audience participation at its most sublime). But to do it during a sombre stage play? It didn't seem appropriate to me.

A second, portly lady in a front-row seat was anxious to let the rest of us to know that she had figured out the plot in advance. 'She's their half-sister!' she cried out, pointing to the maid character on stage. 'It's her, now.'

Two minutes later, the play reached its climax when in the final line, the housemaid confessed to being the illegitimate daughter of the deceased politician: '*He was my father.*'

'See, I told you,' the portly lady commented as the lights dimmed, pleased at her foresight. The cast took a bow, the audience clapped, and my anger imploded into resignation. There was no point hoping for quiet. This was the Lagos way of watching a play, and if I ever wanted to enjoy the city, I simply had to get used to it. In Nigeria, every diamond, even Victoria Island, was fashioned with rough edges.

Across the water from Victoria Island was Tarkwa Bay, a sheltered beach along Lagos Harbour. It wasn't the prettiest of places, but it was a diversion from the city, singled out by my guidebook for its mere existence rather than its attractiveness. In Lagos a trip to the seaside – with all its debris and harsh views of Lagos's industrial harbour – represented a break from the hustling multitudes and non-stop irritation of city life.

After the play, my okada man took me to the western edge of Victoria Island, past the foreign embassy buildings and the armed soldiers idling on chairs beneath a grove of trees by the water's edge. At the jetty, I saw a shaven-headed man with a goatee wrapped around extremely shapely lips. He was sitting at an outdoor desk. As I watched him stand up and walk towards me, I could tell he was a hustler right from the start. Obscuring his shifty eyes behind dark sunglasses, he homed in on me with a swiftness that made his motives clear. He worked in the office near the boats, he told me, helping people apply for visas to the US. Though this bore no connection with the boats, he acted as an intermediary between me and the man in charge of the water transport.

'My name is Sam,' he intoned smoothly, extending his hand to shake mine. 'I can show you around Tarkwa Bay.' His intentions aside, I couldn't help being impressed by his cool, laconic demeanour. He led me to the boat and tried to charm a free ride from the boat man, but the old guy was having none of it.

'You're a thief,' he jibed at Sam, a stern glint piercing his smiley eyes. Sam begrudgingly paid for a full-price ticket.

The motor boat took us and a quartet of Italians through Five Cowrie Creek and out to the Atlantic. We cruised beneath the fly-over bridge separating Victoria Island from Ikoyi, and headed into the choppy blue waters. Lagos's industrial sprawl extended into the lagoon, filling its blue surface with oil tankers and oil pipelines that stretched above our heads. A group of hardened white expats, embracing the industrial aesthetic, sailed among the tankers on their yachts and jet skis.

Once at Tarkwa Bay, everyone waded onto the beach, except me. I stayed on the boat, adamant about keeping my shoes and legs dry. Sam gallantly lifted me up in his arms and carried me onto the beach. I felt his knees buckle briefly.

'Ai, I didn't think you were so heavy,' he said as he tipped me onto my feet.

'I weigh nine and a quarter stone. How heavy *should* I be?'

'You've been eating too much yam,' he informed me, examining my frame at arm's length.

The beach was relatively empty at that time of the day. A bald friend of Sam's bounded up to him, slung an arm around his shoulders and whispered conspiratorially into his ear, eyes darting towards me between giggles. I caught the words '. . . at least ten thousand naira,' and prepared myself for the scheming that was to come.

Sam and I sat down on some chairs near a handful of people beneath a shady tree, opposite a makeshift wooden bar run by a female friend of his. For once, I heard birdsong and the rustle of trees in the breeze. Even the gentle whoosh of the sea waves – normally drowned out by Lagos's noise pollution – was a novelty. I closed my eyes and imagined that we were in the Caribbean, less than 10 kilometres away from Lagos. But my illusions were swiftly demolished when I opened my eyes and turned to face the sea.

Tarkwa Bay sat right in the middle of oil tanker traffic. The huge vessels sailed so close to the beach I thought I was hallucinating. Almost noiseless, they moved along at an unexpectedly fast pace. One minute they were blobs on the horizon, the next minute they were partially obliterating the sunlight as they cruised past like mobile edifices 20 metres from the shore.

Sam and I chatted for an hour or so under the tree. Like me, he was thirty-one years old, an ethnic Birom from central Nigeria, the son of a retired air force pilot. Most of his brothers and sisters were living and working in the US.

'Do you ever want to go to the States?' I asked him. He shrugged his shoulders.

'Maybe one day,' he drawled quietly. 'If God wants it to happen it will happen.' Sam had that preoccupied expression adopted by people who spend time with you solely in the pursuit of money. He wasn't in the mood for conversation. He sat back and stifled a yawn.

'What were you doing last night?' I asked.

'I was in a bar on Lekki with some friends. We watched football, danced . . .' Sam's words petered into silence. I bet he'd seduced a woman or two as well. He had the looks and essence of a success-ful womaniser.

'Are you married?' he asked me. I sighed impatiently. People's curiosity about me could be frustratingly one-dimensional.

'No. Are you?'

'No,' he said. 'I hope God will find me a wife soon. I am tired of sinning.'

'What do you mean, "sinning"?'

'I'm tired of committing fornication,' he said, hanging his head in fake shame. I tried to keep a straight face. He took sips of *ogogoro*, a hot alcoholic drink, and stared dramatically into the sand.

We took a walk along the beach, past a lone, sumptuous-looking house overlooking the water. Sam said it belonged to a European expat.

'My best friend died here,' Sam said out of the blue. He said the oil pipeline at Tarkwa Bay caught fire and exploded, killing hundreds of people. Sam's best friend was one of them. The locals regularly smash holes in the pipes to steal fuel that's otherwise beyond their purchasing power. Nigeria loses millions of barrels of petroleum every year this way from pipelines around the country. The pipes bleed oil until the professionals can repair them. Carelessly lit cigarettes or paraffin lamps can start such fires.

'Ade didn't tell anyone he was stealing oil,' Sam said. 'His wife had a baby girl. The naming ceremony was due ... he needed money to pay for it.'

The fireball engulfed everyone in 900°C flames. Some died within seconds; others, including Ade, staggered towards the beach, ghoulishly charred and disfigured, fighting imminent death.

'The white man who owns that big house took him to hospital, but he died before they reached there. You know, these oil burns are not like normal. They burn *inside* your body.' Sam held back genuine tears. He said Ade's burnt features were still recognisable enough for his corpse to be identified, and he was given a quick Islamic burial in Tarkwa Bay that same day.

It was good to finally put some names, if not faces, to the victims of these tragedies. Foreign media reports on these incidents rarely give descriptions of those who died, and sometimes the accidents' exact locations aren't stated: 'near Lagos' is the vague description provided. It was a stinging reflection of our worth in the eyes of government and, by extension, the world.

Sam and I sat on the smooth, damp sand of a deserted beach. The turquoise surf threw up a mist that blurred the brilliant sunshine and cast an ethereal haze around us. The beach and its palm trees stretched into the distance where the matchstick figure of a man rolled about on the shoreline, waves cresting over his body. He was performing a traditional Yoruba prayer, Sam said. Four hundred kilometres beyond us to the west, I knew that foreign tourists were sunning themselves and taking drum lessons on the beaches of Kokrobite in Ghana, staying in well-run hotels. Why can't Nigeria offer something similar? Our thousands of miles of glorious coastline lay empty and shamefully under-capitalised. Oil saboteurs like Ade should be earning their money from beach tourism and using their disposable income to enjoy the beach more. The only people who seemed to be enjoying this particular stretch of beach that day were a handful of expats – the fat Israeli talking loudly to his friend in Hebrew; the haughty, muscular surfer walking past with his surfboard.

Out on the dazzling horizon, I counted more than fifty tankers. Sam told me that the vessels spend up to six weeks on the water waiting to load and offload their goods at the port, their crews sustained by hawkers and prostitutes who sail out to them in small boats.

By now, Sam's eyes were caressing my face, and his voice had lowered to a pre-coital purr. My ego toyed with the possibility that he was genuinely interested in me, but after factoring in my messy hair, baggy trousers and legs greyed by the dry winds, I knew my wallet was the only thing fanning his gigolo interest. His eyes now bored into mine while I stared into the horizon and made idle chit chat, strategically adjusting my position in order to maintain some daylight between us. When the daylight shrank further, I quickly rose to my feet.

We walked back to the main beach, where the endless stretches of sand were strewn with an ungodly amount of litter. I had recently stopped noticing garbage – after a few days in Lagos, one's eyes surrender to its ubiquity – but suddenly its quantity offended me to the core.

'*Why* don't they clean up all this rubbish?'

'Who will do it?' Sam was surprised that I expected anyone to take responsibility. Not only was there litter everywhere, but there were also a few wooden crosses, which looked like they'd been plonked there unceremoniously. Sam shrugged his shoulders; that's where people chose to bury their dead, he said. Land is used randomly in parts of Lagos.

We returned to Tarkwa Bay's main beach, which was now filling up with expats. Groups of Lebanese men played football and volleyball by the waves. Sam pointed out the very hairy, barrel-chested Arab whose father owns the Eko Hotel, one of Lagos's fanciest places to stay. He was one of the thousands of ethnic Lebanese merchants who came to Nigeria in the early twentieth century, a middle-class stratum that rarely dips its toes in the indigenous gene pool, preferring to marry within itself or fetch partners from the mother country. Their relative wealth and influence, nothing special in absolute terms, shines an embarrassing light on Nigeria's anaemic economy. As the Lebanese men played football on the beach, a Nigerian hawker stood nearby and watched them, a tray of fruit balanced on top of his head. I couldn't tell if he was waiting to sell them something, or whether he was simply fixated by the game; either way, he cut a frustratingly marginalised, shabby figure against their flabby affluence.

When I told Sam I wanted to return to Victoria Island, he stared sadly into my eyes, disappointed that our day out hadn't been more enriching for him. He stood in the water beside me as I sat myself in the boat that would take me back to town.

'I need to see you again,' he murmured, saucing his disappointment with false romantic distress. 'Please . . . I am not an Area Boy.'*

'I know,' I told him, before hugging him goodbye. Even though Sam wasn't a gangster, he didn't deserve any money from me.

On the way back to Victoria Island, Europeans bounced around the boat on jet skis, and from a thatch-roofed balcony overlooking the water, members of an expat boat club sipped drinks and gazed

---

* Area Boys are organised street gangs who extort money from the public and are involved in other crime, such as selling drugs.

at their surroundings, easily gratified by sunshine and sea despite the presence of pipelines and tankers.

It was time to return to the city.

The air had begun to take on a distinctly crepuscular hue. By the time I reached the CMS bus stop on Lagos Island, the city was twinkling beneath the dark night sky. Janice had warned me time and time again never to stay out after sunset, and my guidebook was equally stern ('Never, and I repeat never, stay on Lagos Island after dark'). At this time of day, thieves and armed robbers were on the lookout for hapless commuters. I waited restlessly for the bus to fill.

Finally, the bus began to inch slowly through the dense traffic. The journey was uneventful until we approached Mile Two, where the traffic dispersed and the roads quickly became less clogged. Our teenage driver reacted to this unexpected freedom in the same way that air inside a balloon reacts to a puncture. He stamped on the accelerator and sent us all crashing back into our seats.

'Go small small, o!' a young woman said, begging him to slow down. The rest of us clung silently to the seats in front of us. 'People are not feeling well,' she implored. 'Please . . . think about them.' Her pleas only spurred the driver to go faster. He raced down the expressway, swerving past all other traffic before braking suddenly and slamming all of us into the backs of the chairs in front. Before we had time to recover, the driver resumed top speed with a painful lurch.

'Conductor, please tell him to go small!' another passenger appealed, but the conductor, hanging from the side of the vehicle like a nonchalant bandit, was deaf to their desperation. The mood inside the bus turned from anxiety to heart-stopping rage, and before long everyone was taking turns to insult the boy behind the wheel.

'Idiot!' the young woman shouted.

'How *old* are you?' a man barked rhetorically.

'Are you mad?' fumed another.

'You're going to kill us all, and *yourself*!' an older lady screamed.

Through the rear-view mirror the boy driver cackled as if he were the devil himself. Perhaps he was on drugs. As soon as the bus slowed into another traffic jam, nearly every passenger evacuated the vehicle as though it had just burst into flames. Had I known my way around I would have joined them. But I stayed on, along with a young woman and her boyfriend, to witness the final – and scariest – segment of the journey.

At the spaghetti junction of Mile Two, the driver wanted to switch from one strand of a fork in the road to the other. Getting there involved crossing the V-shaped patch of rocky ground between the two roads. When the danfo tried accelerating over the rocks, it came suddenly to a halt and brought the three of us – and all the bus seats – sliding forwards. The seats were makeshift benches that had been loosely screwed into the floor. Without the weight of any passengers to hold them down they slid in tandem with the danfo, which now accelerated and reversed alternately as the driver tried to overcome the sloping terrain beneath us.

'Hold on to the window!' the guy advised his whimpering girlfriend. Her dark knuckles had turned caramel from gripping the seat so hard. We were batted around the metallic shell of the bus with every forward jerk, like expendable characters in a horror movie. My skin was scratched repeatedly as it bashed against the twisted metal of the bench in front of me. I couldn't quite believe what was happening. A part of me wanted to giggle hysterically, yet I knew I was in the hands of a mad man and could end up badly gashed.

The bus finally heaved itself across to the other section of road and came to a standstill on the busy roadside. I clambered out, shaken and speechless. In the darkness, the expressway was an Inferno of red tail lights that glowed hellishly through the pollution haze, throwing an eerie light on the human shapes still selling food, dodging the traffic and running for buses.

I jumped into the final danfo that would take me to Aunty Janice's house. As we sped along the expressway towards Satellite Town, the sliding door of the bus broke loose from all but one of its hinges. The door dragged along the tarmac road, spewing a screeching shower of sparks. The conductor ordered the driver to stop so that he could re-attach the door.

'I beg, leave the thing now and let's go!' someone shouted at the conductor. Neither he nor the other passengers had time for such trivial hitches. They were anxious to get home and enjoy the scraps of family time not already devoured by their daily five-hour commute. They were also rushing to escape the thieves who lurk in the tall grass flanking that section of the expressway, waiting to pounce on stationary vehicles. Travelling without a car door was preferable to arriving home without one's wallet.

It was 9 p.m. when I returned to Aunty Janice's house.

'*Where* have you been?' she yelled at me. I'd never seen her this angry.

'I went to Tarkwa Bay,' I explained, defensive and irritated. 'Sorry, I didn't realise it was so far away.'

'I told you to *never* stay out in the night. *Never!* I was so worried . . . I called your mother in England!'

'But I sent you a text telling you I was running late.'

'I didn't receive it! If I knew you were returning so late I would never, *never* have allowed you to go!'

Was I to blame for Nigeria's useless telecoms system?

Aunty Janice set my dinner, a truce, on the table. I ate it in worn-out silence, thinking about Victoria Island and what a distant memory it now seemed. In the space of ten hours I felt I had been snatched from its celestial grace, sucked through a wormhole and spat out into the relative purgatory of the mainland evening commute. Lagos had taken me through many emotions that day. I was feeling particularly chastened and disorientated, but at least boredom hadn't come into it: for all its defects the city never failed to deliver buttock-clenching excitement, and I was grateful for that.

I just needed to shed my complacency and learn not to get too cosy on the roads. As much as Aunty Janice loved Lagos, she knew it was no one's friend. She furiously recounted her experiences of night-time robberies when the traffic would slow to an ominous halt, and passengers – accustomed to the drill – scrambled to remove the SIM cards from their phones. The robbers would hop on board and demand phones and cash, slapping the passengers until they relinquished the treasures hidden in their hair, their cleavage and their underwear (thieves knew *all* the tricks). The night throbbed with danger, Aunty Janice chided, and she considered me a fool for staying out after dark, using buses and okadas and dangling myself within tantalising reach of trouble.

For once, at least privately, I agreed with her. Lesson learned, I lay down to sleep and vowed to make early starts from then on.

Later that week, I went on another trip, this time with Mabel. Around Lagos, I kept seeing people who resembled African Americans from TV and film: that same kissing of teeth, the intriguingly similar speech cadences that emphasised certain syllables, the way when they laughed they clapped their hands and collapsed forwards. Yet the idea that some Americans originated from Nigeria via the slave trade barely crossed my childhood mind, especially when most Americans and West Indians were flocking to Ghana in search of their African roots. The author Maya Angelou was one of many African Americans to spend time in Ghana. During the early 1960s, she worked at the University of Ghana's music department, wrote newspaper articles and plays, and learnt the Fante language. English-speaking and politically stable, Ghana has long been more palatable for foreign visitors, and holds firm at the centre of the slave heritage tourism map. As a travel guidebook author, I too had visited its imposing, white coastal slave fort at Elmina where slaves were imprisoned before their journey across the ocean. I had also seen forts in Senegal, which for years has successfully portrayed a hut on its Gorée Island as the fulcrum of the transatlantic trade, and stood on the beaches in Benin where slaves left Africa for the last time. But Nigeria, for all its size and history, seemed a rather quiet player in this context, even though our colonial place name made our slavery links clear: Ghana was the Gold Coast, further west was the Ivory Coast, while Nigeria was unequivocally titled the Slave Coast.

Slavery underpinned economic life in the Lagos region for centuries, its human cargo crossing Lagos harbour almost as frequently as today's barrels of oil. Badagry, a former slave port forty-five minutes west of Lagos, was the focal point of this human flesh trade, a conduit for hundreds of thousands of Nigerians who were shipped across the Atlantic to the Americas. I decided to visit Badagry with Mabel on a day trip, curious as to what the Nigerian version of a slave fort looked like.

We boarded a danfo heading west from Satellite Town. These minibuses rarely come to a complete halt when picking up or dropping off passengers – even women with babies strapped to their backs are expected to jump off ('Sharp, sharp') while the wheels are still moving. One vexed mother, having launched herself and her baby onto the road, gave the conductor a piece of her mind.

'You're crazy!' she screamed.

'Your baby is crazy!' he hit back with a breathtaking lack of empathy or logic. Mabel and I were still laughing when the bus got going again.

We travelled along the coast to Badagry, which lies on the Porto Novo Creek, a slither of water that connects Lagos to the next-door Republic of Benin. Badagry was founded in the early fifteenth century, a part of the Yoruba people's Oyo empire. From the early sixteenth century onwards, the town, blessed (or cursed) with a protected harbour, became a transit point for shipping slaves. More than half a million people were captured in raids from other parts of Nigeria, Benin and Togo, and sent across the Atlantic to the Americas. When the slave trade was banned in the mid-nineteenth century, Badagry became a major exporter of palm oil, and in 1842, the site of Nigeria's first Christian mission. These days, at least in Aunty Janice's eyes, Badagry was a place where lots of witchcraft was 'cooked'. 'Don't go there,' she had warned with a wag of her finger.

We arrived at a quiet road next to the gloriously blue lagoon, a steaming, soporific place that languished in sheepish contrast to its inglorious past. Right by the water, where slaves once crossed to board ships, lay a small garden and a 500-year-old cannon holding vigil over the lagoon. A class of young schoolchildren in brilliant pink uniforms bobbed and fidgeted around the garden's tree, like a flock of flamingos. Further back from the water, across the street, the barracoon – the slave prison – still stood, now locked. Slaves were held there before being transported by canoe across the lagoon and put on ships anchored further out in the ocean.

Mabel and I inspected the Slave Relic Museum across from the prison building. The museum was owned by local Chief Mobee, descended from the long line of chiefs who had presided over the slave trade since Badagry's founding in 1502. The Mobee family still runs the museum, which – I pedantically remarked to Mabel – makes them profiteers of the slave trade still. Guiding us was Shegu Mobee, the chief's grandson, a clean-cut, laid-back nineteen-year-old university student. I asked him whether he was embarrassed about his family's past involvement. His dark serene face displayed not a flicker of guilt.

'Slavery was all over Africa,' he said quietly, pointing to a map and tracing his languid finger north of the Sahara where many sub-Saharans were sent to serve North Africans. That was all he had to say about the subject: slavery was simply a part of life in those days. Between AD 800 and 1900, Muslim empires sought slaves from sub-Saharan Africa and sent them north, to the Middle East and to the Asian subcontinent. Slavery, although a somewhat inaccurate term, was also common among sub-Saharan Africans. Indentured labourers were put to work in the fields, and paid a tribute to their masters. But they usually weren't the personal property of their masters, and could eventually purchase their freedom.

Badagry's Slave Relic Museum was a tiny, low-ceilinged building with dark concrete walls. On one wall hung the Mobee family tree, stretching back to the sixteenth century. By the opposite wall, various original artefacts of the era were displayed, including a metal neck chain worn by the slaves.

'Can I touch it?' I asked Shegu.

'Yes, you can wear it if you want to.' Shegu placed the rusty metal ring around my neck. It bore down so heavily on my shoulders and collar bone that I had to hold it up with my hands to stop it from bruising my flesh. Less than 200 years ago, someone was forced to wear this very chain – without holding it up with their hands – and go about their daily business. Shegu showed me a pair of twin ankle cuffs, designed to be worn by two people simultaneously. Again, I asked if I could try them on. Indulging my masochism, Shegu fixed them around both our ankles. We tried walking together, but the weight of the metal, combined with our lack of coordination, made it too difficult. As he removed the cuffs, I breathed a deep, deep sigh of relief. I felt so incredibly lucky to be born in a prosperous and enlightened era. Discounting family bereavement, I've more or less dodged the bullets of misery and ill health that have rained down on humans throughout history.

Shegu crossed the small room to show me a set of chains worn by disobedient slaves. Connected to the chain was a hook that pierced the slave's toes whenever he or she walked. I didn't fancy trying that one on. Shegu also held up a lip hook, which the slave masters attached to the faces of misbehavers to prevent them from talking and eating. But by far the most barbaric object was the cone-shaped drinking trough, apparently designed for maximum humiliation. The dehydrated slaves, while handcuffed, would drink from the trough like animals, up to forty of them pushing and jostling for access. As the water level lowered, they had to push their heads deeper into the container. Shegu painted a picture of the rusty, sharp edges cutting their faces and chests, and blood flowing into the water, leaving a salty tinge for the other drinkers.

The sadistic treatment of slaves is an eternal mystery to me. Surely it's in every salesman's interest to keep his merchandise in good condition? Car salesmen keep their vehicles gleaming; goose farmers fatten their fowl; London fruit sellers tell you not to 'set those grapes down too hard' after you pick them up for inspection. Yet these slave masters routinely beat the strength out of people whose very muscles lay at the core of their commercial value. Even if such treatment were designed to diminish the slaves' spirit and mental strength, there's a fine line between demoralisation and death; those slave masters tripped over that line so often, it seemed to defy business logic. Their profits, though healthy, could have been a lot healthier.

When the slaves were ready to be shipped abroad, they were led out of the barracoon and onto boats that crossed the lagoon to a beach known as the Point of No Return. Shegu, Mabel and I retraced their steps and boarded a motorised canoe at the waterfront. Two others joined us: a young journalist called Success, and her lanky photographer, Sesi, who took a shine to Mabel. The pair were covering Badagry for a news feature.

A few minutes later, the five of us climbed out of the boat onto empty, grassy land on the other side of the water.

'They should build a bridge across this lagoon,' I commented.

'If they built a bridge, people would come and build houses here,' Sesi replied. The land had a tranquil, bucolic atmosphere, its tall grass munched by a scattered herd of cows. About a kilometre and a half ahead of us, a coconut tree grove rose from the soil. Shegu assured me that the Point of No Return beach from which the slaves departed was behind the trees, but I couldn't envisage it, not when I couldn't smell or see the ocean. As we walked under the raging sun, our laughter dwindled rapidly into grimaces and grunts, the stroll slowing to a pained stagger. Sandy soil swallowed my shoes with every step I took; Success struggled to move along in her tight skirt and corporate stilettos. 'See your shoes!' Sesi teased, as her heels sank into the sand.

Designated slaves walked this very route in bare feet under the same merciless sun, weighed down by neck and ankle chains and handcuffs. The thought of it ought to have put my suffering into perspective, but it didn't. I felt I was slowly dying.

Shegu led us away from the main path towards a rusty old well. He told us it was once filled with a liquid that the slaves were forced to drink. It made them delirious and therefore easier to load onto the ship. 'When they drank it,' Shegu said, perhaps metaphorically, 'they did not know who they were. They forgot their past.'

'They forgot so they can go to America and do their rap.' Mabel smiled enviously. Her mind was firmly in the present, not the past.

The five of us approached the coconut grove, the sea breeze cooling our faces. We emerged from the trees onto a wide, empty beach: the Point of No Return. Palm trees rocked in the wind against the gentle roar of the green-blue waves. Here, the slaves boarded a small schooner and were taken to a ship anchored further out at sea. My mind's eye pictured them chained to the deck on their backs for months on end, squirming in tides of faeces, urine, menses, vomit and brine as the boat rocked along the Atlantic waves. On the other side, I imagined them getting washed down, branded with hot irons and displayed for sale at the slave market where – for one time only – their humanity and personalities were acknowledged: '*hardworking wench*'; '*insolent and untrustworthy young man*'. Survivors of this process went on to live a life of backbreaking toil and ruthless punishments, yet they still managed to continue a lineage that produced the cultures of Brazil, the Caribbean and the US. Although Africans have yet to fulfil our potential, we've proved our strength at the opposite end of the spectrum by enduring some of the harshest abuses.

'It's so nice here,' Success cooed, stretching her arms as if to embrace the beach. 'You could come here and write novels and be inspired.'

The beach was once the venue for the Black Heritage Festival, which the local authorities launched in 2001 to celebrate Nigerian history and its cultural links with the New World. Hundreds of African Americans, Brazilians and Nigerians attended the festival, playing music on the beach and praying. Gathering at the Point of No Return, they danced, re-enacted slave raids and celebrated African culture under the watchful eye of their armed security men (one attendee later told me that the foreigners brought so many gun-toting bodyguards, the beach resembled a war zone).

Near the coconut grove stood a stone slab engraved with the words BLACK HERITAGE FESTIVAL, 2001 near the top. Space had been left to commemorate the festivals in years to come, but apart from the 2001 engraving, the slab was empty. As with many things in Nigeria, the festival didn't last. Shegu told us that someone in government jeopardised it by trying to register the festival under his own company in order to make personal profit. In the end, he succeeded only in dismantling the entire project. So now the engraved stone slab, created as a monument to the Black Heritage Festival, looked more like an epitaph to the idea, a celebration of Nigeria's ineptitude in organising or documenting its culture and history. As with the National Museum, greed and a scarcity of funds and imagination had left a trail of half-baked projects.

The reporter, Success, couldn't understand the concept of people gathering on a beach to remember slavery.

'This Black Heritage Festival,' she said, taking in the surround-
ings with confused eyes, '. . . so people come to sit here and . . . cry?'
She was drawing on familiar images of tearful American visitors to
West African beaches.

The rest of us fell about laughing.

'We should be crying and praying for their souls,' Success
implored with a twinkle in her eye.

Some Americans might have been surprised or appalled by our
flippant reaction to the concept of heritage festivals. But Nigerian
sadness about the past is expressed differently; it is an all-encom-
passing emotion that lies beneath the wry jokes and laughter; it
doesn't attach itself to specific places or objects. As we are not
descended from slaves, slavery didn't inspire the same angst in Mabel,
Success and Sesi as it does among our American cousins. Mabel
envied the lives of African Americans, the source of her beloved hip
hop and R'n'B, who lived in a land of milk and honey, as far as she
was concerned. I wondered whether she and other Lagosians had
time to worry about the slaves' tortuous boat journeys when every
cramped bus ride to work felt like a mini Middle Passage, and people
filled Internet cafés to apply for US green cards. Slavery is seemingly
another of those traumas that falls within our nation's high pain
threshold. We still don't fully understand its effects on our society and psyche.

We returned to Badagry's waterfront and then Mabel, Success,
Sesi and I walked to the first two-storey building built in Nigeria.
Constructed in 1845 by a church missionary, it was also the first
Nigerian parsonage, and was now a school. The teacher, a charis-
matically stern man, led us to a room housing the first ever Bible to
be translated from English to the Yoruba language.

Mabel and I stepped back outside and waited for okadas to take
us to Badagry's motor park. 'These towns . . . they never progress,'
she said as we squinted at the boiling, white-hot sky. 'You look at
them now . . . they're always so quiet.'

Badagry was one of the first places in Nigeria to establish links with outsiders through the slave trade and then nineteenth-century British colonialism. But sub-Saharan Africa's geography and tropical diseases marginalised the continent in the global flow of people and ideas. We fell behind, and by the time foreigners settled on our shores, their advanced technology ensured that the nature of their relationship with us was exploitative rather than mutually beneficial. These days, Badagry has little to show for its early contact with missionaries and the slave trade. It's as shabby and poor and undeveloped as any other town, and Shegu, an indirect beneficiary of slavery, was studying for a degree and trying to make his way through life like everyone else.

3

Total Formula for Victory Over the Hardships of Life

Lagos

Exploring Lagos from my base in Satellite Town – so far away from the heart of the metropolis – required much arduous wading through the city's sweltering, viscous crowds. Satellite Town was a separate universe from the fancy Lagos that I saw in the Sunday newspaper pages, the Lagos where lavish wedding ceremonies are frequented by celebrities, entrepreneurs, senators, royalty and every eminent 'Chief and Mrs' in the vicinity; the Lagos that arranges for American R'n'B superstars to come and perform concerts, where Nigerian hip-hop stars work the red carpet at glamorous award ceremonies, speaking with faux American accents, and underpaid 'Nollywood' actresses feign a wealth and glamour befitting of their cultural status.

Only a few contacts lay between me and that side of the city's life, but reaching that epicentre required far too much physical effort. I felt shackled to the haggard, quotidian side of mainland life and, after three weeks, increasingly comfortable in it, too. Happy to let the tide carry me wherever it pleased, I began taking aimless bus rides around town during my last few days in Lagos.

As I sat on a danfo at a bus stop, a man walked past, pushing a cake-laden trolley. He was drawing the attention of customers by blasting the recording of a baby's screams from loud speakers. He sniggered at my horrified reaction. As my bus waited to fill up with passengers, a beggar hopped on board and faced the passengers. Intoning like a church pastor, he began a very long speech detailing his sad life story in Liberia. But far from drawing sympathy, the beggar's laboured, inarticulate ramblings only irritated the buck-toothed old man next to me.

'I beg, *what* is your point?' he barked at the beggar, who snapped his mouth shut immediately. The old man angrily rummaged his pocket for some naira notes. 'I'm tired of your *mad* talk,' he muttered before pressing hush money into the Liberian's palm. The beggar jumped off the bus, and the old man let out a disgruntled sigh.

'Where are you from?' he asked me once the bus got moving.

'I'm Nigerian,' I said, disappointed that he had discerned that I was a diasporan. 'What makes you think I'm not?'

'You don't look like a Nigerian ... you dress like those YMCA girls,' he said. 'And I can see you staring out of the window ... you are looking around curiously. You cannot come from Lagos.'

YMCA girl? That was a new one. Most passers-by asked me if I was a 'footballer' because I wore running shoes all the time. We chatted all the way back to Satellite Town. We found ourselves disembarking at the same stop, walking down the same side street, through the same market. It turned out the old man – his name was Julius – lived five minutes away from Aunty Janice. He invited me to his house for lunch.

Like all the houses in Satellite Town, Julius's was a modest bungalow fronted by a porch and a tiny yard. A retired civil servant, Julius received his accommodation from the government. His first house, back in the 1970s, had been in Ikoyi, which in those days was still a quiet suburb of Lagos, and nothing like the swarming downtown area it is now. Julius couldn't bear the area's calm. He was later moved to a house in Satellite Town, even further behind the back of beyond.

'In fact, it was worse than Ikoyi,' Julius said as we sat in his small living room. 'You could hear the sound of a bird – that's all. No human traffic . . . nothing!' he laughed. 'It was like being in solitary confinement. You see, I like to *see* human beings. But Ikoyi is better now. Things have improved in terms of human traffic. Ikoyi has improved *tremendously*.' Julius must be the only person who considered the chaos of Ikoyi to be an improvement on the past. He was a Lagos old-timer, at ease with the city's pandemonium. 'I like the hustle and bustle. I'm used to noise!'

'Lagosians do like their noise,' I said.

'I think it's natural with human beings. If you are born in a noisy environment, you are afraid to be taken away from it. What will you do? That's one of the ways of life in Lagos . . . shouting, arguing. A first-time visitor will see Nigerians as mad. *Mad* people coming together,' he gave a closed-lipped chortle. 'So now that you are in Rome, you have to do as the Romans!'

Julius showed me his collection of old naira notes and coins. He poured a bagful of old money onto the coffee table.

'I remember these!' I said, picking up some ₦10 and ₦20 notes. My parents used to give me these low-denomination bills as pocket money when I was child. I could spend the cash on fruit and skewers of *suya* meat, and I still had change to spare. In the 1970s, two naira equalled one British pound sterling. Now the exchange rate was ₦250 to the pound. Over the years, the government has reprinted naira notes in higher denominations to keep up with the naira's declining value. Regardless of their economic value, I cherished those crisp, newly issued notes, which seemed an improvement on the current soggy, bacteria-infested bills.

Julius handed me a one kobo coin, a sure contender for the world's most valueless coin. One hundred of these coins made up one naira. Once upon a time, a few kobo could buy me some sweets; now they wouldn't buy me a mouthful of banana. Julius showed me a ₦2 coin, issued in 2006 by the government in a bizarre imitation of the British £2 coin. The coins were withdrawn from circulation after public protests about their weight: most things cost ₦100 or more; even sachets of 'pure water', the cheapest item, go for ₦5.

Someone of Julius's rank should have been enjoying comfy-slippered retirement. Instead he was topping up his retirement income by selling office furniture and stationery and renting cars to businesses around Lagos. He said he could cheat his clients if he wanted to, but he preferred to enjoy their goodwill instead.

'Was there corruption in the civil service when you worked there?' I asked.

'We had it,' Julius said. 'But when we had it we had what you might call "old level" corruption. You could put it at about 5 per cent. But now it is one *million* per cent. When we were at the civil service there was temptation, even from outside . . . people advising us to steal funds. But we were typically honest.'

'Do some people regret not stealing?' I asked.

'You are correct. The reason why is that some of them say, "We are retired but we have no money, no pension." Successive governments have been very slow in releasing many civil servants' pensions. Many retirees are complaining. They say if they had known, they would have stolen. And now it is the cause of why younger ones are stealing . . . they look at the older ones being punished, not being paid their entitlement. So they wonder if they must suffer the same fate. They are afraid.'

Julius was an appealing character. He was feisty and raw, but had an old-school gentility and charm, a member of that generation who spoke very upright Nigerian English ('Have you got your choice drink?'). Yet he didn't share the intense religiosity of most Nigerians. Sinful thoughts, he believed, were not the same as sinful deeds.

'I don't know about heaven and this afterlife,' he whispered conspiratorially to me, out of earshot from his daughter and her friends,
who were playing loud gospel music. 'You can create a paradise of
the heart.'

'I agree.' We both felt that heaven and hell seem too extreme a
conclusion, and very few people deserve to end up in either place.
God surely calibrates our virtues and sins more finely than that.

But Julius's relative secularism was unusual. After three weeks, I
had resigned myself to Nigerian levels of religious fervour. If there's
a country more religious than Nigeria then I haven't been there.
According to the Bible, God made the earth in six days and took a
rest on the seventh. But by creating Nigerians, he ensured that that
was the last day off he's enjoyed ever since. Twenty-four hours a
day and seven days a week we call upon his services, connecting
with him, singing his praises, establishing dialogue with him (and
extremely loud dialogue at that). In my time in Lagos I had heard
hairdressers singing their hallelujahs at salons; evangelical radio
stations resounding in Internet cafés; bus passengers collectively breaking out into ovine choruses of 'Jeezos is my father . . . he never, never
fail me'.

Television brought little respite. Whenever the electricity mirac-
ulously flowed in Aunty Janice's house, I would flop onto the sofa
to savour a football match or a music show, only to be lulled out of
my square-eyed stupor by a pastor barking down a microphone at
the start of *The Divine Connection Hour* and other such broadcasts.

Night time was no haven either. One morning, as daylight
diluted the inky sky and the humidity had receded enough to allow
me finally to sleep, I was woken by a man walking down the street
outside, preaching the gospel at the top of his voice. Temptations
of the flesh and the evils of promiscuity were the main themes: '. . .
You no want for sexing! . . . You no want for sexing!' he bellowed
in the cool dawn. I couldn't hear the rest of his sermon because he

was sauntering down the street, allowing residents of each house to catch only portions of what he said. Had he been serious about spreading the Good News, he might have chosen to stay in one place and let everyone in the vicinity hear his message in full. But he wasn't concerned about this; the act of *imparting* the message was his main motive, a conspicuous show of piety that bordered on the self-indulgent.

All of this was evidence that God's love is spreading, Christians would say. My view of the situation was less nourishing: years of economic struggle and political corruption seem to have focused Nigerians' attention on God more strongly than before. I noticed these changes in some members of my extended family. Religion anaesthetises the pain of bad transport, low wages, stuffed ballot boxes and candlelit nights. People's anger seems to have faded into a muted resignation that shies away from staging street protests. Instead, they develop strategies to earn more money: selling items on the side, begging relatives and friends for loans and donations. But above all, they pray for salvation from life's tribulations.

Half of Nigeria's population – concentrated in the north – is Muslim, but among the other half, evangelical Christianity, especially the Pentecostal kind, is thriving. This charismatic, fundamentalist form of Christianity originated in the 1920s. Focusing on a direct relationship with God, its adherents affirm their faith through the baptism of the Holy Spirit and speaking in 'tongues', a strange babble understood only by God. Their interpretation of the Bible is a more literal one, with a strong emphasis on abstaining from alcohol, gambling, extramarital sex and other vices.

Charismatic Pentecostalism began to flourish in the 1980s as Nigeria tumbled into an economic abyss. On IMF orders, General Babangida had introduced a harsh economic structural adjustment policy aimed at cutting government spending and opening Nigeria's markets to imports. It ended the decadence of the oil boom years and brought on a nightmare of high unemployment and even

deeper poverty for the ordinary man. Out of this emerged an educated elite with a strong, highly conservative message. These
Pentecostal Christians believed that by being 'Born Again', i.e.
living a life of spiritual purity free from sin, one could be 'saved'
from going to hell – like the rest of humanity – and enjoy a healthy
and successful life on earth.

Pentecostals set up new churches that branched away from the
colonial Catholic and Anglican churches. The preachers were entre-
preneurially savvy and well qualified, often former lawyers,
professors and doctors. Inspired by American televangelists, they ran
their churches like businesses. Worshippers were promised that by
becoming Born Again and making generous donations to the
church, they would be blessed with health, wealth and good luck.
Pentecostal ministers are seen as prophetic figures, responsible for
passing on God's words to followers. They are self-styled faith heal-
ers, problem-solvers, doctors, philosophers and economists all rolled
into one. They offer the gospel as a cure-all for every ill, their services focusing on divine healing, exorcisms and the performance of
miracles.

Call it what you will – Prosperity Christianity, Health and Wealth
Gospel – Nigerians are highly receptive to its message. Around 20
million people now belong to a Pentecostal church, pouring money
into its bulging coffers, and turning some churches into highly
lucrative concerns. The ministries (some of which may specialise in
certain types of healing, such as finances or fertility) are run like
commercial enterprises: they manufacture books, CDs, DVDs and
merchandise stamped with their own logos.

These churches have proliferated like mice. A handful of large
ones enjoy million-strong congregations, but the other thousand or
so ministries are generally tiny, established by anyone who wills it.
For every legitimate ministry, several are run by charlatans seeking
enrichment of the non-spiritual variety. Competition for adherents
is fierce. Yet their wealth isn't frowned upon. My sister Zina once

came across an article in the Nigerian society magazine *Ovation* titled the 'Jet Set Pastor', in which a wealthy church leader posed for photographers in the plush interiors of his mansion. His wealth may very well have been legitimate, but such affluence often evades suspicion because, much like in the gold-encrusted churches of sixteenth-century Europe and South America, in the Pentecostal mind wealth and virtue are intertwined.

Pentecostal pastors are nearly always the founders of their church and the focus of attention. Thousands of worshippers gather in stadiums or convention centres to listen to their sermons. The preachers prowl and strut around the stage like R'n'B stars, using their charisma to spread the gospel and rouse the congregation into a frenzied, spiritual orgy. The 'miracles' they perform are something to behold: the blind can suddenly see, sex freaks discover monogamy, paraplegics stagger out of their wheelchairs for the first time since their car accident. Amen!

In Lagos, not a week goes by without one of these evangelical events taking place somewhere. They're promoted like rock concerts and given lavishly worded, pseudo-intellectual titles, such as the 'Expository and Systematic Revelation of Victory Over Worry and Anxiety'. On the streets are countless billboards featuring these star preachers, looking extremely dapper in their silk ties and boxy Italian suits, handkerchiefs poking neatly from their breast pockets. Their shiny faces stared down at me with toothy, camera-ready smiles that might twinkle if I stared at them long enough. Such stylishness seemed rather disquieting. After all, Jesus, the Prophet Mohammed, Nelson Mandela, Mahatma Gandhi and Aung San Suu Kyi aren't renowned for their snappy dress sense.

The preachers' presentation is unmistakeably American in influence, though some intellectuals argue that their message of prosperity is rooted in traditional African animist religion, which has always sought material gain from the gods. Either way, many Nigerians see Christianity as a fail-safe conduit to financial prosperity. On a bus one day, a man sitting beside me was reading a book titled *Unlocking Your Finances Through Faith*. Intrigued as to how prayer can produce money, I read a section of it over his shoulder. The American author had identified a certain aspect of finance, making capital gains, for example, and followed it with a quote from the Bible to demonstrate how such wealth could be obtained via scripture. He leapt from one concept to another without offering any real structural or logical connection between the two. The man reading the book had underlined the biblical quotes in biro. I wondered what he would do with those quotes? Repeat them in his prayers? Then what?

'Ninety per cent of literate Nigerians have only ever read the Bible or the Koran,' my brother told me. Only half of the country is even literate. Most of the books published each year by domestic publishers are religious in some way. The conventional wisdom is that Nigerians are too poor to read novels or general non-fiction, hence the thriving trade in religious tomes. But surely it costs just as much to publish a religious book as it does to produce a new novel? Same paper, different content, that's all. The demand for Christian reading simply obliterates all other genres. I worry that so much uncultivated intellect will breed more poverty and push Nigeria along a downward spiral. Already, I could feel the creeping philistinism smothering the country like a hot, wet blanket.

The media, too, is being saturated. Churches are buying up TV and radio airtime and newspaper advertising space with zeal. The government-run media owes around two-fifths of its advertising revenue to the Church, and allows ministries to occupy large portions of its broadcasting time. By law, religious programming should not exceed 10 per cent of output, but the Nigerian Television Authority swept aside that limit, and dropped the concept of free, state-funded religious broadcasting altogether. Smaller church denominations can't afford to get on air.

But for all Nigerian religion's flaws, I couldn't imagine Nigerians surviving without it. By following the path of Jesus, people told me, they were paving their way to an afterlife of everlasting peace and happiness. Knowledge of this helps them endure the constant anxiety over financial survival. It makes them very happy. Their faces reflect a genuine euphoria as they calmly negotiate Lagos's nightmare streets.

'We are the happiest people in the world!' Aunty Janice gleefully informed me. She had read the World Values Survey, which showed that Nigerians are indeed the most satisfied, contented people on earth; they know that beyond the power cuts and food rationing, beautiful heaven awaits.

Faith in God imbues Nigerians with an optimism that I rarely see anywhere else in the world. It is reflected in the names of businesses, such as the Winners Express bus line, the Victory Be Sure Academy, the Correct Restaurant or the club night featuring DJ Humility. The Christian half of the country seems to be fuelled by the 'ecstasy of sanctimony', to borrow a phrase from Philip Roth.

But all this Christian passion still competes with pre-Christian beliefs. Paganism takes time to capitulate completely to Christianity in any society – Americans were still burning 'witches' more than 1,000 years after Christianity came to Europe, and Nigerians are unlikely to shake off our paganism only 150 years after the missionaries arrived. While we replaced our benevolent gods with Jesus, we're still convinced that the traditional, malevolent spirits are out to get us, a part of that universal human obsession with the 'dark side'. And so Christianity in Nigeria partly supplements our traditional religions; Jesus is often incorporated not as a new belief system but as a potent new force to combat those ancient evil spirits.

Consequently, the lexicon of Nigerian Christianity is highly defensive and combative. Our pastors talk incessantly about 'satanic agendas' and 'war against satanic manipulation'. Buildings are draped in religious banners, printed with phrases such as 'I am blessed beyond satanic manipulation'; small stickers on bus windows say:

'No weapon fashioned against me shall prosper'; people learn the Bible in institutions with names like the Weapons of Warfare Healing School.

With attack considered to be the best form of defence, our churches are now filled with 'prayer warriors' who use the gospel to fight off evil. They've changed the nature and style of other denominations, too. Gone are the days when Catholics murmured in lethargic unison about sinning 'in thought and word and deed'. Now they're shouting the Lord's praises and defeating evil. Many people, Aunty Janice included, have left these traditional denominations altogether and switched to Pentecostalism.

'Why did you leave the Catholic Church?' I asked her.

'The prayers were not effective,' she replied, as though describing a brand of medicine. 'They were not *hot*.'

Religion is by far the greatest manipulator and regulator of our thoughts and behaviour. Recognising this in their own societies, British taskmasters successfully incorporated the 'work ethic' into Christianity as a way of boosting worker productivity in the 'dark satanic mills' of the Industrial Revolution. If only the same had occurred in Africa. Had I been a missionary or imam in nineteenth-century Nigeria, I might have adopted a similar strategy and taught Babangida and Abacha's ancestors to associate corruption with evil spirits, thus striking fear into the hearts of their thieving progeny.

Then I would have declared pounded yam to be the food of the devil, so I would never have been forced to eat it as a child.

The strength of Nigerian spirituality was fully brought home to me on the bus one day when another preacher-salesman stood up to promote his self-written pamphlet, entitled: *Total Formula for Victory Over the Hardships of Life*.

'I am not hungry,' the man said, assuring us that this was no money-making scam. 'I am a qualified university doctor,' he said. 'I am doing it purely for my new-found love of Christ ... You are speaking to a former occultic general ... the man who rejected Jeezos is now praising Jeezos today!'

I bought one of his pamphlets for ₦400 and flicked through it. Printed on the front page were his contact details. In order to pass himself off as a university professor, the man had incorporated the University of Lagos domain name ('unilag') into the first half of his Yahoo e-mail address. Evidently, he was hungry. I opened a page at random, in which the 'doctor' was discussing the causes of female infertility. I was startled to see the following statement: 'A woman is infertile because the vagina is an elephant's ear or anus of a bird ...'

That evening, just after the electricity cut out, I asked Mabel whether she believed in the supernatural and believed this theory about infertility and bird-anus vaginas. Scepticism must have been written all over my torch-lit face.

'Were you there when God created the world?' she challenged pre-emptively. 'Do you believe that God created the world?' I cowered in silence. I'd never seen her so assertive. 'Listen,' she continued, 'I know this guy who slept with a woman who was a prostitute or something like that. Afterwards, she told him he would never have children. And now he has trouble getting an erection.'

'But maybe his problem is psychological,' I suggested, monitoring Mabel's swelling impatience. 'If he believed what the woman said, then it might've affected his brain and made him impotent.' She shook her head. 'You studied psychology, right?' I asked.

Mabel kissed her teeth. 'I'm a Christian psychologist.'

'What ... so you studied Christian psychology?'

'*No*, psychology. But I'm a Christian. I didn't agree with everything I studied. Anyway,' she placed a candle on the table, 'these scientists don't always know what they're talking about. Science can only explain so much. You know, most of them don't believe in God,' she added disdainfully.

'So do you also believe that a woman is infertile because her vagina has turned into the anus of a bird?' I asked.

'It's not that her vagina is *actually* an elephant's ear or anus of a bird,' Mabel replied. 'It looks like a vagina, but in the spirit realm it's an elephant's ear or whatever.'

She gave me an example.

'I know this woman who's still not married even though she is pretty, has money ... everything. She's reached a certain age but still hasn't married. It's because in the spirit realm she is a man, so when men see her they see another man. They don't ask her to marry them. They just stay as her friends ... but she looks like a woman.'

Still not satisfied, I returned to the theme of female fertility. 'But there are women in England who are infertile, then they go to the doctor and the condition is cured.'

Mabel impatiently agreed. 'Yes, of *course* that happens. I'm not saying people *can't* be cured by doctors. But there are things you cannot see in the spirit world.'

Her belief in both doctors and spirits confused me. The next day I went online to research the issue of metaphors in religion. One philosopher, Sam Keen, says that religious language describes 'a spiritual experience that transcends verifiable knowledge and is very imaginative, poetic, metaphoric and inexact'. After some thought, I could see that bird anuses and elephant ears of the spirit realm were just metaphors that were referred to in a very literal, anatomically exact, way. Perhaps the ex-occultic general on the bus wasn't as insane as I thought.

Still, I was disconcerted that people could think in such terms – metaphors can enjoy a logic all of their own. And who knows how many people actually interpret metaphors literally? If American evangelicals, with all their education and cultural sophistication, can still believe in Noah's Ark and use it to resist twenty-first-century scientific theory, I didn't rate Nigeria's chances of modernising enough to raise our living standards.

*

Aunty Janice and Mabel's faith was a profession in itself, in which prayer was conducted with industrious intensity. Attending church three times a week didn't always suffice – sometimes they needed to focus exclusively on the Lord for several days at a time. Prayer City was the place to do it, Aunty Janice told me, a city entirely devoted to supplication, all day every day. Mabel had recently attended the 'Weekend Deliverance' for workers who can't make it during the week. Intrigued, I asked her to accompany me there on a visit.

Our danfo trundled along the Lagos to Ibadan highway. Lagos clung unceasingly to the road, which seemed to be secretly bending and folding in on itself like a maze, trapping us in the metropolis. Among the endless hanging laundry and signposts, I caught sight of a religious banner draped on a building. It was praising the Lord, using a Nigerian turn of phrase that's supposed to flatter but, when literally interpreted, actually spoke my mind. It read: GOD IS TOO MUCH.

Finally, the city gave way to quiet grasses. We disembarked next to a long high wall, the words PRAYER CITY painted on it in giant white letters. Prayer City is owned by the Ministry of Fire and Miracles (MFM), one of the biggest evangelical organisations. MFM, like other large churches, bought a large tract of land where adherents can stay for days on end and participate in prayerful activities. Prayer City also contains a school, a bank and a hospital, all commercially sponsored.

Mabel and I entered the City through a checkpoint that was manned by policemen, who were also ministry members. They looked me up and down, casting a censorious eye over my trousers, earrings and short-sleeved T-shirt. The MFM bans women from wearing these items. Female trousers are considered a form of ungodly transvestism, jewellery is too flashy and tight clothing is a distraction for MFM menfolk who might salivate rather than pray. The MFM guards excused my faux pas on the grounds that I was from abroad.

Mabel and I walked down a tarmac pathway that cut through quiet, sprawling acres of grass, stretching as far as the eye could see. To one side there was a large terrace filled with countless white plastic chairs. They were occupied on the weekends by thousands of worshippers talking in tongues and creating a febrile din of prayers, a unified spiritual climax.

In the distance stood several low-rise hotel buildings where visitors stay. Every social background and problem presented itself here: families wanting to resolve conflicts; young mothers whose ex-boyfriends won't accept paternity of their babies.

Mabel and I walked along streets with names like Salvation Close, past the cheap dormitories with floor mattresses, and the pricey suites for wealthier worshippers. According to Aunty Janice, any guest checking into the hotel is grilled at reception about which church group or division of MFM they belong to. The ministry doesn't want people coming to Prayer City simply to put a roof over their heads. It's called Prayer City for good reason: guests are expected to pray and fast, day and night, and the staff and security guards will make sure that they do.

'You've come to bother God,' Aunty Janice had explained earlier in the day. 'You don't give God any *rest*.' Prayer City's staff will ring bells along the corridors to call people to prayer, she said. If a guest spends three days at the City without praying, their stay won't be extended, and no guest can stay for longer than one month, no matter how dire their circumstances. Aunty Janice knew this from experience. Years ago, she took refuge at the City during her lowest ebb when she was penniless and homeless. She slept on the cheapest dorm mattresses and devoted her days to non-stop supplication, yet after a few weeks the ministry told her, 'Madam, you must leave.' Such a harsh policy was designed to guard against potential thieves and the indigent hoards who might use its facilities as a permanent base.

Mabel and I strolled through the grounds, past the cybercafé, the business centre and the restaurant. We stopped at the branch of a major bank chain to withdraw money. I was curious about what the upmarket suites looked like. The hotel receptionist was a picture of implacable hauteur: hair scraped back into a severe bun, and a neatly pressed purple skirt suit that signified an intent to stick to the rules with holy-minded relish. I had to cajole her into letting me see one of the rooms. Only guests were allowed to see them, apparently. While she kept vigil in the doorway, I peeked into the suite's spotless bathroom and surveyed the thick purple carpet in the bedroom. This accommodation was better than most in Lagos in its $70 per night price range.

Afterwards, Mabel and I walked towards Prayer City's restaurant. On the way, a man roughly the same age as me approached us. His face wore a knowing, friendly grin. Mabel rolled her eyes. 'He *always* wants to talk to me,' she whispered. The man, Emmanuel, had been staying at Prayer City for a few weeks. His round face seemed ravaged by untold hardships, and he was clearly suffering from depression. His conversation – a stream of manic consciousness – was a predominantly one-way affair.

'Do you like it here?' I asked him.

'It is an advantageous environment. I feel as if I am walking on the moon ... You live in *Jand*?' he asked (*Jand* is the slang name for 'overseas'). 'I want to go there. My parents were going to take me when I was five years old but we weren't able to go ... my friend is in the US. He says he will help me get a visa. We have a business ... we export T-shirts ... we are music producers.'

Mabel and I nodded patiently. The three of us walked to the restaurant, a shaded outdoor area with tables and chairs and biblical Nollywood film posters lining one wall. A suspicious-looking man, sitting with idle vigilance, watched us from a corner. Perhaps he was one of the plain-clothed security guards who patrol the City to ensure that visitors are obeying the rules.

'Do you want some food?' I asked Emmanuel as he sat with us

at a table. He declined, and leaned forward to continue talking at us while we ate rice and stew.

'Education is very important,' he declared. 'Did you go to university?'

'No,' I lied, trying to avoid being roped into more conversation.

'Me neither,' he said. 'Getting a degree is not enough. Your degree is only 10 per cent of it . . . it won't bring you money . . . it's not like putting your card in ATM. You must try and create your own job, not sit and wait for someone to employ you.'

Emmanuel's ambitions included song production, IT management and church administration. He was sane enough to recognise the diversity of his plans. It was justified, he said. He cited a successful pastor who had gained five degrees and applied his multiple skills to running his ministry. Emmanuel's thinking flashed with occasional clarity. He was an intelligent guy suffering from a mental illness. But I felt he needed urgent medical treatment, not prayers. By staying here in Prayer City, I worried that his fundamental problems, like Nigeria's, were going unsolved.

Emmanuel spent his days attending daily prayer classes and prayer services where the pastor issues prophetic utterances to members of the congregation ('God will give you a child; God will bless you with a new job soon!').

'The prayer makes me feel good,' Emmanuel smiled. 'It gives me purpose and destiny.'

It didn't give him good mental health or a job, though. But perhaps I was being unfair in demanding pragmatism from a society that had suffered so much. Applying practical solutions is next to impossible when corruption strangles all aspects of life. Bona fide evangelical ministries do a lot for the community, providing facilities that the government and private sectors don't. The Church collects money from people more effectively than the taxman, and builds on its assets (many of the gleaming vans or cars seen on the roads had Church ministry logos painted on their sides).

In many ways, the Church reflected Nigerian society at its most functional. Prayer City's orderliness was the product of hundreds of thousands of people with similar cultural values subscribing to a common vision, contributing towards it, and having a leadership that executes that vision. Our non-governmental institutions – the village, the Church, the family – tend to work more smoothly than the state: bring government into the frame, and everything goes to the dogs.

After a fortnight of staying at Aunty Janice's, eating by candlelight and collecting water from a well, I now worshipped the miracles of daylight and rain, and wanted to kiss Mother Nature's hand for providing them free of charge. Mabel and I set off one day to the local NEPA office in Satellite Town to pay the electricity bill. In her hand was a cheque for ₦4,000, NEPA's fee for giving us less than four hours of electricity that month. The NEPA man sat in a tiny office, watching an evangelical church service on his portable DVD player. The device was powered by batteries since there was no electricity in the building. The man accepted Mabel's cheque – her compulsory payment for a month of almost total darkness – and wished us a good day.

The two of us took a danfo to Victoria Island and ate ice cream. Later on, Mabel headed to her office and left me alone to explore the Galleria shopping mall, wide-eyed with veneration. After dodging ditches in the street markets of Satellite Town, the gleaming, stock-rich shininess of a mundane shopping mall became a thing of beauty. In other countries I marvel at ancient ruins found among their modern streets, but in Nigeria, a modern jewel among our ruins was deeply impressive: vanilla ice cream, glossy magazines and other banal consumer items never seemed more enchanting. The Galleria on Victoria Island excited me in particular. It housed Nigeria's first multiplex cinema, which – praise be – was showing a Nigerian 'Nollywood' movie. I never thought I'd see the day when Nigeria would make its own films and show them at such a venue. Twenty years ago our film industry didn't even exist. Today, Nollywood thrives, but mainly on DVDs in homes and restaurants – cinemas are a rarity, especially in Southern Nigeria. Having seen a handful of Nollywood movies myself on DVD, I couldn't resist the novelty of experiencing Nollywood on the giant silver screen. I was intrigued as to whether the film quality would match the grandeur of the venue.

I settled down in an almost empty afternoon auditorium, a bag of popcorn between my knees, and munched excitedly as the opening credits of *Mission to Nowhere* illuminated the screen. A woman a few rows ahead of me chatted on her mobile phone, while two stewards talked audibly in the front corner – a veritable whisper by Lagos standards.

The film was the best Nollywood movie I'd seen, in terms of cinematography: good close-up camera angles and cameras held steady on tripods, even though the sound was still rather tinny, as if boom mikes were absent. The film's murder mystery plot wasn't particularly Nigerian, the musical score was American, and the characters all had English names: there was a heavy US influence throughout. The plot, which unfolded through the police detective's eyes in a first-person narrative, was linear to say the very least: each murder suspect and other characters were introduced to the audience only at the time of their arrest. Still, the unusual technique had a surprisingly suspenseful effect.

I was thrilled when Mabel used her contacts to arrange a meeting with *Mission to Nowhere*'s director, Teco Benson. We travelled by okada to his offices in the mainland district of Surulere, the movie-making capital. Like downtown Lagos, Surulere had an appealingly urban aesthetic. Narrow streets funnelled through mid-rise colonial buildings, segmenting them like chunks of a cake. The air clanged with the productivity of sewing machinists, shoe repairers, bike mechanics and food merchants.

Benson's offices were on the upper floors of an unassuming four-storey building. We waited in a reception room furnished with a suite of pneumatic red-and-black leather armchairs. On one of them sat a voluptuous woman, breastfeeding a baby.

'That's my wife and our fourth child,' Teco smiled as he invited me into his office. His quietly spoken courteousness softened his stocky, almost thuggish aspect. A devout Christian in his mid-thirties, Teco left his civil service job in 1994 to become an actor and then producer. He was now one of Nollywood's most successful directors. Posters of his movies decorated the wall of his small office, which was dominated by a large desk. The sounds of street traffic roared through the windows.

'Where did you learn to make films?' I asked Teco.

'I taught myself. I travelled to different countries, attended film festivals. I read books about movie production. Nigeria has no film schools, so I had to teach myself the camera work and lighting and all that.'

Nollywood is still mostly an amateur affair. It barely existed in my childhood. Nigerians watched American films, and they had a curious penchant for Indian Bollywood movies too. I remember a cousin of mine played me one of her favourite Indian films years ago. A singing man caged a female love interest by hurling wooden fencing into the ground around her. While he constructed this four-walled prison, the woman stood there in a feminine fluster, needlessly rooted to the spot. Such theatricality wasn't to my taste, but many Nigerians were keen on it – in the absence of our own indigenous films, Bollywood tapped into something they weren't getting from Hollywood.

Unbeknownst to me, in the late 1980s, the seeds of Nigeria's film industry were germinating. Yoruba creatives who had previously worked in the travelling theatre began shooting self-scripted films on video, a relatively new technology. But then Nigeria's economy suffered under a painful structural adjustment imposed by the IMF.

Government spending went down, and unemployment went up. Celluloid film became too expensive to produce, forcing film-makers to adopt the video format instead.

One of the first Nollywood directors was Kenneth Nnebue, an electronics dealer who began selling these Yoruba films on video cassettes. Viewers could now watch the films at home on their VCRs instead of going to public cinemas, which had become decrepit and were based in cities that had become too dangerous at night (many cinemas have now been converted to churches).

The ease of shooting on video inspired dozens of film-makers to emulate Nnebue and create films that were made cheaply and quickly, and distributed informally. In the twenty years since Nnebue produced his first film, Nollywood has grown into the third largest film industry in the world in terms of output, churning out three movies every day. It's a money-making business, run largely by fast-buck entrepreneurs without a creative bone in their collective bodies but a strong knowledge of their market. Companies with names like Get-Rich Productions shoot the films in under a week on home-movie budgets before selling them to an unfussy, undis-cerning audience.

Teco's film – a one-man effort – was especially impressive, con-sidering the collaborative requirements of film production. Nigerian cinema, unlike that of Senegal and other francophone countries, has no colonial sponsorship or tutelage. It's purely indigenous, financed by local producers and marketers (including Pentecostal churches), who demand a strong 'Nigerianness' to the storylines. The speed of production and distribution makes it possible for films to cover topical issues while they're still hot. Largely uninterested in accept-ance by global cinema, Nollywood film-makers tap into audiences' aspirations and concerns: domestic strife, sex scandals, marital infi-delity, financial swindling, Christianity, witchcraft. Storylines like these, which guarantee profits, are demanded by the predominantly Igbo marketers who control much of the films' distribution. Teco Benson, however, was part of a minority of film-makers with higher aspirations for the art.

'I had a strong vision about film,' he told me. 'I wanted to be an agent of change for people in the village. They weren't getting proper news, only state newspapers. They cheered their corrupt kinsmen but would stone them if they knew the truth. I have no access to the pulpit or political power, but I can tell the truth through my films.'

Teco gave me copies of his DVDs. They were American-influenced films with dramatic names such as *Blood Diamonds* and *False Alarm*. The cover blurb of *Explosion: Now or Never* read: 'Just out of prison, Steve discovered to his shock that the gang he suffered to protect wiped out his family. Having given his life to Christ, he is left in a dilemma. To revenge the killing, or hand them over to God.'

'Are you into making films about witchcraft?' I asked him.

'No, I'm not so interested in those type of films. I made a witchcraft film called *End of the Wicked*, but I like to explore themes like gangsters, 419 scams [fraudulent letters or emails used to extort money from people] and religion.'

On Teco's desk was a non-fiction book, written by a pastor who claimed that if people dream about sex in their sleep, it is because evil spirits are having sex with them in the night. I hoped he was speaking metaphorically.

'Do you have dream about having sex?' he asked me.

'No,' I replied defensively. Teco warned me against it, and suggested I read the book. I don't know why his religiosity still surprised me – being in the creative arts didn't make a Nigerian any less devout.

Supernatural forces, so strongly rooted in the psyches of some Nigerians, dominate and drive the film plots. The characters' circumstances are often controlled and changed via the spiritual: a mother who disapproves of her daughter's fiancé will cast a spell on

the girl in order to change her romantic choices; a man makes financial gains through ritual sacrifice, then suffers retribution at the hands
of mysterious invisible forces. Guilt, epiphanies and the court of law
rarely feature in any plot line. Character development is an alien
concept.

Yet the films are so popular they're watched across English-
speaking Africa. The once-thriving Ghanaian film industry withered
in the shadows of Nollywood. Our films play on television screens
in Southern Africa and the Caribbean, and Nigerian slang can be
heard in the slums of other African cities.

Nollywood is popular despite its startlingly shoddy production
quality. Convulsive camera work and poor lighting are de rigueur.
Tinny, electronic synthesiser music often drowns out the dialogue,
recorded without a boom mike. The characters speak with a slightly
alien, non-Nigerian vernacular ('For crying out loud!'), sometimes
adopting highly un-Nigerian mannerisms, from insipid laughter to
slow, stilted dialogue. The only exceptions to this rule are anger and
disdain – Nollywood actors always convey those sentiments
convincingly.

I found the poor production standards of these movies even more
entertaining than the plots themselves. One film used exterior shots
of a street in Cape Town – complete with sunshine and palm trees –
to depict 'London, England'. Other directors on constrained budgets see no shame in shooting two different films in the same house
('Hold on, didn't I see that room, that car, in the other film?' Mabel
once exclaimed). Editing discipline is loose; they shoot very long
scenes that do nothing to take the plot forward. No activity is too
mundane. In one film, the central character drives to the market to
purchase some clothes in an eight-minute sequence so dull it was
captivating.

The poor standard of these films embarrasses many Nigerians,
but I'm proud of Nollywood in some ways. It is one of Nigeria's
few indigenous, non-oil industries, and it represents a certain

independence of mind and spirit, while generating jobs for poster designers, distributors, journalists and promoters. Nollywood speaks to its audience and maintains cultural ownership without bending to Western cinematic values. On the other hand, surely there are cinematic rules that shouldn't *ever* be flouted? Aren't scene length and camera angles dictated by innate, universal human responses and aesthetic values? Maybe Nigerian viewers differ from the rest of the world. Perhaps all those electricity blackouts and traffic go-slows have stretched Nigerians' attention spans and raised our tolerance threshold to the point that we're comfortable with poor sound and picture quality, comfortable with interminably long film scenes, and *positively* in favour of supernatural conclusions or any finale involving the comeuppance of women.

Then again, audiences throughout the world seem to find ways of ignoring bad production quality, sieving it out and distilling a film to its basic essence: the human story. Knowing this, the producers of trashy Western soap operas such as *Eastenders* and *Sunset Beach* use it to win the shameless loyalty of some of my most intelligent British friends. Nigerians will watch Nollywood films, no matter how bad, because everyone likes to see their own culture played back to them. Watching ourselves on screen makes for a pleasant change after being bombarded with foreign stories and images.

Some of the superior Nollywood films have begun to appear at small international festivals. Teco showed one of his at an Israeli film festival. A framed newspaper article about the event hung on his wall.

'Did they like the film?' I asked.

'Oh yes, they liked it. They were very encouraging. People came up to me afterwards and congratulated me. They were pleased to see Nigerians making films.'

Things were improving, Teco said. The more sophisticated directors are looking at more esoteric aspects of Nigerian life. The well-known film-maker Aquila Njamah made *After the Vow*, which followed a young couple discovering new aspects of one another's personalities after their wedding. Another of his films, *Widows*, explored the mistreatment of widows in rural areas. Njamah placed quality above quantity, producing movies at a relatively work-shy rate of two per year. His latest, *The Rivals*, had recently won Best International Drama at the New York International Independent Film and Video Festival.

But constant bootlegging may stall Nollywood's artistic evolution. I wondered how our film production could keep improving when profits often vanish into the streets.

'We're trying to stop it,' Teco said. 'I've been speaking to distributors and making agreements with them.' He didn't specify how he hoped to control those bootleggers who offered me DVDs at a tenth of the original price. Their copying machines, shamelessly positioned in the market stalls, churn out numerous DVDs, the sleeves littered with incriminating spelling mistakes and smudgy photos. For a small 'dash', the police look away and conduct raids once or twice a year for show.

The actors and actresses' incomes still don't match their huge fame, and certain celebrity faces must endure the ignominy of riding around town by modest means. 'Hold on, didn't I see her in that film?' Mabel once asked, as a famous actress trundled past on an okada. But money is not the objective. Even a few famous Nigerians, football stars included, have appeared in Nollywood movies.

'You could act in one of my films,' Teco suggested.

'Really?'

'Introducing Noo Saro-Wiwa,' he said, drawing imaginary opening credits with his hands.

Once upon a time I might have laughed at the offer. Now, I swelled with hubris. A fantasy reel spooled through my mind, my metre-long face emoting on a cinema screen. Hollywood meant nothing. Why be a plankton in the ocean when I could be a big fish in an emerging pond? Nollywood now seemed a more dignified enterprise, something I could take seriously. Directors like Teco Benson breathed life into the possibility that it might transcend its amateurism and produce international-standard films one day.

I returned to the streets of Surulere, imagining myself with a copper-coloured hair weave, preparing my Oscar acceptance speech.

A few days later, Mabel and I dragged my heavy bag through Mile Two's sandy streets to a 'motor park', a terminal for minibus taxis destined for all parts of the country. A driver wedged my luggage forcefully between two other suitcases, then flattened it beneath a colossal old TV set before closing the door on all of it with the full thrust of his body weight. Sandwiched between the window and a plump lady, I waved Mabel goodbye as the vehicle pulled out onto the road to Ibadan. I wasn't completely done with Lagos, but, after three weeks in the city, I was worn out. I thought I'd take a deep breath and see the rest of the country before returning here at the end of my journey.

4

Under the Light of Fading Stars

Ibadan

Ibadan. I had always liked the name. It sounded unusual – not Nigerian, not English; almost Arabic. Ibadan was the city where my father attended university. Its name brought back memories of him conversing with his friends; of loud, intellectual gripes that hung in the tobacco clouds above the clink of brandy glasses. Academic books were read as fervently as the Bible back then, a distant era of enlightenment, before the colonial baton of educational progress had been fumbled and dropped.

The Yorubas, Ibadan's dominant ethnic group, were among the first people to mix with European missionaries, and consequently became the most educated Nigerians. Among them was Samuel Ajayi Crowther, born in 1809, the first African bishop and one of the first Nigerians to receive higher education. Yorubas embraced literacy and education, and by the late 1950s, a million of their children were enrolled in primary schools in the south-west. Grammar schools and universities were built, transforming Ibadan into the intellectual heart of Nigeria. The University of Ibadan, where my father studied in the early 1960s, became one of the finest academic establishments in the developing world, a refinery for our newly tapped intellect. We didn't visit Ibadan during our 1988 trip. Too far west, my father said. So I was particularly keen to visit the city now and see where he studied all those years ago.

Ibadan lay three hours north of Lagos on the highway, just beyond shouting distance of Lagos and its residents. It was a smaller, less labyrinthine city, set in gentle hills that elevate it above Lagos's sea-level humidity. The large golden dome of a mosque rose above streets crowded with vendors and markets and more nondescript modernist architecture, much like Lagos. But there was no question I was still in mouthy Yorubaland, where bedfellows bark at each other as if separated by a busy river.

I checked into an ageing hotel perched aloofly on a hill. The receptionist commented on my non-Nigerian 'intonation' and asked me where I was from. When he saw the name Saro-Wiwa on my check-in form, he gushed. I looked nothing like my father, apparently.

'You look like footballer,' he said, glancing down at my trainers.

A porter carried my bags to my room. This was the first time I had stayed in a Nigerian hotel at my own expense. At my price range, I wasn't sure exactly what to expect, although what I found didn't surprise me: an old carpet, a cold shower and a 1980s TV set emitting crackly images of a Nollywood movie. After flopping onto the jelly-springed crater of a bed, I decided to visit the university rather than risk injury to my spine.

I jumped on an okada. During a traffic go-slow near the market, my driver took issue with the driver in front of us for having the temerity to wait three seconds before moving forward with the traffic. To my driver, this had caused an unforgivable delay to our journey. He pulled up alongside the idiot time-waster to give him a piece of his mind with all the diplomacy of a drill sergeant. The pair of them argued, roared and wagged fingers at one another for half a mile, ignoring my screams for them to watch the road. Eventually they went their separate ways, and I was deposited in my usual fluster outside the gates of the University of Ibadan.

Entering its grounds was like stepping into a new dimension: no smog, no noise, no crowds. From the main gate I walked towards the campus buildings down a long quiet road, flanked by smooth lawns and with colourful flowers running along its centre. The university, known as UI, was established by the British in 1948 as an external college of the University of London. Some of Nigeria's most influential people sharpened their minds here: the author Chinua Achebe; the writer and Nobel Prize-winner Wole Soyinka; Jacob Ade Ajayi (one of Africa's best historians), and a stream of lawyers, engineers and doctors. My father gained his English degree here in the early 1960s, just before the college became independent from the University of London.

Education mattered to my father. He *worshipped* the concept. Giving his children a good education, he believed, was the pinnacle of his achievements as a parent, even if he wasn't so good at the everyday displays of affection: on my birthdays he would summon me to his desk to wish me a perfunctory happy birthday, signing my card while I stood and watched. He would stick the card inside an envelope without bothering to seal it, and then hand it over to me, puffing his pipe between unsmiling lips. But when it came to cultivating our minds, we couldn't ask for a more nurturing parent.

Education enabled him to transcend his rural roots. As a ten-year-old boy selling palm wine on the streets of the tiny town of Bori, he won a scholarship to the best local government secondary school, and later enrolled at UI as an undergraduate, then a postgraduate. As one of only two Ogoni students on campus, he encountered what he described as the 'cankerworm' of tribalism. By his reckoning, voters overlooked him in the Student Union elections because he was an ethnic minority. Regardless, he was part of the 'High Table', a mixed group of postgrads who met regularly at the refectory to discuss Nigeria's feared demise. It was the 1960s, and student minds had to focus on dissertations amid the distractions of military coups, a civil war, dawn-to-dusk curfews and tense radio news updates. Yet in spite of the political turbulence, the university maintained academic excellence – an almost enviable inverse of today when standards are sinking in front of a placid backdrop of democracy.

Were my father still alive I'm not sure he would recognise life on campus today. The buildings still looked the same, but the placard erected near the bookshop was undoubtedly a sign of modern times: 'University of Ibadan says: Cultism puts you in bondage. Renounce and denounce it so that you can enjoy your God-given freedom. Cultism is evil and destructive. DO NOT be part of it.'

University cults are a big problem in Nigerian universities. They began as fraternities or 'confraternities', harmless social clubs for male students. At UI in the 1950s, Wole Soyinka was a member of the Pyrates Confraternity, which comprised idealists who wanted to rid UI of its elitism. But by the 1980s, the nature of confraternities had morphed into something more sinister. After the coup of Ibrahim Babangida in 1985, military leaders began supplying the confraternities with weapons to subdue pro-democracy protests by students and university staff.

Around the same time, some of the confraternities were evolving into aggressive cults. They engaged in traditional religious rites and voodoo-type practices, giving themselves names such as the Campus Mafia and Brotherhood of the Blood. Their initiation ceremonies consisted of harsh beatings, the drinking of liquid mixed with blood, or even the raping of female students. But it wasn't only the men who joined them. The Black Brazier, Daughters of Jezebel and other all-women cults germinated in the late 1990s, joining forces with their male counterparts and running prostitution syndicates. The cult members also became academic 'high-fliers': by vandalising lecturers' property or abducting their relatives, they ensured that they received enhanced grades.

When their activities diversified to kidnapping, armed robbery and the murder of rival cult members, universities throughout

Nigeria started a campaign denouncing cultism. They expelled the cults and granted amnesties to students who renounced their membership. But this simply shifted the cults' activities away from campus and onto the streets. The universities also failed to police themselves properly, which eventually led to the return of cultism to the campuses, except that these cults now had off-campus links to the criminal world.

Newspaper reports have alleged that politicians used cults to intimidate their political opponents. And the cults are involved in the kidnapping of foreign oil workers in the oil-rich Niger Delta region. They've fought alongside militant groups such as the Movement for the Emancipation of the Niger Delta (MEND), and even joined these organisations. The cults' influence has extended into government, with some State Assembly members belonging to them. Their power is becoming so extensive – and the networking opportunities so agreeable – that cult membership can further a student's job prospects more than any degree qualification.

My father would be mortified. I carried on walking, past the student halls of residence where lines of laundry hung out to dry on the balconies of grimy, whitewashed buildings leached grey by rain. It had been a while since I was in a place where almost the entire population was educated. I discerned a difference in the way the students carried themselves compared to the vendors who sold them fruits and peanuts from wooden stalls outside the faculty buildings. Their movements were sprightlier, sharper. Perhaps the students were less passive to the mysteries of the world around them now that they understood them better.

In the humanities wing I passed students chatting in a central courtyard and climbed the stairs to the English department where my father once studied. These days, a degree from most Nigerian universities is worth less than a high-school qualification in other parts of the world. Budgets have fallen, standards have fallen, many of the best academics have moved abroad to South Africa, the US and the UK. But is Ibadan still the academic gold standard in West African education?

'Of *course*,' replied one lecturer in the English department head's office. I didn't know if he was being defensive. It would have been rude to probe: they'd kindly given me some of their time; my father was a great man, they told me, and they were honoured to meet me.

Faith Odele, the president of the Student Association, was disgusted by the current state of affairs. 'What is the basis of calling ourselves the best?' she asked. 'Are we living on past glories or are we comparing ourselves with the best today?' She was a quiet, slim girl whose graceful neck held up a pretty face etched with permanent anxiety.

'The curriculum needs to be more relevant to society,' she said, pouring forth on the university's defects. 'The lecturers were more dedicated to work then than they are now. They used to reward excellence, but now people read to pass. They no longer read to know. We turn out graduates that cannot meet with world standards unless they do their own work privately ... I think the teachers stifle creativity. Some lecturers don't allow you to do your own thinking ... the timetable doesn't give you time to do your work. You lose interest when time is squeezed ... they fix lecture times to suit their own personal schedules. It's not easy to plan your time.'

Faith showed me the English department's library. Housed in a room the size of a small classroom, the shelves lining the four walls contained fewer books than I will personally accrue in my lifetime.

'There are recent books that you cannot find in the library,' Faith said.

'How do you get hold of the books you need?'

'We had classes on *The Color Purple* and they told us to write an essay about it ...' Faith paused disdainfully. 'I have not seen the book.'

Lecturers were reduced to photocopying literature and selling it to students. They devoted significant proportions of their time and mental energy trying to supplement their measly incomes. Teaching students is no longer the sole focus when the department struggles even to afford a handful of new books.

'We should make deals with publishers to give us access to books,' Faith said. 'But lecturers don't do that. They're not interested.'

Faith said the lecturers give themselves priority access to the department's sole computer. It has a constant power supply, but only the faculty are allowed to use its Internet twenty-four hours a day. 'They say it's for writing their papers, but *we* need it too,' she complained. However, university life had its positives, Faith insisted. Since attending UI, she had learned how to write poetry, and had quickly outgrown her childlike diffidence and gone on to become student president. 'I didn't know I could be a leader until I came to UI,' she said. 'I saw a need. No one was contesting the election, and I thought, "Do I just leave it to anyone who wants it, or do I make a difference?" I was scared of failure but I decided to conquer that fear.' After graduation, Faith hoped to be a professional poet, writing essays and dramas 'for the people', but she doubted whether living in Nigeria would allow her to realise her dreams.

'It seems that Nigerian writers who make it are from the diaspora. I want to write a book, but I'm scared. Will I be able to publish it? People don't seem to want to read books by Nigerians living in Nigeria. Do I have to travel abroad for people to like my work?' Faith was referring to successful US-based writers such as Chimamanda Adichie and Helon Habila. She cited Kaine Agary's *Yellow-Yellow* as a book that's similar to Adichie's but didn't enjoy the same publicity. 'If Agary had published the book in the US, Nigerians would have taken an interest in it.'

Faith wasn't sure how successful she could be within Nigeria when people can't afford books. Adichie's award-winning *Half of a*

Yellow Sun costs ₦1,500 – half a day's salary for some. 'Because of that the reading culture is poor. People say, "I don't have enough money to eat … you expect me to spend ₦2,000 on a book that I will finish in three days?"' Faith wanted to leave Nigeria to pursue her writing ambitions. Her dream was to take the GRE exams and get a master's degree in the US. Achieving that, however, was a mountainous proposition both financially and in light of academic standards.

In my student days, my plans and ambitions were unfettered by any sense of limitation. I felt able to do anything, travel anywhere, pursue any line of work. Age has reduced my hubris and eroded my optimism to a more realistic level, but Faith appeared to have bypassed all that, and had the anxieties and resignation of someone much older than twenty. Tears collected in her eyes when she told me that a cult member had thrown acid in her sister's face after she refused to date one of his friends.

'Do you want to get married soon?' she asked me out of the blue.

'When the right person comes along,' I told her. 'Do you?'

She looked down at the ground. 'I've not seen an example of marriage that makes me want to settle down. People have so many expectations from other people. We don't know how to manage with what we get. We see Hollywood movies and we expect to get what we see from them. But the reality is hard.'

We strolled along the campus's spacious open-air corridors. The optimism of the 1960s still lingered in its modernist architecture. A bespectacled student called Ifisayo joined us and showed me around their halls of residence, built in 1948 but not expanded to accommodate the country's swelling student population. Two students occupied rooms that had originally been singles, while four people were herded into twins. Ifisayo shared his single room with two others. During the day they stacked their mattresses on top of one another to create breathing space and a chance to sit at his computer.

'Private investors should build student accommodation,' Faith suggested.

The balconies were strewn with laundry lines and old stoves where the students cooked food if their floor lacked a kitchenette. We stared out over the courtyard. Undergraduates were chatting happily, carrying the burden of their financial worries lightly. Nearly all of them spent their spare time raising cash. A few of the girls walked around campus with a triumphant, coquettish bounce in their stride. They're the ones who are flown by politicians and corporate Big Men to Abuja and Lagos to accessorise their parties and provide sexual services. A weekend and a few blow jobs later, these girls return to campus wearing fancy clothes and fresh hair weaves. The majority of students find other ways to raise cash: making beads, baking cakes, selling mobile phone recharge cards, typing and photocopying for colleagues, printing and designing fliers, travelling across the country to beg wealthier relatives to assist them with their ₦50,000 annual tuition fees.

Was it possible to enjoy student life under the circumstances?

'Oh yes,' Faith smiled. 'We don't want to let things take their toll on us.'

'So what do you do for fun?'

'If you come tomorrow we're putting on a dog show on campus.'

I returned to UI the next morning, a dewy, sun-drenched Saturday. The campus reverberated with the sounds of smacked cricket and basketballs, and tae kwon do groups grunting and kicking the air. I was excited about watching a dog show, although I'm not a lover of dogs. I find little charm in their excitability, funky-smelling fur, hot fetid breath, and eyes that glisten with an irritating mawkishness. It's always been a source of personal pride that Nigerians don't love dogs quite the way the English do. Nigerian canines know their place and, thankfully, are emotionally independent. They trot around the margins of society without bothering anyone around them, in refreshing contrast to their Western counterparts who will bound up to any random stranger for a hug, tummy tickle or breathless French kiss.

Learning that Ibadan students were partaking in the dog-loving madness should have disappointed me, but after the previous day's tour of the university's decline, I needed confirmation that the apocalypse was at arm's length.

For several years now, the university's veterinary students have held a dog show at the end of each academic year, sponsored by a dog food company. They had ring-fenced a section of the playing fields with a line of colourful triangular flags. At the registration desk I met the lead organiser, a fresh-faced student called Oyelami Oyetunde.

'Ken Saro-Wiwa was my idol at school,' he told me. He said he enjoyed reading *Mr. B Goes to Lagos*, one of my father's children's books. It was heartening to know that someone as young as him knew who my father was.

'What do you think of UI?' Oyelami asked.

'I like it,' I replied. 'It's nice to see everyone carry on as normal despite the financial hardship.'

'Well, we have to.' Oyelami smiled.

All the students looked like they were having fun. The hip-hop song 'Who Let the Dogs Out' thundered out of loud speakers, followed by D'banj's ubiquitous 'Booty Call' – I must have heard that song at least five times a day on my trip so far. A student danced to it, shaking his arse in front of a female friend who looked on in mock disdain. As their classmates play-fought one another and giggled endlessly, a boy of around seven wandered among them carrying a tray of peanuts on his head. He was so much younger than the students, yet comparatively sombre in demeanour, his instinct for horseplay overridden by his need to earn a living. For him, Saturday was just an ordinary workday.

Nearly two hours after the show was scheduled to begin, competitors began arriving with their dogs at the registration desk. A particularly vicious pit bull, which had lunged violently at a student earlier on, paced around the gated verandah of a nearby building. Thankfully, it was kept on a chain leash.

On the edge of the field, a muscular man with 'Prosperity' tattooed on his shoulder swaggered about with his large alter-ego of a bull mastiff. I realised then that nearly all the dogs entered in the competition were either rottweilers, pit bull terriers, Alsatians or mastiffs, many of which were tethered by metal chain leashes; there were very few toy breeds about.

'Why are all the dogs aggressive breeds?' I asked Tobi Opanuga, the dark, stocky event coordinator.

'I don't know. I think maybe rottweilers and Alsatians are cheaper,' he suggested as the animals growled at each other and salivated menacingly. The white pit bull lunged at someone for a second time near the pyramid of canned dog food.

'Please, take your dogs back,' a student organiser advised.

'I'm not comfortable with that,' said a buck-toothed girl, nervously eyeing the dog.

'Just relax!' her colleague told her with a carefree giggle.

At the registration desk, the organisers recorded the dogs' weight. They did this by first weighing the owner on a set of bathroom scales, then asking the owners to cradle their pets and recording their combined weights. One student crouched cheekily on all fours while his classmates tied a pink ribbon around his neck and lifted him onto the scales. Their fun was disrupted when the mastiff lunged at the pit bull. It put everyone on edge. We eyed the pit bull anxiously as its owner muzzled its white face and held it on the scales. Then a massive Alsatian jerked its head under the registration desk, prompting two girls to scoop up their chairs in panic and step back, tittering nervously.

A crowd of about 500 spectators gathered behind the cordon

lines in the sports field. The music stopped playing, and the MC (one of the veterinary students) asked everyone to pray before the competition began. During the initial confirmation stage, each owner brought their dog to the judges' table to be inspected for pedigree and appearance. I expected the dogs to adopt the fastidious positioning I'd seen at dog shows in Britain, their heads held at a regal angle and their hind legs stretched backwards. But, true to Nigerian tradition, the dogs weren't trained to stand still, let alone pose, which made an entertaining change from the exactitudes of the UK Kennel Club.

The first dog, a boar bull called Razor, casually urinated during her inspection. Thoroughly amused, the crowd cheered as she and her owner paraded past them afterwards. Razor was followed by a pit bull terrier that I'd seen fighting with one of the Alsatians earlier. The extremely po-faced owner of three fat rottweilers brought his dogs up for inspection, one by one. A more serious dog handler, he had trained his pets well: each of them stood still for several seconds in the correct pose. But as the man walked his trio around the field, one of them, a mean-looking mutt called Tom Cruise, broke free from his leash and ran towards the crowd. Two dozen people turned and fled towards the cricket pavilion.

'I beg, don't run, o!' the MC implored down the mike. 'The dog will pursue you if you run!'

Thankfully, Tom Cruise's owner caught up and brought him to heel before he could 'mingle' with the crowd. After the rottweilers, a long-tailed American pit bull completed his corpulent trot in front of the audience before the MC introduced the first Alsatian.

'These are known as "police dogs" in Africa,' he said. 'If you've been to Heathrow or Gatwick Airports, you'll know they use these dogs to sniff Nigerians.' Wry laughter rippled through the crowd. People were familiar with the humiliating drug inspection at British airports.

'This dog is very clean, cleaner than most of you,' the MC joked, announcing a small terrier. 'This dog baths every day . . . more than those of you who don't have running water in your house!'

Two orange-coated mastiffs paraded around the field, followed by a small shitsu, which had the crowd cooing in admiration. 'It's *so* cute,' a disembodied voice sighed from behind me. Cute? This wasn't the Nigeria I knew.

'People in Ibadan are getting crazy about dogs,' Tobi enthused. 'Many of them have never seen these breeds before.' He theorised that this dog-loving was down to the American and British films and TV shows on satellite television. All around me I witnessed people indulging this strange obsession: a professional dog breeder handed out fliers and let spectators peruse his *Dog World* magazine while he informed a friend that 'dogs are not used as a method of security in Ibadan banks'; three young children pored over a veterinary lecturer's copy of the *Encyclopaedia of Dog Breeds*. And over to one side, a small crowd jostled to stroke a tiny Alsatian puppy on offer as first prize in the raffle.

After the interlude, the organisers resumed the proceedings by announcing the discipline segment of the competition. Everyone quietened down. We watched the white pit bull with a curly tail jump through a rubber tyre held by its owner.

'Audience, what do you think of this dog?' asked the MC. The audience had been granted a 40 per cent share of the vote in this section of the show.

'Yeeesss!' everyone cheered.

A man entered the field with a tiny terrier. He tossed a ball for the dog to fetch, but the miniscule animal couldn't retrieve it because the ball was too big for its mouth. For a full minute, the dog tensed its legs and ground its little face against the ball, struggling to wrap its jaws around it. The crowd fell into a concentrated silence and willed the terrier on. Its owner swallowed with anxiety. Finally, the terrier succeeded, and scuttled towards its owner with the ball in its mouth. The crowd roared in congratulation.

Next up was the aggressive pit bull, which held up its paw for an uncharacteristically friendly 'handshake'. A friend of its owner then baited it with a stick and ran towards the crowd. The owner let go of the leash and allowed the dog to chase his friend. The snarling beast sprinted towards my section of the crowd near the judges' table. I mentally prepared myself to dive behind someone. Others stood, tense, ready to flee. But seconds before the pit bull ploughed into us, its owner suddenly commanded it to stop. It did. Nobody was impressed. The crowd, shaken and disapproving, remained silent, unable to muster even the laughter of sweet relief.

'Audience, what do you think?' asked the MC. We responded with a smattering of uncomfortable applause.

Afterwards, spectators were invited to photograph the dogs in the centre of the field while the judges deliberated on the results. In the end, they declared Samurai, the long-tailed pit bull terrier, to be the best dog in show. I walked off the field, back to my hotel, while the crowd poured onto the field to mingle with the dogs. As they stroked the animals and snapped their cameras, I envisaged a Nigeria where dogs were widely affordable, pet food was a billion-dollar industry, and people took their animals on leisurely strolls without fear of being hit by okadas or stumbling into the ubiquitous open sewage drains. I hoped the country would become like that one day.

For now, though, this dog show was good enough. It was the Nigeria I wished I'd seen in my teens, scenes of normality that poured sugar on the bitterness of military dictatorships and made the country seem a more sane place.

5

Transwonderland

Ibadan

As a child, amusement parks symbolised everything that I liked about the West. My desire to spend holidays in the US centred around fantasies of a Disney-esque promised land that was lustrous, modern, kitsch and fun. Artifice impressed me a lot. I favoured rank hot dogs over tasty plantain, the smoothness of a plastic toy over the soft frond of a palm tree, the garish green of Kermit the Frog over the brilliant white of an egret. Creating these fake textures and colours – transcending nature – seemed the ultimate achievement. And Nigeria was distinctly lacking in this.

I'd long outgrown such thinking, but I still had a residual urge for Nigeria to 'achieve' and be a place that people admired and want to visit; a credible tourist destination. So when Ibadan's Transwonderland Amusement Park was described by one of my outdated guidebooks as 'the closest thing Nigeria has to Disney World', I knew I had to pay it a visit. I was intrigued. My perceptions of Nigeria had never really accommodated the concept of amusement park rides – our downtime usually involves sitting sedately on white plastic chairs, eating food and dancing a little; I couldn't quite envisage Nigerians screaming goggle-eyed in giant spinning teacups or roller coasters.

My arrival at Transwonderland's entrance vindicated those

preconceptions. In the car park a marquee was filled with dozens of well-dressed men and women sitting on white plastic chairs and chatting among mounds of jollof rice, a rice dish cooked in tomato sauce, with onions, vegetables and meat. Loud Nigerian pop music pounded the air and mingled with the screams of children who chased each other between the tables. This wedding reception wasn't quite the kind of 'amusement' I was hoping for, but it appeared to be all the action I was going to get, since its vivacity contrasted sharply with Transwonderland itself.

Stepping through the turnstile, I was confronted with a forlorn landscape of motionless machinery. Rides including the 'Chair-o-Plane', 'The Dragon' roller coaster, dodgem cars, a Ferris wheel and merry-go-round stood rusting amid the tall grass. Only the tumbleweed was missing. A handful of people walked around the decrepit park, surveying the desolation. One of them, a quiet skinny man, approached me and asked if I wanted to go on any of the rides. Was he being serious? None of them appeared to be working.

'They are working,' the man assured me. He led me to the Ferris wheel and ushered me into a seat stained with solidified bird shit. He switched on a button, and the wheel slowly groaned into motion, lifting me high into the air. Ibadan's small buildings undulated in all directions towards the horizon. A small crowd, including a middle-class couple and a trio of street kids in torn clothes, gathered on the ground below to watch me. Sitting alone on the empty ride made me feel self-conscious. Should I smile or look serious? I couldn't decide. Smiling would make me look a little foolish and deranged, but keeping a straight face made me look inappropriately solemn, if not *more* foolish and deranged. I think I settled for an embarrassed grimace.

Next, I asked the man to switch on the Chair-o-Plane, a ride containing spinning metal spokes with chairs attached to the ends that swung through the air in a circular motion, as if flying. Again, the same small crowd migrated below and craned their necks to watch me. This time I couldn't help but smile as my chair swooped down towards the ground, my legs dangling dangerously close to the metal fencing on the ground. I saw flashes of the street boys' big, crooked teeth grinning up at me.

The boys seemed eager to have a go, so I bought them tickets for The Dragon, a relatively gentle roller-coaster ride. I was surprised to see the middle-class couple hop on too. We lowered the metallic safety bars across our laps and waited for the man to press the start button. The carriage started with an ominous creek. My distrust for Nigerian machine maintenance, combined with my love of danger, was a thrilling combination – roller coasters are no fun if one feels 100 per cent safe. The Dragon ride wasn't particularly high, fast or convoluted, but it was exciting. We screamed as the rusting carriages rattled and plunged precariously along the ageing tracks. Each sideways jerk offered the tantalising possibility of catastrophe, but before my stomach had a chance to turn, the man brought it all to an end. Dismounting, the boys smiled and crouched to touch the ground, a local, traditional show of thanks.

The dodgem cars didn't interest me. I paid for the three boys to have a go, while I watched from the sidelines. The manager of the ride was a tall Muslim man who seemed oblivious to the pleasurable aspect of these rides. He directed the movement of the cars as if he were a policeman on traffic duty. Draped in a long blue djellaba, he barked impatient instructions to the drivers: 'Reverse! ... Turn ... Turn around!' When one boy failed to extricate himself from a jam with two other cars, the manager mocked the boy's intelligence with a cantankerous tap of his own forehead. Cowering beneath this taskmaster's gaze, the boys drove the cars studiously and unsmilingly, flashing each other glares of quiet outrage whenever they collided. Because the old, overhead electric netting gaped with holes, the cars stopped moving whenever their aerials strayed into these openings. As the manager repeatedly stepped onto the platform to push the cars along, I wondered why nothing ever lasts in Nigeria, and how

institutions like Transwonderland kept going long after their economic viability had expired, like twitching corpses that refuse to die.
The amusement park must have prolonged its wretched existence
through the life-support of slave wages, power conservation and
minimal maintenance.

The park had no facilities for emptying my bladder or filling my
stomach, so I decided to leave. Towards the car park, next to the
gates, I noticed a plaque that read: TRANSWONDERLAND NIGERIA
LTD. THIS ULTRA-MODERN TRANSWONDERLAND AMUSEMENT PARK
WAS COMMISSIONED BY MRS. MIRIAM BABANGIDA, NIGERIA'S FIRST
LADY, ON 21ST DECEMBER 1989. Right in front of the plaque, a
group of men were hand-washing clown costumes, making an
unwitting mockery of the plaque's pretensions. Babangida was a
comic Roman emperor too inept to provide for his people, yet
equally incapable of offering them a long-lasting distraction from
their poverty. And so the Transwonderland Amusement Park stood
there, rusting and waiting to be gobbled up and strangled by the
long grass of economic stagnancy. My childhood dreams of a
modern, artificial Nigeria were stalled for the time being. But the
key was not to rely on guidebooks written four years previously;
change happens quickly here. Somewhere in the country, another
amusement park will no doubt have been built.

I walked into the car park, aware of the sound of footsteps shuffling behind me. When I turned around, the three boys and two
more of their friends were holding out their hands for food, or at
least money to buy some. For the first time I noticed how bony
their limbs were. Somehow the amusement rides had distracted me
(and perhaps them, too) from their penury. Rooting around in my
wallet, I realised I only had enough money for an okada ride back
to my hotel – all my spare cash had gone on treating these kids to
rides that churned their empty stomachs. Now *I* felt like a Mrs
Babangida, the empress with confused priorities. How could I
explain my situation to the boys? They spoke no English. All I could

do was apologetically give them my last ₦20 note, then rush to mediate as the five of them squabbled over the cash.

Stiff with guilt, I mounted an okada and asked to be taken to my hotel. As the bike sped off, the boys watched me, confused about why they deserved a ride on the dodgem cars but not a plate of rice.

The next morning, wobbly with sleepiness, I took an okada to one of Ibadan's main motor parks. Dozens of inter-city minibuses were lined up in rows, waiting for passengers. The merry-go-round of informal trading whirled about me: the man selling matchsticks to the woman who sells bananas to the person who sells candles to the matchstick seller, and so forth. Untaxed, unsupported with bank loans, unable to expand, this virtual bartering system – the lifeblood of the Nigerian economy – pins down the uneducated but ambitious trader. How they survive was a mystery to me. I imagined all their profits being swallowed up by the bus fare at day's end.

I sat in the front seat of a vehicle bound for Osogbo, three hours north of Ibadan, to see a sacred shrine there – a Yoruba religious site that is a UNESCO World Heritage Site and one of Nigeria's main attractions. After the inglorious kitsch of Transwonderland, I was curious – and hopeful – about how Nigeria presented its more authentic sights. I glowed with the satisfaction of being the first passenger on board, and thus able to pick the best seat. Before long, a man dressed in a neat blue shirt and navy trousers sat down beside me and began a stressed phone conversation in fluent Italian.

'How come you speak Italian so well?' I asked after he'd hung up.

'I live there,' he explained. 'I came to Nigeria to visit my family, but now I cannot get a visa again to enter Italy. I was telling my boss I will not be at work this week.'

The man told me that he'd flown back to Nigeria via various European airports. He'd been endlessly questioned by Italian and Spanish visa officials who decided, after leafing suspiciously through his passport, not to grant him re-entry to Europe. Tension bulged behind his bloodshot eyes. The stress of his predicament had taken him close to depression, and my simple question unleashed a torrent of manic storytelling.

His name was Michael, and he was a graphic designer who had grown tired of grafting for nothing in Nigeria and had chosen to migrate to Europe illegally. In 2005, he and a dozen other people squeezed into a truck bound for Libya. The journey across the Sahara lasted a week. Michael and his co-passengers huddled inside the vehicle like jarred pickles, grinding their teeth against invasive grains of sand by day and shivering by cloudless night.

'Was the journey hot?' I asked him. Stupid question. I was externalising my obsession with uncomfortable heat. Michael screwed up his face, kissed his teeth and eyeballed me with a wordless, almost comical, intensity. He and his fellow passengers rationed one vat of water, he said, which amounted to around one litre per person – tiny, disciplined sips, spread out over seven long, parched, bone-jarring days. Once the migrants reached Libya, they piled into a prearranged boat and sailed across the Mediterranean towards Italy's porous coastline.

'The coastguards caught us,' Michael said. 'They took us to refugee camps. I call them concentration camps. They are not refugee camps, they are *concentration* camps. You have guards who let you in and out ... they are concentration camps! They sent me back to Libya. I tried to return to Nigeria but my money it finished. I was trapped in Niger for four months. I had no job, no money. I was walking in the street, begging like a Hausa man!' he hollered.

With the passing generosities of a thousand strangers, Michael gathered enough money to make a repeat attempt. This time, he took with him 4 litres of his own water and joined twenty other people in a Land Cruiser, riding the Saharan sand dunes towards Libya and its Mediterranean coast. They made it to Italy, landing at night on the empty shores of Crotone province, not a coastguard in sight.

'The sky is the limit,' Michael told me, pointing a finger upwards in triumph. 'No ... the sky is the *start* of the journey!'

It was an ignominious start. Local children threw stones and spat at him as he walked the streets of southern Italy. He migrated further north where he obtained refugee status by pretending to be a Sierra Leonean fleeing war. The fighting had actually ended in Sierra Leone, but the 'foolish' immigration officials weren't aware of that. In time, Michael bought a fake Italian passport and found a job picking tomatoes alongside Romanian and Bulgarian girls. Eastern Bloc migrants were streaming into the country, he said, and they were driving wages down for people like him. Now he was working in a farm factory and living in a small apartment, which he shared with other immigrants.

'Do Italians like Africans?' I asked.

'They hate Nigerians more than anyone else.' That didn't surprise me. Nigerians have a special talent for landing in people's bad books all around the world. We're louder, brasher, more noticeable than other Africans, who seem mild and timid in comparison.

'Africans from French-speaking countries, they are cowards,' Michael sneered. 'The French colonised them and taught them to become French. But the British came to Nigeria and just wanted to make their money. They left us alone. They said, "Go do your own thing." Nigerians are not scared of anyone. We push to succeed ... we are *making* it.'

'Maybe', I tentatively suggested, 'the Italians don't like us because we've got a reputation for doing illegal things – like forging immigration documents?'

'They are hypocrites!' Michael exploded, extending his fury to the West in general. 'They came to Africa without anybody's permission. Mungo Park, Lord Lugard ... did they ask us if they could enter here? No!' I laughed in partial agreement. Park was a nineteenth-century Scotsman who explored the Niger River. Lord Lugard had been Nigeria's governor-general during the First World War. I couldn't help but admire Michael's energetic sense of entitlement and determination. Through his migration he had gained a lot of skills and life experiences, too: he could speak Italian, Yoruba and English, and had worked on farms and factories. He had overcome deserts, destitution, a language barrier and humiliating stonings on his journey into a different sort of 'heart of darkness'. Except that today he was judged not by the skill and tenacity of his activities but by their legality. The Mungo Parks of the world, by contrast, were judged by their fortitude and adventurousness. And their intentions were just as self-serving, their legacy just as ambiguous as Michael's.

Michael was a product of Nigeria's densely populated poverty, which is so desperate and competitive it cultivates an energetic drive that spills across our borders to the rest of the world.

'Is life better for you in Italy or—'

'Italy,' he retorted. 'I make money, I'm taking care of my family . . . I can travel back here for holidays. One day I will be able to return to Nigeria and build a house.'

'How much longer do you want to stay there?' The suggestion that his plans could be restricted by a timeframe brought on a huffy, theatrical glower.

'I will go when I *want* to go. If I want to stay five, six, seven, nine years, I will *stay*!'

We reached Osogbo surprisingly quickly: Michael's captivating chatter made the journey feel a lot shorter. Reluctantly, I cut short the conversation and said goodbye to him. I disembarked from the minibus and took an okada to the Osun-Osogbo Sacred Grove. Getting there wasn't without the expected hassles. I couldn't speak a word of Yoruba, and the first two okada men whom I flagged down spoke no English, mistaking 'sacred' for 'secretariat'. After two infuriating round trips to the local government office, a third man finally brought me to the Grove.

The 600-year-old Sacred Grove is one of the last existing forest shrines of the Yoruba religion. It contains the shrine of the Yoruba river goddess, Osun, founder of Osogbo and bringer of fertility to barren women. The entire grove was devoted to worshipping the pantheon of Yoruba gods. Set in 27 peaceful hectares of virgin forest, its tranquillity immediately drained my body of all its urban tensions.

The ground was dappled with the shadows of swaying foliage. I walked through trees that rustled furtively with white-throated monkeys and small antelopes – animals the Yoruba people regard as embodiments of Osun. Lining the pathway were dozens of abstract, humanoid sculptures with facial tribal markings, in different shapes and sizes. Art and nature were sublimely intertwined.

Sacred groves like Osogbo were once a central and ubiquitous part of Yoruba life. These holy places were reserved for religious purposes. By the 1950s, the groves were overrun by urban development and disparaged as 'black magic' by the locals who had converted to Islam in the early nineteenth century, or Christianity under British rule.

It took the exotic passions of an Austrian artist to resurrect the Osun–Osogbo Sacred Grove in the 1960s. Suzanne Wenger had visited Nigeria in 1950 and fallen in love with Yoruba culture. She met a high priest who initiated her into the Yoruba religion, according to which each person is destined to be unified in spirit with Olorun, the divine creator. The world is divided into the physical realm and the spiritual realm, with every individual striving to reach Orun Rere (the 'good' heaven), as opposed to Orun Apadi (the realm of the forsaken). Spiritual growth, involving meditation and the veneration of the gods, is the key to reaching Orun Rere. Life and death are stages along the path to heaven.

Though the Yoruba high priest spoke no English and Wenger spoke no Yoruba, they communicated through the 'language of the trees', she once said in an interview. Wenger, who always lamented the West's indifference towards the spirit world, was dismayed at the neglect of Yoruba traditions. The number of traditional priests was dwindling, looters were targeting the shrines' antiquities, and people had begun fishing in the Osun River and hunting the grove's animals. On top of this, the colonial Department of Forestry and Agriculture began clearing areas of the grove for agricultural experiments. Wenger went on to become an *olorisha* (high priestess), and dedicated her life to resurrecting the Osogbo shrine.

She and several Yoruba artists set up the New Sacred Art group. Together they crafted dozens of sculptures of varying sizes, each effigy depicting one of the many anthropomorphic Yoruba gods. According to the religion, there is one super god, Olorun, and several lesser gods (*orishas*), such as Ogun, the fearsome god of war and retribution, Eshu, the trickster god, Shango, the god of thunder, Obatala, the god who forms the human body, and Shokpona, the god of smallpox.

According to legend, a local *oba* (king) called Larooye was building a new settlement in the area. One of his men cut down a tree that fell in the river. The river goddess Osun complained that it had broken one of her pots. Larooye apologised to her, and Osun advised him and his people to move further away from the river to avoid annual floods, which they did. Wanting to appease Osun, Larooye later returned to the river where the pots were smashed, and made sacrifices to the goddess. To this day, the people of Oshogbo have made annual sacrifices to Osun at the river in order to receive her protection and fertility blessings.

Suzanne Wenger's sculptures represent Osun and many other gods. All around me, I saw small figurines nestled in the undergrowth. A bug-eyed mother cradled her baby; another very small, squat effigy of an unidentified god sat on some rocks by the Osun River, which twisted and meandered listlessly through the trees, its creaseless surface gently disturbed by a snake.

Walking deeper into the forest, I came across grander, towering statues. In a small clearing among the trees, a slender, insect-like figure stood 6 metres high, with long grasshopper arms raised to the sky as if imploring the gods. This was the effigy of Obaluaye, a messenger of Osun. Beneath Obaluaye were the entwined, root-like bodies of several figures, apparently bent over in supplication. The curvy figure shone brilliantly in the sunlight, a larger version of the traditional sculptures of Yoruba shrines, which were fashioned from wood. Many of Wenger's sculptures were a product of artistic licence, modern behemoths made from a mix of iron, mud and cement – heavy materials that would deter the theft of the sculptures. Nearby, the huge statue of Lyamaro, another messenger of Osun, spread its numerous straight arms and legs like octopus tentacles towards the ground. Local people bring food to these orisha effigies and pour alcohol on them, asking for blessings.

The sculptures were ageing, unkempt and fading, but this had the effect of blending them into the surrounding forest colours. Although based on traditional African abstract design, they also bore Wenger's distinct artistic style. Apparently, such fluid interpretation is acceptable because the Yoruba religion is based on oral tradition, the mythology varying from town to town.

During the annual week-long Osun Festival in August, Yoruba society throws off its Muslim and Christian top layers and congregates at the shrine to worship the goddess and ask for her blessings. Men, women and children converge here in their thousands, bathing in the river and praying for fertility, respite from malaria, or money to pay next month's rent. A virgin carries a symbolic presence of the river goddess inside a calabash. To affirm the connection between the people and Osun, the girl carries the calabash to Osun's shrine, a Gaudi-esque thatched-roof building supported by wood-carved columns. Inside it is a sacred stone stool, on which Larooye is said to have first sat. Food is tossed into the river as an offering to the goddess. The crowds follow the virgin girl en masse, their faces contorted in prayer.

But nothing is too sacred to entrepreneurs. Soft drinks companies circle the festival crowds like mosquitoes, telling people that the gods will bless those who use their beverages for libation rituals. And the Sacred Grove itself is being buffeted by both the indifference of capitalism and bad government: in recent decades the authorities illegally sold off portions of it to property developers, who chopped down trees and dislodged some of the sculptures during construction. Trees were also sacrificed when a paved road was laid down through the forest, inching the Grove closer to extinction.

Wenger herself was disgusted by the state of affairs. By the time she died in 2009, she was furious at the condition of the Sacred Grove and its sculptures, which were decaying as relentlessly as Ibadan's Transwonderland Amusement Park. Maintaining a site like this under today's circumstances requires a certain assiduousness, of which Wenger had plenty in her younger decades. So intense was her passion for Yoruba culture, she even prevented her children (whom she adopted locally) from receiving a Western-style education for fear of contmabelting their spiritual purity. 'Neo-Tarzanism' is how Wole Soyinka once described this foreign reverence for our past traditions. Some of those children, now grown adults, remain illiterate to this day. As literacy and modern education tend to erode traditional religious practices, Wenger believed that keeping her children 'native' was the only true way of sustaining the Yoruba religion. In her mind, modernity and tradition were two immiscible concepts, the former compromising the latter.

I understood Wenger's concerns. My foreign upbringing and education had diluted my cultural identity. Yet it had also given me certain advantages that Wenger herself enjoyed too – her education and worldliness had given her the wherewithal to travel to Nigeria in the first place and revive the Yoruba cult. Was westernisation the Sacred Grove's nemesis or saviour? I couldn't decide. Anyway, the peace and tranquillity the grove exuded was nourishing enough for me. I just hoped that the water would keep flowing, the trees would keep rustling, and the animals would continue living among it all.

6

In the Chop House

Abuja

I first visited Abuja in 1988. My father, in the city on business, deposited us in a hotel, and ordered us to write essays about Abuja while he was at work. Idle hands were the devil's hands, he said. But how could I describe emptiness? I managed 300 words of half-hearted gibberish about the numerous construction cranes and the mosque's shiny golden dome, which sparkled in the vista from our hotel window. But that was it. I couldn't articulate the sense of inauthenticity and fabrication, the 1970s architecture, the blandness of the street names plucked by town planners from an encyclopae-dia and inspired by every African leader, capital city or river in the world: Amazon Street, Mandela Street. Danube had been given the Africanised pronunciation 'Da-noo-bey'.

Abuja was the type of city I dreamed about during my school holidays in Port Harcourt. Back then, after the electricity blackout interrupted the movie we were watching, Zina, Tedum and I would take to our beds with a flop and a moan, and fantasise about how Nigeria *ought* to be. As children, we believed that fixing a country's aesthetic was all that was required for it to become orderly and suc-cessful. We mentally drew up clean streets and fancy shopping malls, populated by smartly dressed people who had been taught how to wear good make-up (Zina's main objective), frequented fancy sweet shops (my personal goal) and drove plush cars (Tedum's ultimate vision).

That fantasy of Abuja as an upmarket urban paradise had been partially realised. I flew to the city, emerging from the plane into the fresh whiteness of its domestic airport. It was like a dream. Large windows revealed the shafts of modern architectural beams outside. The interior's relative newness and cleanliness was uncompromised by hawkers or 1970s-fonted wall signs or disoriented wildlife; the smell of neglect was absent. I struggled to stay awake as the taxi cruised along the pristine highway, its immaculate centre lined with trees that continued for several miles with stupefying monotony, like the background landscape of a Formula 1 computer game. But as the streets rolled by, I found its featurelessness a relaxing antidote to my usual anxiety when arriving in a new place. I felt even more at ease knowing that I would be staying with my brother.

Abuja was a relatively new metropolis and the cleanest, most orderly one in Nigeria. In the late 1970s, the government anointed it as the new capital city, stripping this status from the incorrigible, Yoruba-dominated Lagos, and moving it to a central region not overrun by any of our three biggest ethnic groups. And so today the local cars' number plates carry the motto 'Centre of Unity', which describes Abuja perfectly, since the city seems to have united Nigerians in the view that it's the dullest place on earth.

'God forbid I spend Christmas in Abuja,' Mabel had declared when considering whether to visit her brother during the previous year's holidays. In her eyes, the city had no soul, no organic flavour. I could see what she meant. Abuja's fundamental character hadn't changed in the eighteen years since I was last here, when it was nothing but a network of empty highways and big hotels pleading for humanity to breathe life into them.

As I toured the city by car that day, on my way to my brother's house, it still seemed like a work in progress, although it has begun to grow into its big-city pretensions. The traffic-free highways coursed past shopping malls and cuboid buildings made of reflective glass that gleamed with passé futurism. There were no indecently exposed sewage drains and, following a government ban, not an okada in sight. Nigerians and expats jogged or walked their dogs along real sidewalks in the cool, smog-free mornings; a flat TV screen broadcast commercials from a street corner. Islamic, calm, rich, tidy: Abuja was the opposite of my home town of Port Harcourt. I felt an outsider. In an unexpected show of civic pride, my taxi driver even ordered me to both fasten my seatbelt and desist from throwing my orange peel out of the window.

Reminders of the real Nigeria were everywhere: certain motorists still converted the pavements into extra lanes, or sounded their horns impatiently if the cars in front hadn't moved within two seconds of the lights going green; nomadic Fulani farmers still herded their cattle along the sides of the roads. For the most part, however, Abuja exuded cleanliness and dreary order, populated by transitory government ministers and civil servants, who often prefer to keep their hearts and families in the bedlam of Lagos, where the real partying is done.

It's ironic that this city – a place that confounds Nigeria's reputation as a hotbed of chaos and dysfunction – is partly funded by the very corruption that created that reputation. After siphoning Nigeria's assets, politicians and other thieves bring the loot to Abuja, where they've created a panorama of semi-laundered splendour – a world-class stadium, the manicured Millennium Park, the elegant golden dome of the National Mosque, the huge church, the world-class IBB Golf Course and millionaire mansions with giant model aeroplanes playfully attached to their rooftops.

But a strong conservative undercurrent yanks constantly at Abuja's ambitions for world-class status. The city is the gateway to the Islamic north of the country, where men dominate public life

and women operate less noisily behind life's curtains. The Miss
World beauty contest, hosted here in 1999, was abandoned after
Islamic youths protested violently against the perceived debauchery
of the pageant. A few years later, the city was accused of lagging
behind the times, losing its bid to host the 2014 Commonwealth
Games because of the government's intolerance towards homo-
sexuality. Try as it might, Abuja hasn't quite reached that ever-shifting
benchmark of 'modernity'.

Next morning, I luxuriated on my brother's sofa, savouring the
novelty of cable TV and a well-stocked fridge – such simple pleas-
ures were rarely available during those ascetic holidays with my
father. I was staying with my eldest brother Ken, or 'Junior' as we
call him. He worked as an assistant adviser to the president on environmental affairs, and was currently compiling a report on the
double threat faced by Nigeria's environment: rising sea levels
threaten to submerge our coastal cities, while the swelling Sahara is
gradually snuffing out the vegetation and lakes in the north as sand-
storms dump sand across people's farms. The felling of trees for
firewood is speeding up desertification even more, allowing sand
dunes to push people further south, chasing them towards the eye
of a land-shortage storm.

Junior had lived in Abuja for a couple of years, shuttling back and
forth between there and his family in London. Working for the
government was for him the culmination of years spent reintegrat-
ing into Nigerian life after the death of our father. He'd grown up
in England since he was nine years old, and had been heading
towards a career as a sports journalist before circumstances elbowed
him off his chosen life path. Aged twenty-seven, he took control of
the small family businesses in Port Harcourt before being offered a
government job in 2007 as part of the new democratic government's
reconciliation process.

I saw him regularly in England, but this was the first time I had observed him in his Nigerian habitat. The transformation was intriguing. Once upon a time in London, he was known as Mr Public Transport due to his encyclopaedic knowledge of the city's bus system. Now he travelled around Abuja in the back seat of a car, and I nearly laughed when I heard his maid address him as 'sir' after he'd ordered her (in a slightly Nigerianised accent) to wash his shirts. Siblings often retain old conceptions of one another, unaware of each other's full maturation: my brother was now an *oga*, complete with minions and authority and responsibilities; a more laid-back incarnation of our father.

Junior had built a wide network of friends in Nigeria, including Nini, a girl I went to school with in England. She now worked in government too, and dropped by for a visit later that day. We hadn't seen each other in two decades, when I was eleven years old and she was a seemingly adult fifteen. Back then, Nini was unusually popular with both younger students *and* older ones, blessed with a charm that was impossible to deconstruct or emulate. More than anything, I remembered her as an extremely fast runner, an Olympic champion in the making who at fifteen was already sprinting 100 metres in 12.3 seconds. Nike saw her potential and gave her free running shoes for training sessions with a top athletics coach. It was all going so well.

Then her father suddenly withdrew her from school and sent her back to Nigeria. Her fate was many a diaspora child's worst nightmare, a punishment my father routinely threatened whenever I was naughty.

'I didn't want to be in Nigeria,' Nini said. 'I was *so* upset. I fell ill . . . they put me on a drip.' She finished her education in Nigeria, attending the University of Benin where she continued to run competitively. By her early twenties she was clocking 11.4 seconds in the 100m, often beating her training mate who went on to compete at the Olympics.

'But my parents didn't want me to be an athlete,' Nini said.

'Were they scared you wouldn't earn enough money?' I asked.

'No, they're just conservative. Many Nigerian parents are. They don't want you to go into music or sports or anything like that. My brother wanted to go into the music industry but they weren't happy about it.'

Now in her mid-thirties, Nini hadn't lost any of the magnetism that so bedazzled everyone at school. Giving birth to her four children hadn't diminished her speed either: she had recently raced a male friend for a bet, and won. But instead of being a world-class champion athlete, her pockets bulging with endorsement dollars, Nini was working in the foreign service at the Nigerian vice-president's office, known locally as 'Villa'. Her husband, having finished his master's degree in law at a Scottish university, was searching for work in a city where personal connections count more than professional qualifications. Nini was the family's temporary breadwinner, stretching her salary to cover their children's school fees.

'In my village they think I'm evil because I'm working in Villa and not giving them millions,' she smiled ruefully. Although Nini's experience of leaving England for a life in Nigeria was one of my biggest adolescent fears, she said it had worked out for the best. Despite the uncertainties, she had carved out a life of typically Nigerian fabulousness, a carousel of constant fashion shows, weddings, birthday parties and barbeques. 'I'm glad I came back,' she said. 'I'm not groping like you diasporans!'

Junior chuckled; it had taken him years of 'groping' to reacquaint himself with Nigeria and understand the workings of life here. Nini suggested I come back too. But I wasn't sure. I didn't think I could ever grasp the complex mechanics of the economy, the networking rules, the corruption that makes the UK system seem comparatively meritocratic and straightforward. I told Nini about a conversation I once had with an acquaintance concerning how government contracts are obtained. If I ran a hypothetical construction company in

Nigeria and wanted to bid for a contract, how would I go about securing it?

The acquaintance had described the widely known process. Securing a meeting to bid for a government contract requires giving the minister a hefty payment, perhaps as much as $250,000. When you tell the minister of your plans to build something like a gas plant, you must include details of his kickback. It's standard procedure. If you don't, he will pretend to listen to you, end the meeting on a positive note, and quietly dismiss your proposal without your knowledge.

'You see?' I moaned to Nini. 'You have to *know* things like that before you can live here. If I'd gone for that contract, I would've come out of that meeting thinking everything was OK!'

Junior and Nini burst out laughing. They weren't in a position to confirm or deny the story.

I knew so little about the rules of Nigerian life, and how to make money here. Nini was trying to figure out how to make money too. She reclined in a chair and stared at the ceiling, considering her finances. I suggested buying shares but she was nervous about the risk.

She wasn't nearly as optimistic as my cousins, Ledum and Ketiwe, who also dropped by for a visit that afternoon. Of all my cousins, they were closest to me in age, and I knew them best. Ledum was at law school, and Ketiwe was a qualified doctor, looking for a job in Abuja after recently moving there to live with her mother. Again, in both those professions, finding work was all about whom one knew. But neither of them seemed daunted by the challenge.

'My classmates say they should make friends with the people whose fathers are governors,' Ledum joked. Ketiwe was looking for a job specialising in haematology but, like Ledum, she planned to do business on the side to earn cash.

'You need to do three, four or five businesses. You've got to *diversify*,' Ledum smiled, splaying her fingers with optimistic zeal. Their drive was striking and alien, a new development since we'd last spent time together in our teens. They didn't seem too worried about the financial precariousness of Nigerian life.

'You should come and live in Nigeria,' Ketiwe proposed. 'It's good here.'

She and Ledum raided the fridge while painting a picture of my potential life. 'You can marry one of those Big Men,' they cooed. 'And you could be Minister for Culture and Tourism! They will like this your accent.'

'No,' I said. 'I'd change it. It doesn't sound right in Nigeria.' I didn't like having a foreign accent here. It marked me out and robbed my words of their venom and authority, especially when arguing with okada men or fellow bus passengers.

'No!' Ledum insisted. 'They like real English accents, not like those fake ones.' Radio and television broadcasters in Nigeria sometimes strive for English pronunciation but often end up simulating a hybrid of Dutch and drunk Nigerian. A broadcaster trying to say, 'I will give you the information on Saturday,' in an English accent usually ends up sounding something like this: 'Ay weel gif you thee informaiyshon on Saahtordayy.'

The right accent was all very well, but did I have the qualifications to become a government minister? Ledum and Keti said that having a foreign degree of *any* sort would get me any government job, regardless of my experience. Their enthusiasm opened a door to a macrocosm of exciting possibilities, and for a moment I seriously considered living in Nigeria. But I didn't have the appetite for struggling financially. Ketiwe was still looking for work and had no place of her own. Doctors in Abuja are paid ₦50,000 per month, around £200. Ketiwe and her fellow young doctors blamed their low pay on the older generation of medics. In order to cut hospital costs, the chairman of the Medical Association had recently called for interns to stop being paid. Boosting hospital budgets at the

expense of junior staff was a more viable option than asking the government or patients for extra money. I wasn't sure if I was prepared
to live in a country where qualified doctors can't find employment
easily. The system seemed too difficult and unpredictable; I might
flounder without meritocracy's comforting crutch.

But the system's fluidity can be liberating if one is able to ride it
rather than being steamrollered by it. Sitting in my brother's sun-
saturated living room, eating lunch prepared by the cook, I could
see the positive side of living in Nigeria: more living space, lots of
family support, not being a racial minority, enjoying a certain freedom that comes from being restricted in one's choices and
expectations. I wouldn't have to explain myself if I declined alcohol on a night out, and I could grow old and fat without losing my
social standing.

Nini and Junior invited me to see their offices at Villa, the vice-president's complex. The buildings are scattered in a compound beneath
Aso Rock, the iconic inselberg that looms over Abuja like a giant
steak-and-kidney pudding. Millions of years of wind and water erosion had worn down the ground in the Abuja region, except for a
few chunks of resistant rock that now erupted from the landscape
in great mounds.

After passing through security gates of the government compound,
my taxi steered along palm-lined avenues, past several clusters of
buildings, with chauffeurs and armed security men leaning against
lustrous 4 x 4s outside. Disdain for politics in general didn't stop
me feeling like a cowed and shabby speck in the face of so much
officialdom. This was also enemy territory I was invading – the
military dictatorship that killed my father was based at Aso Rock.
Walking around it sent a chill of hostility through me even though
my brother now worked here under a new dispensation.

Junior's office was startlingly shabby compared to the ostentation
outside. The ceiling tiles bulged with age, the faux-marble floor begged

to be cleaned, and dusty leather armchairs cluttered the unmanned reception area. I had expected a classier outfit for someone in Junior's position as an assistant adviser to the president, but in the Nigerian government ethnicity and budget are intertwined: our federal republic is modelled on the US political system, with representatives and senators from each of our thirty-six states. As an assistant adviser to the president, Junior had no official attachment to any federal state, yet his budget still came from the Rivers State government because that's where Ogonis come from. Ethnicity pervades a lot more of government structure than I'd imagined.

Nini's offices were further down the road in Villa itself, a handsome, new-looking edifice designed in a neo-Islamic style, with white walls that deflected the brilliant sunshine. How ironic that this seat of government, so pristine and fetching, presided over Nigeria's disarray.

The new government had inspired tentative optimism among some people. The general elections, held in April 2007, brought a new president (under the same PDP ruling party) into power. But the elections were said to be sullied with irregularities and vote-rigging. Politicians allegedly bribed electoral officials to turn a blind eye to the fiddling or stuffing of ballots. Observers were beaten up or turned away from polling stations by policemen and gang members. In some areas, reported voter turnouts outnumbered the ballots. The PDP won 70 per cent of the vote. But it was the first time Nigeria had passed from one democracy to another without a military coup. People were mildly grateful for that.

The new president, Umaru Musa Yar'Adua was a quiet aristocrat from the Fulani ethnic group. An obscure former chemistry lecturer, he had barely travelled outside Nigeria before becoming president, although his late brother was vice-president under Obasanjo in the 1970s. Rarely for a politician, Yar'Adua had no history of corruption (he was the first Nigerian president to declare his assets), but some suspect that as a friend and possible

puppet of his predecessor, Obasanjo, he was unlikely to bring genuine change.

In 2003, the government tasked the Economic and Financial
Crimes Commission (EFCC) with investigating political corruption.
In the early days of the new administration, several governors were
charged by the EFCC, but when a powerful politician from Delta
State was accused of financial misdemeanours, the head of the
EFCC, Nuhu Ribadu, was suddenly removed from his post and
bundled away on 'study leave'. The EFCC charges appeared to be
selective, letting several governors off the hook. The public, some
of whom were initially optimistic, was disgusted but unsurprised. It
appeared to be a witch-hunt for lesser politicians who had fallen out
of favour with the top echelons.

When I arrived at Villa, all these state governors were attending an important meeting. They clambered out of shiny black 4 x 4s,
wearing sunglasses and traditional *agbada* robes. 'Your Excellency'
is how these politicians are hubristically addressed. They moved
with the ease of people who know they're accountable to no one.
I believe that you can tell from a politician's walk whether they're
part of a true democracy or not: to me, the catwalk swagger of
Russia's Vladimir Putin contrasts tellingly with British politicians
who mince self-consciously past disparaging camera lenses, slaves
to public opinion. Many of the Nigerian politicians I saw before
me seemed old, patrician and slow – the very opposite of the
caffeinated, productive vigour of Washington, DC or London
lobbyism.

Nigeria's rumour mills spun a picture of our politicians as play-
ers in a game of intrigue, strategising, mutual back-scratching and
back-stabbing. Ministers try to manoeuvre ahead of one another,
mindful of the skeletons in each other's closets. Allegiances, created
out of short-term expediency, run the constant risk of collapsing
into a betrayal of some kind. Somehow these politicians find a
strength and appetite for it all. I wondered whether the endless

power struggles have selectively bred politicians to become more cunning with every new decade. A cousin of mine once described the power-hunger of politicians by relaying a conversation he had with a friend about wealth and power. When my cousin quoted Shakespeare's 'Uneasy lies the head that wears a crown,' his friend replied, 'Give me the crown and I'll take the uneasy.'

Nigeria's political system reminded me of my school canteen, when we'd line up to take biscuits from the pile on a tray in the dining room. All it took was for one child (often myself, I confess) to step out of line and snatch a handful before the entire process degenerated into a no-rules scramble.

'The state has completely collapsed,' my cousin told me. 'Nobody trusts it any more.'

Nigeria's chaos wasn't an embarrassment to our politicians. I was starting to think the disorder was vital to their operations, the ideal context for power and enrichment. I heard angry speculation that the people who sell generators will bribe NEPA workers to sabotage the electricity grid in order to boost demand for home power supplies. Whether it was true or not, our grafting politicians always find ways of living with such appalling infrastructure: emergency airlifts to European hospitals for heart bypass surgery, or private helicopter rides to avoid dangerous roads. All very convenient, but where's the joy in owning a fancy car when it has to travel over potholed roads? What was the attraction in living in a palace powered by noisy private generators instead of the state electricity supply? I couldn't understand why these kleptomaniacs preferred to be kings of a slum rather than live amongst equals in paradise.

I asked people what was wrong with Nigerian politicians. 'They're just selfish,' I was repeatedly told; 'They're bush,' one family friend said, referring to the politicians' uncivilised acceptance of squalor; 'You're assuming they have your civic-mindedness and sense of national pride,' the friend went on. 'That mindset comes naturally to *you*, but it doesn't to *them*.' The reason why is anybody's guess.

Some people believe that criminals have infiltrated Nigerian politics. Others, however, view corruption in Nigeria as a continuation of a traditional system of patronage that's been around for centuries. Traditionally in Nigeria power and money were controlled by Big Men who wielded huge influence by bestowing status and resources on a sycophantic 'clientele'. Chiefs dished out gifts, food and titles, and projected their power through ostentation and conspicuous consumption: gold jewellery, sprawling palaces, a harem of wives and dozens of children; theirs was a life of leopard-printed, ivory-tusked, divinely sanctioned opulence. And bureaucrats served this power structure – they weren't independent actors working for whichever political system governed them. Politics and resource control were firmly intertwined.

This ancient mode of relations stubbornly persists to this day, resisting attempts by colonialism and Western-style politics to sweep it away. Added to the problem are Nigeria's size and ethnic heterogeneity. Judging by Transparency International's annual corruption surveys, the world's least corrupt nations tend to have small, homogeneous populations in which mutual trust is higher. But Nigeria's 300-odd ethnic groups were prodded by the British into an arranged marriage to form a 'unified' nation state. Thrown into this bonfire were – among others – centralised feudalistic Muslim states, decentralised confederate-style Igbo kingdoms, and cattle-herding nomads, all of whom suddenly became 'fellow citizens' in a political entity represented by an alien coat of arms.

In Europe, the nation state followed ethnic boundaries (established through centuries of war) more closely. But in Nigeria, this nation-state concept has flopped. We haven't yet dismantled centuries of extended family and ethnic bonds that have served us well through famine and drought. The system has its benefits: had my father not paid his younger siblings' school fees, my aunts and uncles wouldn't have become lawyers, doctors and entrepreneurs. And my mother's support keeps the breadline at bay for certain members of her extended kin. But providing for his extended family put massive pressure on my father. Asking him for new clothes was always a tentative, dreaded task for me and my brothers and sister. After fielding constant money requests from his siblings and cousins, he gritted his teeth at having to bankroll our teenage growth spurts too.

For all its benefits, the social fabric of extended family doesn't wash well in a free-market economy; it hinders it badly, I think. Corruption and nepotism increase when pressure is placed on successful individuals to look after dozens of clinging family members. Many a Nigerian office is staffed with unqualified cousins and uncles who bring little innovation and creativity. Hard graft wins few prizes, and workers in government institutions will gladly raid the coffers partly to placate the upturned palms of demanding relatives. Bribery lubricates the cogs of everyday life: police won't take action without a small dash, and licences sometimes are not granted until money exchanges hands. All our civic institutions are irritatingly slow and ineffectual as a result.

The idea of civic institutions – a concept invented by Europe where family bonds are weaker – still mystifies certain Nigerians. We never needed them traditionally. People relied on extended family support, which was given on the assumption that the favour would be returned; a genetically based system of trust and reciprocity. Rarely did we extend such support systems beyond our kinship groups. As a result, trust and a sense of duty towards our 'fellow Nigerians' hasn't fully settled in the collective psyche. Moral and ethical standards, so prevalent at village level, disappear on the national stage where many politicians feel no obligation to work for the common good.

Nigeria's cycle of corruption and eroded trust locks the country in a tailspin. Nigerians have become pessimistic about their chances

of succeeding through normal channels, yet wealth remains a culturally important goal. This coupling of ambition with non-opportunity
seems to have fuelled corruption even further. Politics becomes the
only route to enrichment, and once the ministers have clubbed, kicked
and clawed their way to power, they plunge elbow-deep into our
government tills with breathtaking abandon.

Former dictator Sani Abacha helped himself to an estimated $6
billion. The EFCC uncovered a catalogue of financial skulduggery.
Joshua Dariye, a governor of Plateau State, reportedly stole nearly
$35 million, which he kept in twenty-five different bank accounts
in London. Bayelsa State governor Diepreye Alamieyeseigha was
arrested in London where he was allegedly found to have properties worth £10 million, plus £1 million of cash stashed in one of his
bedrooms. Another £2 million lay in a British bank account, it was
reported. This was in addition to bank accounts traced to Cyprus,
Denmark, USA and the Bahamas.

Some researchers say that dishonest politicians use this money to
maintain patronage and influence in Nigeria; much of the rest is
stashed overseas rather than invested in Nigeria's economy. In some
Asian countries such as South Korea, investing ill-gotten money
abroad is considered to be virtually an act of treason – South Koreans
keep their money within their borders and use it to maintain the
world's fourth largest economy.

My father never bought into the Nigerian system of corruption.
I was blind to the virtue behind our modest home and few holidays,
and I resented his frugality and non-materialism. I craved a luxuri-
ous lifestyle. But he held an intense disdain for such things. Once,
when I was eleven years old, I told him the names of all the
Nigerian girls at my school. One girl's name stuck out.

'Her father is a very bad man,' my father murmured between
puffs of his pipe. I asked him why. Silently, he stared ahead, refusing to elaborate on it. 'I will tell you when you're older,' he said.
He was killed before he had the chance to fill me in, though his

murder was an answer of sorts. Seeing the crude lengths to which politicians were prepared to go to protect their wealth dented my idealism rather abruptly. Up until age nineteen, I thought the world was a more malleable place, that the difference between poverty and prosperity was 'change', which simply required willing and tenacious agents. Life hadn't yet taught me how sociopathic greed can be. But after my father's murder, I realised that corruption was a monster that could vanquish even the toughest moral warriors.

7

Spiderman, Rock Stars and Gigolos

Abuja

I stepped out onto the expressway to flag down a taxi. The pale tarred road was broad and clean and quiet, except for the occasional zoom of a passing car. The government had also introduced zero-tolerance planning laws, which it exercised ruthlessly, demolishing any buildings that fell foul of the Land Use Act. This, coupled with the okada ban, bestowed Abuja's uncluttered streets with an eerie and thoroughly un-Nigerian serenity. Pleasant as the effect was, it seemed a shame that the city could only achieve its orderliness by stripping itself of everyday Nigerian life.

My taxi driver dropped me off at the Wonderland Amusement Park on the edge of town. Like most places in Abuja, this amusement park was gleaming and modern, a sparklingly redemptive jewel that obscured all memory of Ibadan's Transwonderland. Beyond the fairy-tale castle entrance and water fountain, a few families ate ice cream and strolled through the largely empty park. A diaspora teenager, perhaps the child of a diplomat or businessman, chatted on her cell phone in a strong Californian accent as she strolled with her brunette friend. Despite the 37°C heat, a man dressed head to toe in a Spiderman outfit (including a completely covered face) sold balloons and paced about the place with the speed and zeal of a street hawker, squeaking and hissing for customers' attention.

'Aren't you hot in that outfit?' I asked him. He stalked off without answering, annoyed that I wasn't buying a balloon.

I lined up for the roller coaster. It consisted of one carriage with space for a lone individual. I watched it zip along the track, soaring and diving in all directions. Curiously, the boy passenger was burying his head between his knees throughout the ride. At the end, he disembarked, looking shaken.

I soon discovered why. My carriage started along the uphill track with a jolt so forceful it instantly wiped the smile off my face. The 'protective' metal crossbar lay nearly a metre in front of me, meaning I had to lean forward in order to grasp it. And though the aircraft-style safety belt kept my thighs securely in place, it left my shoulders and back completely exposed. Each time the carriage turned a violent corner, I had to clutch the crossbar with all my strength to stop my torso being flung over the side. The ride turned out to be a white-knuckle battle to avoid injury, typically and amusingly Nigerian in its disregard for comfort and safety.

Nursing a slightly sore back, I took a cab to the Garki district, once an indigenous village but now swallowed up by Abuja. The residents weren't wealthy. Here, Abuja gave up on its pretensions to be a modern city with good infrastructure for all. One street, the aptly named Lagos Crescent, was a tatty confection of potholes, giant rainwater puddles and cheap shop stalls, a surprise oasis of the real Nigeria. Abuja came alive here.

On a leafy street corner, I encountered a group of youngish men engaged in a loud, animated conversation.

'I want to live in Russia!' one of them shouted. 'Because there is plenty of vodka there. Vodka, I *like* . . . there is no *vodka* in my life!' The man launched into a theory about Russia becoming the world's superpower this century. His friends and I disagreed.

'What makes you think so?' I asked, inviting myself into what I thought was a refreshingly intellectual conversation.

'Russia is an ally of the Arabs, so it will become a superpower soon,' he replied. 'It says so in the Bible.'

I walked on.

My bus rolled north out of Abuja and circulated endlessly through the spaghetti junction, still sparse and new-looking after all these years. The road uncoiled into the highway towards Zaria, cutting through sandy, scrubby plains that continued for miles, providing ample space for Abuja's urban expansion. We passed Abuja Model City, a gated community of brand-new houses organised in tidy, toy-like rows in the midst of this semi-desert, like pioneers in a brave new world of orderliness. I wondered how long Model City would last before sinking into the quicksand of Nigerian urban decline.

I was on my way to Zuma Rock, a large, dome-shaped volcanic inselberg, known as the 'Ayers Rock of Nigeria', an iconic symbol of the central region. Zuma Rock was one of the few places from 1988 that I remembered clearly. My father, brother, sister and I had climbed out of the car and stood on the empty highway to observe the giant monolith. My father said you could see a man's face on the rock, a quirk of natural erosion. Everyone except me seemed able to spot it.

'Can't you see the eye?' my brother Tedum asked incredulously. 'It's there . . . *there!*' I thought they were all hallucinating.

Perhaps I would see it this time around. For the last portion of my journey from Abuja, I switched to an okada. After going a week without these bikes, I realised how much I loved them. Though fraught with danger and often ridden by reckless drunks in a hurry, okadas were exciting, liberating and cheap, and they appealed to a downwardly mobile side to my character I hadn't known existed. I would use this form of transport even if I were a billionaire.

Minutes later, as we crested a hill, Zuma Rock rose suddenly and magnificently out of the otherwise featureless, yellowy landscape. Its dark, striated dome stood several hundred metres high and held dominion over the scenery for miles around. After days in Abuja's flatness, my eyes needed to adjust to this topographical excitement. Back in 1988, the surrounding landscape was a flat and barely populated expanse of trees and sandy soil. Now, traffic in the area around the rock droned more densely, and the previously deserted plateau shone with corrugated rooftops.

This time, my eyes could decipher the outline of a cone-headed alien with a dark round eye. I wanted to phone Tedum and tell him I could finally see the 'man' on the rock. But there was nobody to call: five years after first visiting here, he died suddenly from heart failure, two years before our father was killed. My sister is now the only living link with that day. Revisiting Zuma Rock by myself felt like a physical expression of the family's loss, and all morning I had been worried that coming here might disrupt whatever amnesia may have protected me from my pain these past dozen years. Fortunately, my melancholy was swept aside by some unusual activity in the area.

As my okada approached the stone dome, I could see that dozens of parked motorcycles and two, maybe three, hundred people were clustered on the side of the highway. Everyone stared and pointed fixedly at the dome, which loomed 300 metres away. The focus of all this fuss? Two Europeans in sports gear and helmets slowly abseiling down the rock.

The roadside spectators chattered excitedly on their mobile phones as they urged their friends in the nearby town to come and watch. Most of the crowd were dark-skinned, sharp-featured Muslim men wearing flowing white boubous and *kufi* hats. I and a handful of peanut-selling girls were the only females there.

Police patrolled the roadside, directing traffic and shepherding everyone away from the highway. One helmeted officer with massive aviator sunglasses rode the fanciest patrol motorcycle I'd seen in

Nigeria, a shiny, high-spec machine fitted with a windshield, siren lights and loud speakers. He knew he looked like a Californian patrolman, and he was loving it.

'Kommot for de side of the road!' he boomed down the speaker at a driver who had stopped his car to observe the spectacle. 'Look me well, o.' But the driver was too busy staring at Zuma Rock to acknowledge the officer's command.

Why all this attention for such a simple leisure activity? Were the abseilers famous? A very tall and irritable second policeman with tribal markings radiating from his nose gruffly ordered me to keep away from the road. I hoped he might know something about these foreigners.

'Who are they?' I asked him.

'They are human beings like you, and they are white,' he sneered, brushing past me as if I were a lowly she-goat. Rudeness aside, I admired his ability to keep things in perspective. Everyone else ogled the scene as if aliens had just landed.

One of the abseilers, a girl, was stranded midway down the steep rock face. Her partner was several metres away and slowly struggled to scale across and reach her. No-one had witnessed abseiling before, or even heard of it. But, this being Nigeria, there was an expert at hand to expound on the subject.

'I can climb Zuma Rock,' a man boasted, his arms folded across his chest. 'I don't need all these things.' He cast a belittling eye on the abseilers' harnesses and belay devices.

A superstitious man standing next to me proclaimed he wouldn't touch Zuma Rock, 'not even for a million naira'.

'Why?' I asked.

'I fear it,' he said. I later found out that in the old days, young girls were sacrificed near the rock to appease its evil spirits. He mistrusted those abseilers too. 'They use other things,' he said. 'It's not just rope.'

I asked him what 'things'. He didn't know exactly.

'Do you mean voodoo?'

He shrugged his shoulders without expanding on the matter. 'It's not safe,' he said, grimacing with fearful disapproval.

'They have equipment to stop them from falling,' I assured him.

'Are you with them?' he asked.

'No.'

'Are you a Nigerian?'

'Yes.'

'But you don't talk like a Nigerian.'

'That's because I live in London.' *Was my Nigerian accent that bad?*

He smiled suspiciously. 'I think you are with them.'

'I'm not!'

'Why did you come here to Zuma Rock like this?'

'I just came to see it. I didn't know all this was happening.' It was indeed odd that I managed to catch this event. The coincidence was bizarre, but I was glad of it. Nobody had ever abseiled down Zuma Rock before.

The male abseiler finally reached his friend and rescued her from her predicament. Both of them were descending the rock more rapidly now. As they approached the bottom, the spectators fizzed with excitement. One middle-aged man abruptly launched himself into the scrubby bush and strode authoritatively towards the rock as if he were personally connected to the adventurists. A second guy copied him, and soon a trickle of people began wading through the foliage. The trickle graduated into a steady current, which within a minute exploded into a mad rush. Nearly everybody was now racing towards the base of the rock. Stick-legged boys with ringwormed scalps and ragged clothes giggled and bounced through the scrub; little girls, still carrying trays of groundnuts on their heads, gathered their dresses with their free hands and sprinted in aim of God knows what; the men's long djellaba garments billowed like sails as they hot-footed it with everyone else.

A part of me almost joined in the madness, but the thought of running in that heat dissuaded me. I stood with the handful of people still left on the highway.

'Nigeriaah . . .' one man chortled ruefully.

'You cannot see such a thing outside of Nigeria,' the rock-fearer said to me.

Five minutes later the abseiling pair emerged through the trees and walked towards the highway, surrounded by the panting welcome committee. A police vehicle was parked on the highway, ready to collect them. The girl walked several paces in front of her friend. As she approached the 4 x 4, the onlookers parted to make way for her, like the sea fanning out for Moses. This tiny, red-headed slip of a thing looked exhausted as she cut a self-conscious swathe through the crowd. Everyone kept a respectful distance and watched her in silence. You could have heard a groundnut drop, it was so quiet. Her male friend, however, enjoyed a very different reception. This guy was the hero. He'd saved the girl.

'Yaaaaay!' the men all cheered as he strode through, a strange display of male solidarity that I wasn't privy to. They tousled his blond, shoulder-length locks, patted his back and shook his shoulders until the police led him into the back of the police 4 x 4 like a rock star. The car zoomed off into the horizon, chauffering him and his friend back to wherever they had come from.

Their abseiling was not the only new thing happening on Zuma Rock. The government plans to build a $500 million, five-star tourist resort nearby to 'boost' the area's economic development. There will be a cable car and walkway to Zuma's summit, and an artificial waterfall tumbling luxuriantly from the top. Already I could glimpse what looked like either a golf course or well-tended lawn just north of the base of the rock. I was all in favour of improving tourism, but how would this playground for the rich energise the local economy and educate people enough to stop 'fearing' the rock? It all seemed like sweet icing on a rather stale cake, an imitation of Western economies and their big service sectors. I wished that the government would focus on creating manufacturing jobs on a mass scale, too.

Now that the show was over, the hoards of spectators crossed the highway to mount their motorcycles. I ran from person to person, begging them to give me a lift to the nearby town of Suleja where I could catch a bus back to Abuja. A man eventually agreed in exchange for a few naira. I hopped on and we sped towards the town.

Back in Abuja that evening, I had to get a taxi back to Junior's house. I rather resented having to resume this form of transport, but it was the only means of getting around the city. Every fare had to be negotiated, and it often involved more wahala than I cared for. After getting into the vehicle, my driver opened the proceedings with a warning that the place was 'far' and it would cost me ₦500. I baulked and suggested ₦150. Stamping his foot on the brake, he ordered me out of the vehicle in theatrical disgust. Angrily, I concurred, slamming the door shut and glaring into the middle distance, pretending to look for another taxi. This ritual dance of strategic posturing, kissing of teeth and mutual outrage was exhausting. Life in Nigeria was an unending negotiation, with few guarantees.

'₦250,' the driver said through the rolled-down window. 'I am not cheating you.' *Story.* I declined with a haughty silence, and watched him drive away very slowly. After 10 metres, he opened the passenger door to offer a reconciliatory ₦200. I climbed back in and we resumed the journey back to the house.

'Hausa men are the nicest,' my cousin Ketiwe said, referring to the biggest ethnic group in Northern Nigeria. We were ambling through stalls separated by tidy alleyways in Wuse Market, west of the city. 'They buy you things, they take care of you when you're dating. If you run out of water they buy you a whole crate of bottled water.'

She and I were indulging in some silly ethno-romantic profiling. After witnessing the Hausa men's silence towards the female tourist at Zuma Rock, I had gender relations on my mind.

'What about Igbos?' I asked Ketiwe.

'An Igbo man takes care of his wife,' she smiled. 'She will dress like a queen while he wears ordinary clothes. If they only have one car he'll say, "It's OK, you can take it into town."'

Ketiwe was dating a Yoruba man from Kwara State in the west. She joked that our men from Rivers State were to be avoided because they're sexist philanderers. But marriage anywhere in the country seemed a minefield of infidelity, jealousy, intrigue and money fights; a clash between modern values and traditional ideas, between men (such as my father) calling themselves 'traditional' polygamists, and women (such as my mother) labelling them as mere philanderers.

The Sunday newspapers gave a highly entertaining insight into the Nigerian dating scene. The messages in the 'Lonelyhearts', 'Friendships' and 'Relationships' pages differed sharply from British ones, where pithy humour is welcomed but stating a strong intent for marriage is taken as a sign of madness. Nigerian lonely hearts contributors, by contrast, get straight to the point:

Oke, 24, female, needs a guy that is ready for marriage, aged between 30–33.

Others had more exacting requirements:

Kay, 28, resident in Port Harcourt, needs a tall, slim, disciplined, God-fearing lady for a relationship that will lead to marriage.

And:

Hakeem, lawyer, needs a young Muslim lady for a serious relationship. She must be dark complexioned, pretty, and of
Yoruba origin.

Then there was this brazen offering:

Prince, 45, handsome, married, kind, needs a romantic lady
with a fear of God.

I think Prince forgot to add 'hypocrite' to his list of qualities.

The 'Friendships' and 'Relationships' sections were surprisingly
short, occupying less than one-third of the page. The rest of the
spread was devoted to a compelling section called 'Sugar Cares',
where men looking for sugar mummies made their demands
extremely plain:

Uche, 27, needs a wealthy lady for marriage.

22-year-old fun-loving guy, seeks a financially stable older lady
aged between 40–55.

Felix, 27, graduate, romantic, needs a rich, sexy sugar mummy,
aged between 35–55, from any part of the country.

Tony, 27, undergraduate, needs a caring, independent, neat
and comfortable sugar mummy who needs sexual satisfaction
(preferably single parent, divorcée or widow).

Brown, 23, needs a mature, lonely lady, resident in Lagos,
Benin or Port Harcourt.

Victor from Port Harcourt needs a fat sugar mummy with big
boobs. He promises to satisfy her needs.

Julius, 28, needs a rich, sexy single sugar mummy, aged between 30–45 for financial support in exchange for the fun of her life.

I was intrigued. Pretending to be a prospective sugar mummy, I picked up my phone and dialled one of the numbers.

John, a 'cute, handsome undergraduate' picked up the phone. I explained to him that I was new to this sort of thing and wanted to know more before taking the plunge.

'Have you had a sugar mummy before?' I asked.

'Yes,' he replied, 'I've had just one.'

'How old was she?'

'Hmmm, she was about forty.'

'Why did it end?'

'I promised to make her happy. But she disappointed me. We agreed not to cheat on each other. But she cheated on me ... I didn't like that. I obeyed her rules very well but she was a liar.'

'What happened?'

'I wanted to know if she was unfaithful. I thought I'll ask her in a playful way. She said no. But my friend told me he saw her in a hotel with another man, so I changed my appearance. I put on head scarf and went to the hotel. I saw she had parked her car in a hidden place. So I bribed the waiter with money and he gave me her room number. I was waiting for some hours until she came out. When she saw me she was shocked. I told her I can't continue with this. I was angry because I sacrificed myself, my faith.'

I asked John how much money she gave him. He never really counted, he said. He was a student at the time. She bought him clothes and meals. Sometimes she transferred money into his account. When the money ran out, she checked with someone at his university to verify his financial situation, he claimed. On his birthday, she bought him a ₦60,000 Nokia phone. John said the lowest amount he ever received from her was ₦30,000 (perhaps he was exaggerating the figure, knowing that I was a prospective sugar mummy).

'That's why it was painful for me when we ended the relationship,' John said. 'I have no money now.'

'What if you don't find me attractive?' I asked.

'It doesn't matter. As long as you look good when we go out. I just want someone to love me, take care of me, have fun. As long as she can take care of me and her heart is clean. Are you hearing me? If she tells me, "This is what I want," I will do it.'

The next guy I rang – a twenty-three-year-old, self-described 'worker' called Dan – was less romantic. This time, I pretended to be a fifty-three-year-old divorcee looking for my first ever toy boy.

'You're fifty-three? . . . Wow,' he stammered nervously. But it took him less than a second to digest the information and shift into an aggressive, transactional frame of mind. 'You have to satisfy me,' he demanded. 'I don't care if you are fifty-three years old, we have to be together.'

'What are you looking for in a sugar mummy?'

'I need assistance from people like you, you understand? I want to further my studies.'

'Have you had a sugar mummy before?' I asked.

'You'll be the first person I've been seeing. Women have approached me before but they were not serious, they were beating about the bush . . . I need a dedication of your time.'

'I've never done this sort of thing before. How much money would you expect me to give you?'

'I won't ask you. Give me what you have . . . whatever you think is good for me. I'm not doing this because of pleasure. I want to further my studies . . . I need cash. If you are rich, I will satisfy you.'

'But can you satisfy me if you don't find me attractive?'

'Blood flows in my veins,' he said impatiently. 'I'm not a statue. You're going to have *feeling* . . . I promise. You can use oil to make it more crazy. You are pushing your menopause, right? So I would advise you to use oil.'

I asked Dan for his philosophical perspective on male pride and the power dynamic in sugar relationships.

'I just want your security, your loyalty,' he insisted. 'I won't ask you for money. It's like dating a young girl . . . you have to give her what she needs. You just have to apply that situation to this. So when are we going to meet?'

I put down the phone. His enthusiasm was overwhelming.

Sugar mummying isn't rife in Nigeria, but when men start commodifying their bodies, one senses that the economy must be in a bad way. Money was subverting Nigeria's social norms in surprising ways. I'd always regarded gigolos as something confined to a film fantasy or photo-less confessions in a British Saturday magazine, but they existed in Nigeria too. Peeping through this hole in our pious veil gave me a glimpse of the future, perhaps; the wobbling first steps towards gender equality, the end of polygamy, or some other kind of social change. It was comforting, because if there was one thing deterring me from living in this part of the world, it was fear of rigid, old-fashioned social structures.

I spent my last day in Abuja plotting my journey around Northern Nigeria. I knew little about the Islamic, northern half of the country. Ketiwe had helped me buy a long, flowing djellaba gown that I would wear out there. In Wuse Market we had consulted with some stall owners, five old Muslim men, about whether I needed to wear one. They said I didn't have to wear a djellaba, but if I respected myself and I wanted respect from others, then I should wear one.

The north was a very different place, foreign enough to make me feel like a true tourist. Without family connections here, I planned on exploring the region as if I were on one of my guidebook-writing trips. As a pure tourist I could replace my increasing emotional baggage with a (metaphorical) knapsack and travel lightly. That was the plan, at least.

Saying goodbye to Abuja would be a wrench, however. I'd gotten rather comfortable here. Leaving my brother's home felt like an ejection from the warmth of a duvet into the cold of the bedroom air, and I slightly dreaded having to reorient myself in a new city once again.

8

Straddling Modernity's Kofar

Kano

The harmattan mist still clogged the city the next morning. Abuja was a sandy-grey haze of immaculate, sleeping buildings. In these cool, early hours, things weren't much quieter than in the afternoons – the city slumbers, then stirs, never fully waking.

I boarded a Peugeot 505 bound for Kano, five hours north of Abuja. We zoomed along the highway through sparsely vegetated plains interrupted by the occasional dome-shaped, rocky inselberg. The driver, a pretty, feline man, wore smoky eyeliner (a Hausa tradition), spoke no English and barely moved a muscle, save for his fingers tapping to the Hausa music that jangled from a cassette tape. His stereo was set to maximum treble and minimum bass. The music's repetitive bassline and percussion were overlain with Hindi-style singing, which combined with the blazing sun and sandy landscape to mesmerise me into a deep slumber.

Part way through the journey, I was yanked out of sleep when the car swerved violently to the left of the road. Coming towards us was a government car with a wailing siren, tailed by a convoy of five or six other vehicles, including police cars. They veered into our lane in order to overtake the vehicles in their own lane, but the length of the convoy meant that regular cars in both directions were sent screeching onto the hard shoulder in panic. Senior politicians enjoy travelling this way, their sirens screaming non-stop through-out long intercity journeys as they move with an urgency that's manufactured to flaunt their importance.

Five hours later, I woke up in a motor park somewhere on the edge of Kano city. My Peugeot was descended upon by taxi men competing to take me to a hotel. They were all ebony-skinned Muslims, wearing djellabas and kufi hats, and speaking in rapid Hausa filled with Arabic-sounding glottal stops and rolled Rs. Our shared nationality seemed a rather abstract and unreal concept. The only man among them to have a smattering of English won my custom and loaded my bags into his car.

Dusk closed in on us as we drove through Kano's streets. The aroma of skewered meat breezed through the car. Several minarets extended into the ochre sky, adding a touch of elegance to a city that was otherwise draped in that homogenising Nigerian blanket of street hawkers, okadas, litter and eye-watering smog. But I hadn't seen quite this many mosques in one metropolis before. No matter how tiny and poor, they adhered to an Islamic architectural style, with minarets and domes, albeit more blocky and angular than the Middle-Eastern style. Nigerian churches, by contrast, are free-form and modern, often lacking the defining Christian spires and stained-glass window features.

The city felt new and unfamiliar, but it wasn't my first visit. I had spent a week here with one of my aunts and some cousins in the 1980s. As on most family visits, I played indoors most of the time. I didn't see much of Kano. My only memory was of an exotic haze of orange mud walls and kufi hats, and my father pointing ahead and telling us that our next-door country, Niger, was over there. I thought he'd meant it was literally behind the wall.

Kano is the oldest city in West Africa, a once-glorious ancient city at the crossroads of trans-Saharan trade, established as one of seven walled city states of the Hausa people more than 1,000 years ago. It became strategically important in the trade route, and established connections with Mali and North Africa. People from these parts, and Muslim Fulani herders from the Senegal valley, migrated to Kano, bringing artisanal skills and Islam, which arrived some time between the twelfth and fourteenth centuries. The Fulani integrated with the Hausa people as an educated elite. By the sixteenth century the city had became a centre of Islamic scholarship, and was ringed by a large wall. Kano's traders travelled as far as the Mediterranean, modern-day Ghana and Gabon to exchange leather, pottery, metal works and cloth in return for salt, silks, spices, perfume, Islamic books and weapons. At the height of its powers in the seventeenth and eighteenth centuries, the city state was sending 300-camel loads of cloth to Timbuktu. By the nineteenth century, Kano was receiving cloth from Manchester in England, silk and sugar from France, clothing from Tunisia and Egypt, and reading glasses from Venice.

By taking part in the global exchange of goods and ideas that much of Africa missed out on, Kano enjoyed high levels of literacy and architectural sophistication – its Malian-influenced Islamic mud-walled buildings contained vaulted ceilings, pinnacled buttresses and elaborately carved wooden gates. Even the British, who captured Kano in 1903, eschewed their customary destructiveness and instead converted one of Kano's palaces into their central administration office.

By the year 2000, the city was enforcing Islamic sharia law, the strict Islamic legal code, more widely than usual, prescribing lashings and amputations for thieves and miscreants. Women were temporarily banned from riding okadas (too much spreading of legs) and ordered to sit at the back of buses instead. Religious hostilities surfaced in 2007 when a rally to protest the killings of Muslims by Christians in central parts of the country lurched into violence. Muslim mobs burned and looted Christian-owned properties and businesses in Kano; up to 600 people were killed.

Now the city was at peace again. But I felt particularly alone here. I had entered the true north. The uniformity of dress code, the forest of minarets and the weaker Western cultural influence were very foreign to me. My relatively brasher southern energies felt straitjacketed by Hausa's rigidity and poise. Here, I was very much an Ogoni and a Christian. Not that I felt threatened by it, but Kano seemed to me to be underpinned by a tight power structure based on a male-dominated ethnic kinship far removed from my identity. I felt an uncharacteristic urge to 'fit in'.

The next morning, I walked down the street in an ankle-length djellaba, sweating beneath my headscarf. The inflexible hem restricted my stride, forcing me to walk at a slow, demure pace. I cut a foolish figure in my trainers, Ray-Ban sunglasses and less than demure demeanour, which singled me out as flagrantly as full-frontal nudity. When I tried to mount an okada, the stiff hemline forced me to raise the garment to the tops of my thighs, a rather counter-productive move. I subsequently ran back to my room – at a Christian guest house – and slipped a pair of trousers on underneath. God knows what the receptionist thought of it all.

Once out and about in the drier Saharan air, I began to wonder whether adopting Islamic dress code was necessary. Most women were modestly covered up, but I spotted quite a few individuals wearing T-shirts, trousers and no headscarves – and not a dirty look or stoning mob in sight. Any evidence of religious tension had vanished. Islam, established here long before Christianity arrived, was an older and more languid affair, free of evangelism's teenage fervour. Christianity confronted you and pummelled, whereas Islam lay under your feet, underpinning every aspect of society in its quietly dictatorial way. Everyone appeared laid-back. The Hausa people took such a supine approach to life, I found it hard to read their emotions or motives. As a child I mistook their leisured stature for laziness. They were disproportionately prone to begging, I believed. Now I realised it was a trick of the mind – Hausas are simply more noticeable than other beggars because of their Islamic dress.

The boys who rode okadas (or *achabas* as they're known here), possessed none of the competitive, time-pushed zeal of the southern okada men. They sat on their bikes, looking utterly passive, as though someone had physically deposited them on the seats, wrapped their fingers around the handlebars and turned the ignition keys for them. None of them spoke English. And some of them didn't bother letting me know this. They would nod at my destination request without understanding me, then take me to entirely the wrong place. My subsequent tongue lashings were greeted with a vacant stare or gentle shrug of the shoulders; a mule would give a more animated reaction.

Eventually, someone delivered me to the old city wall, which was first erected in the tenth century and fortified in the fifteenth century. The adobe structure had crumbled long ago, but part of it is being restored with assistance from the German government. I walked past a small completed section of it, 4.5 metres of beautifully compacted mud, water and straw. The traditional gates, or *kofars*, leading into the city are still in use, but they're signified by modern hoardings rather than the elaborately carved wooden doors of old. These kofars made for handy geographical reference points when travelling about town, especially as the achaba men rarely knew non-Hausa street names or hospital names.

I asked an achaba man to drop me at Kofar Mata, next to the old indigo dye pits. Cloth has been dyed in these pits for 500 years, largely by the same family. In the courtyard, three wizened, red-eyed men dipped cloths inside circles of brilliant indigo pools that twinkled in the sunlight. They mix natural dyes and ash in water and pour the mixture into the pits. Indigo plant sticks are added and the dye mixture is left to ferment for two or three days. Potassium and more indigo are added to the dye, which is fermented again for a further three days until the dye is ready. By the side of the courtyard, inside a dark room, several young men were pounding dyed clothes with wooden clubs to give the cloth a beautiful sheen. By the back wall several pieces of dyed cloth imprinted with patterns and swirls had been hung out to dry. Local chiefs still wear them as ceremonial robes.

Afterwards, I visited Kurmi Market, in the centre of the old city, where people have traded for nearly 1,000 years. The market was a dense warren of stalls packed tightly enough to partially block out the sunlight. My eyes struggled to take in the piles of henna, spices, eyeliner (worn by men and women), and ink balls for writing books. The place buzzed with artisanal activity, all of it handled by men. They calmly but firmly urged me to examine exquisitely woven rugs, raffia mats and beaded necklaces, the intricate feminine designs draped over their thick manly fingers.

The harmattan wind infused the narrow passageways with the pungent odour of handcrafted leather. I bought beautiful snakeskin handbags and leather sandals, and when the trader placed another of his purses in my hand, I willingly, reluctantly, happily accepted it at a silly price. It was far easier, though, to say no to the modern, Africa-shaped leather pendants, those tacky symbols of Pan-Africanism.

Afterwards I took an achaba towards Dala Hill, the highest point in Kano. The bike weaved through the Old City, which, like the market, consisted of narrow alleyways flanked by flat-roofed, one-storey buildings, some of them centuries old. The occasional satellite dish poked out above the rooftops, but for the most part any shiny gloss of modernity was dulled by the fast-encroaching Saharan sands, which blended with the ochre houses, tree branches, human skin and soil to form a kaleidoscope of brown.

A few people rode through the streets on horseback. I saw flashes of women and girls in brilliantly coloured headscarves, materialising between buildings like shy tropical birds. Their colourful veils – lemons, pinks, bright oranges, lilacs – made my all-black hijab seem needlessly austere and dull. I questioned why I bothered wearing it; I also questioned whether headscarves actually protected Nigerian women's modesty. Our coiffeurs aren't the focus of our sex appeal. If anything, Muslim African women should hide the curve of their backsides from the gaze of men, not their hair.

Kano women were a mystery to me, an inconspicuous, penumbral presence in the city, partaking little in public activity. Men appeared to do everything: they made up the entirety of cinema audiences, dominated the basketball courts, repaired clothes and sold all the fruit on the roadside.

'Ninety per cent of my friends in the north don't work,' said Rabi Isa, from her desk at the British Council in the centre of town. 'Many of them have degrees but they got married and started having children straight after graduation.'

Rabi was an unusual specimen – an employed Hausa woman who wore T-shirts and jeans, but kept the headscarf on. She didn't bend completely to sharia law or other religious rules. A few of her friends wanted to start earning money now that their marriages were in trouble, she said, but most of them still preferred to defer to men.

'I tried to organise a debate about women running for the presidency. I wanted to invite an eminent female professor to speak in favour of the notion, but she declined because she didn't believe in the idea of a female president.'

Rabi said that another woman, a state commissioner, also declined her invitation on the basis that she was happy to occupy a high-status position so long as she could answer to a man above her.

'Is sharia law still being enforced?' I asked.

'Not really. Sharia was mainly for political gain,' Rabi believed. 'The present governor got lots of grassroots support for it, especially in the rural areas.'

In the late 1990s, military rule had ended, and legions of poor Muslims were anxious to combat the corruption, poverty, elitism and baggy-jeaned hip hop threatening their culture. Sharia law was introduced in several northern states around that time. Emboldened conservatives pushed for it to be introduced in Kano, which though

Islamic, considered itself too complex and diverse to lurch in such a conservative direction. But intense local support, backed by Islamic preachers and scholars, compelled the Kano government to gradually introduce the new law.

Women were banned from riding achabas and alcohol was prohibited in all areas. A sharia police force known as the Hisbah patrolled the streets and enforced the new rules, sometimes very enthusiastically. By some reports, they raided a wedding suspected of conducting un-Islamic activities, and invaded certain private homes for the same reason. Although sharia applies to Muslims only, Christian women seen straddling achabas were beaten, and so too were their hapless drivers. The government was forced to relax the achaba ban after vehement public protests.

The Hisbah also made themselves unpopular with the secular police force, which bristled at having to share its authority with them. The forces clashed regularly. While the Hisbah confiscated alcohol, the secular police were escorting lorry shipments of liquor in exchange for tips. This convinced the Hisbah that the secular police were deliberately undermining sharia law in collusion with the government, which had implemented the Islamic code reluctantly. The government had failed fully to fund provision of sharia reference books to train new judges, or to pay existing judges on time. Consequently, sharia never established itself as strongly as hoped (or feared) in Kano. The hand amputation machines said to have been imported from Saudi Arabia were never used, adulterers were never stoned and sharia courts took too long to process legal cases anyway.

The secular government neutered the Hisbah's powers even further by introducing its own compliant Hisbah force, thus splitting sharia policing in two, and giving the secular police the option of ignoring cases brought by the non-government Hisbah. As sharia's influence waned, the prostitution and alcohol consumption it helped to reduce tiptoed back into Kano life.

Supporters of sharia law accused the authorities of equivocating about the more serious issues. The ordinary poor folk watched corrupt politicians get richer, while the sharia authorities focused on the fripperies of film censorship and dress codes.

'Sharia is hypocritical,' Rabi said. 'There's one rule for men and another for women. It was basically introduced as a way of controlling women. Men can do what they like. There's an area just here, near Government House. Prostitutes congregate there every night. The politicians know they're there but they don't do anything about it. If sharia is anti-corruption, why don't those corrupt politicians get their eighty lashes?'

That night, I walked around the Sabon Gari ('foreign quarter'), a section of town where non-Muslims are traditionally exempt from Islamic laws and customs. While the rest of the city fell dark and silent, the Ibo Road hummed with life. For the first time that day, I observed men and women socialising freely. Further along the street, the silhouettes of Hausa men in their fez-style kufi hats fronted tiny, light-filled street taverns crammed with bottles. Suya barbecue smoke mingled with the exhaust fumes of passing cars, and the cars' red tail lights complemented the occasional red light bulb hanging above a front door. At a table outside one restaurant, four animated men drank and joked in the presence of a scantily dressed woman who sat sulkily beside them, an inanimate accessory to their chatter. I wondered if she was dreading 'dessert' with her client. Hedonism, the flip side of the piety coin, had reasserted itself in Kano.

I realised that the power struggle between Islam and Christianity here requires enormous dexterity, like conducting a wrestling match on a tightrope. Compromise is key. Prior to the elections of 2007, after much internal infighting, political parties running for office included Muslims and Christians on their tickets. And in the 2006 national census, questions about religious affiliation were left out altogether, such is the sensitivity of the issue. Revealing the true sizes of the Christian and Muslim populations was considered too great a risk.

Maintaining our ethno-religious Pangaea requires skilful manoeuvring and compromise, something that Nigerian politics – for all its evils – has achieved. On some level, I admired the adeptness with which our society handles its cultural fault lines – especially when compared to the British angst over its tiny Muslim minority. Our sporadic flashes of violence don't reflect complete failure, I realised, but instead the occasional spewings of an active volcano that Nigerian society has done remarkably well to contain.

Back in my bed at the guest house, I watched TV. Many of the shows and commercials were dubbed or subtitled in the Arabic tones of Hausa. English-language TV and Nollywood movies aren't as popular in the north since English isn't as widely spoken here. The movies' witchcraft themes also hold less appeal, I was told, because pre-Islamic animism was severely dented during the Fulani jihads, which swept across the Hausa states in the nineteenth century. Many Hausas prefer culturally similar Bollywood movies over Nollywood films.

The nationwide cable channel still broadcasts Nollywood movies, however. A film called *Long John* came on, the best and funniest Nollywood film I'd seen. The eponymous central character (played by my favourite actor, Nkem Owoh) storms around his village, raging at the immorality he witnesses around him.

In one scene, Long John encounters a member of the village committee canoodling with a woman by a tree. When the couple realise that Long John is approaching them, the woman hides in front of the man.

'What are you doing?' Long John enquires aggressively.

'I'm just urinating,' the terrified man tells him, keeping his back to Long John. 'I'll ... I'll see you at the meeting.'

But Long John spots a piece of the lady's clothing dangling between the tall man's legs.

'Are you wearing apron?' he sarcastically asks the man. 'Are you urinating white silk? . . . Ah, I go see legs, o! You are urinating a whole human being.'

The tall man bribes Long John with alcohol to keep quiet about this sexual indiscretion. Long John accepts the bribe, then says he'll still report the incident to the village elders. The next we see of him, he's drunkenly complaining to a goat about how rogues, his 'fellow goats', have entered Nigerian politics.

Long John brilliantly captures the archetypal mouthy Nigerian who hollers pious, rapid-fire invective, reducing his victims to quivering little children. His rage, his hypocrisy, and the dialogue – delivered in typically starchy, vernacular English – was hilariously authentic. He reminded me of Michael Douglas's character in the Hollywood film *Falling Down*, whose frustration at society sends him on a wanton, self-destructive warpath around the city.

Long John later catches another couple canoodling. He accuses the man of being too lustful ('Even a she-goat is in trouble with you') and advises him to 'offload the burden around your waist and discharge it' by the tree. 'I can see you want this place to be germinating ground for bastards,' he spits disdainfully.

Next, Long John staggers drunk into a meeting of the council of elders and demands that from then on everyone should speak to him in 'Queen's English'. He turns to the chief. 'You have no manhood between your testicles,' he tells the old man before accusing him of embezzling public money. The other elders agree, and accuse the chief of living a rich lifestyle: quaffing only expensive bottled water, and 'masticating fruit like *mad*'.

The film goes on like this, a series of scenes covering everything from the sexual indiscretions of church members to theft (increasingly on Long John's part). We see him capitulate further to his own vices when he tries to seduce his friend's pretty niece. Long John steals his own wife's clothes and offers them to the niece as 'brand new' presents – at which point, the film suddenly ends.

Nollywood movies are notorious for dividing themselves into three one-hour-long instalments, designed to create more money for producers. Unless one watches every segment, it's not always possible to understand the plots and overarching messages. Not once can I remember completing a Nollywood film from start to finish. I could only guess what message *Long John*'s director was imparting. Even so, the brilliance of the script and relatively high-quality cinematography gave me another glimpse of what Nigerian cinema could achieve one day. Uplifted, I fell into a deep sleep.

When the British overran Kano in 1903, they took over Gidan Makama, the home of a member of the Hausa aristocracy ('Gidan' means 'house' and 'Makama' means 'heir apparent' to the emir). The colonialists used the building as their administrative headquarters. The Malian-style edifice had cool interiors and rounded turrets protruding from sloping, sturdy mud walls, its exterior printed with the interlocking Hausa-Fulani symbol. Today, Gidan Makama is used as the city's main museum.

I met my guide inside the dark, cool interior. He was a lovely Hausa man who spoke broken English. I never asked him his name, so I'll call him Amadu. We walked through the first room, which contained black-and-white photos of old Kano, still walled, still separated from the outside world by wooden doors, also decorated with carvings of the Hausa-Fulani motif. The museum's collection of artefacts demonstrated Kano's early sophistication and connections with the outside world: arrow-proof battle shields made from elephant hide; wooden guns manufactured by Kano citizens in the sixteenth century; horned animal masks used as decoys for hunters; various examples of Mali-style, turreted mud-wall architecture.

Beyond the courtyard, in a second set of rooms, a cabinet

displayed the emir's clothes, including a pair of ornately designed trousers that must have been 2.5 metres wide between the legs. Amadu laughed with me. He explained that the emir used the excess fabric as a cushion to prevent saddle-soreness during long journeys on horseback.

Another room showed two sacks printed with the Barclays Bank logo and filled with groundnuts. Until fairly recently, groundnuts were used as a form of currency in Kano, each bag representing the equivalent of £100.

'My mother could not adjust to the use of notes and coins,' Amadu told me. 'When I told her something cost ₦1,000, she asked me, "How many bags is that?" Groundnut was our cash crop in those days. In the south you had palm oil and cocoa. Now it's all oil. I think the government do not take an interest in tourism because of oil.'

Across town was a camel market. In a cavernous warehouse several men were standing and watching a carcass being cleaned. When they saw me they ushered me in with startling readiness. None of them questioned why a random woman was sniffing around an abattoir. Instead, they offered me an impromptu tour.

'You know, nothing comes for free,' the tallest man announced, grinning coyly.

'I know,' I replied, grinning sourly. In Nigeria, even curiosity has a price; people seem permanently poised to turn any situation, no matter how banal, into a profitable one. The tall man was called Ibrahim. His friend, also called Ibrahim, was a congenial older man whose teeth erupted from his mouth at all angles. The two of them guided me around the abattoir, casually treading in the pools of blood on the floor. Toothy Ibrahim laughed at me as I held up my trousers and minced along in distaste. In the room next door, water bled from a pierced hosepipe and seeped beneath the head of a cow. The cow's head lay next to its chopped legs and a chunk of its neck, which had a huge artery sticking out of it. Just a few metres away, a man maintained superhuman stillness while getting his hair cut inside a cloud of buzzing flies.

The Ibrahims led me out of the door towards the back of the warehouse. We entered an open space where twenty-odd camels stood or sat on the straw-strewn ground, a haughty yet foolish expression on their faces. I wanted to know where the animals came from, but the camel dealer, an old man, refused to answer my translated question. He murmured something to Toothy Ibrahim in terse Hausa.

Ibrahim turned to me. 'He is thinking that you want to start your own camel business and compete with him.'

'No, no,' I reassured him. 'I'm just curious.' Toothy Ibrahim explained that the animals are imported by foot from Libya or Cameroon at a cost of ₦100,000 each. 'What do you do with them?' I asked.

'They are for eating,' Toothy replied.

'Which part?'

'The *whole* camel.'

'Do you eat the eye?'

'Yes.'

'The ears?'

'Yes,' he nodded vociferously.

'The tongue?'

'We eat *everything*.'

In Northern Nigeria there is no animal more useful than the camel: they're edible, biddable, strong and can be rented out to other farmers to transport their produce. As the Sahara encroaches, many farmers in the north are using camels instead of oxen to plough their fields. Camels are cheaper to feed as they'll eat shrubs, herbs, leaves and fruit of any quality, and the kind of semi-desert vegetation that other hoofed animals won't sniff at.

The camel dealer stood behind a table piled with brown oval-shaped camel droppings. Tall Ibrahim explained that people mix the droppings with water and pour the mixture into their their ears to treat infections. Camel urine is also drunk to cure coughs. Traditional remedies are still popular here because modern medicine fails people so often; Nigeria is awash with placebos and chemically dubious medication. There was a logic behind our traditionalism, I realised – cultural stubbornness wasn't always the reason.

But a lack of progress and education, evidence of fallow brain power, was evident all around me. On the way back to my hotel, I stopped off at one of the many bookstalls lining a busy main street. While I examined the book spines, the English-speaking stall owner thrust a random selection of books in my direction: self-help, psychology, statistics. Oblivious to the subject matter, he offered me each book as though it were a piece of fruit.

'I'm looking for a novel,' I explained. He pointed me to the children's section. 'No, that's not what I'm looking for,' I said. 'I want a novel.'

The man reached across the cabin and pulled out *The Gynaecological Guide for Women*.

That evening, I checked my e-mail at a Lebanese-run Internet café opposite the desiccated lawns of the Kano golf club. I was still dressed in my hijab and headscarf, but it didn't stop the Indian man sitting next to me surmising that I was a diasporan. His name was Ravi. He was a restaurateur, born and raised in Kano, a descendant of Indians who migrated to Nigeria in the colonial era to work at the tin mines in Plateau State.

Ravi showed me online photographs of a restaurant in London. He had plans to refurbish his own Kano eatery in the same style. After chatting for a few minutes, we drove across town to have a drink.

'Nobody makes rogan josh like me, if I may say so myself,' Ravi smiled, a flash of humour penetrating his general dourness. He was jaded, he said, on the verge of 'burning out'. Running a restaurant six days a week was taking its toll, and so was life in Nigeria. 'I was considering getting Nigerian citizenship in 2001 but I changed my mind. This country is going down,' he said, his fingers itemising the decay, overpopulation and corruption.

'People tell me that if they went into government they would go chop [steal government funds]. Everyone is corrupt. Even that Ken Saro-Wiwa. I've heard he wasn't honest either.'

'Ken Saro-Wiwa was my father.'

Ravi's face fell. 'I'm sorry—'

'You shouldn't believe everything you hear. My father left everything he had to his children. If he were rich, then *I'd* be rich. And I'm not.'

'OK, I'm sorry. I didn't realise . . . sorry.'

We sat in silence for a while. Ravi's cynicism trawled across all things Nigerian, snagging everything in its net, including my father. I was irritated but unsurprised – Nigerians have very little trust in our public figures.

'I hate driving in rush hour. It's so stressful,' Ravi sighed, resting his arms on the steering wheel and staring at the bedlam of traffic. 'Everyone is on a mission. Look at that woman on the okada. She's on a mission to get home without falling off that thing . . . her driver is on a mission to get her there as fast as possible and then find another customer . . . *everyone* is on a mission.'

We parked outside the members-only Kano Motor Club, a colonial vestige frequented by foreign expats and older Hausa men. The club's interior had burnt down two days earlier, 'Probably because of some shitty, cheap Chinese appliance,' Ravi grumbled. We took seats by the undamaged bar looking out on to the gardens. Ravi introduced me briefly to a big Scotsman, the club's manager. Surrounding us were blue-collar English men drinking beer, and a beefy Italian with a vest and gold chain nestled in a forest of chest hair. Colonial exclusivity isn't what it used to be. A couple of silent, heavily made-up Nigerian women sat by the men, while several Hausa men chatted and sipped beer at a nearby table.

'Sharia law is just a political gimmick,' Ravi said, staring into his whisky. He freely sold alcohol at his restaurant.

'You don't get caught?' I asked.

'The police come round sometimes.'

'And what happens?'

'I tip them,' Ravi replied.

I asked him if there was anything interesting that I should see in Kano. He shrugged his shoulders. He'd seen it all, done it all: the Durbar festival, the wrestling, the museums. He wanted to go to India or Pakistan on holiday.

'I haven't been abroad on holiday in seven years. I can't afford it.' He told me he had run out of money after reluctantly paying for his wife and children to fly to the US to visit his mother-in-law.

'Why don't you go somewhere nice within Nigeria, like that bird sanctuary up in Nguru?'

'I've heard it's not very good.'

'What about Obudu Ranch?'

'It's too expensive.'

'It'd be cheaper than going to Pakistan or India.'

'I need a break from *Nigeria*,' he sighed, a rush of blood rouging his tired eye whites. 'I want different food, different mentality, different lifestyle.'

Perhaps being Indian enhanced Ravi's sense of entrapment, his foreignness making him less stoic than indigenous Nigerians in his predicament. I shuddered at the thought that I might end up like him if I lived in Nigeria, unable to leave, unable to achieve financial security or simply satisfy my cravings for foreign cuisine. Western prosperity had made me less hardy, and given me a sense of entitlement to easy mobility that I was terrified of losing. I felt a renewed gratitude towards my parents for giving me the life that I had.

I asked Ravi if he was going to the Durbar that week. 'I've seen it a thousand times,' he muttered, his weariness mopping up my enthusiasm like a sponge. The Durbar was the highlight of the Hausa-Fulani cultural calendar and the highlight of my Kano visit. I'd been counting down the days. Every year, the Emir of Kano invites military chiefs for a military parade at his palace, where finely costumed regiments showcase their loyalty in a magnificent display of horsemanship. The parade goes back to the days when each noble household was expected to contribute a regiment to the defence of Kano's emirate.

The day of the Durbar – held on the eleventh day after the hajj to celebrate the culmination of Eid-ul-Fitr and Eid-el-Kabir Muslim festivals – was a cloudy one. A jolt of adrenalin woke me up prematurely. The harmattan winds seemed to express their own excitement by throwing up an unusually dusty haze over the entire city. It lent an extra magical air to the day. My achaba cruised towards the Old City on traffic-free roads, flanked by policemen and drummers.

The Emir's Palace was an old but renovated green-and-white building with an expansive, sandy courtyard in the middle. I took a seat in the northern royal stands alongside well-to-do Nigerians and foreigners. The expats were mainly diplomats and company workers who fanned their flushed faces and chatted in low voices. They had smartened up for the occasion in suits and hats and dresses, an unusual show of deference to Nigerian culture. The cost of a seat in the royal stands, a paltry ₦2,000, was enough to grant us privilege over ordinary Kano citizens who lined the streets nearby. In order to get a good view of the courtyard, some of them perched on a wall of the Central Mosque opposite the palace. Dozens of others clambered onto the rooftops of nearby buildings. How wrong it seemed that outsiders like myself should enjoy privileged views of the Durbar while ordinary Hausas and Fulanis couldn't.

'They know their place,' said the buxomly elegant, fifty-something woman sitting next to me. 'They'd never force their way over here. Hausas like protocol and respect.'

The woman had an American accent. Regally swathed in bright red Senegalese cloth, she looked like she had lived in Nigeria for a long time. Her name was Nadira, she told me, and she had converted to Islam thirty years earlier, back home in Miami, long before she came to Nigeria and met her husband and settled here.

'I never felt that I belonged in America,' Nadira said. 'I went to the Caribbean, tried living there for a while, but it wasn't what I wanted. Something was missing.'

'Do you know what it was?'

'Freedom,' Nadira replied. 'I can come and go as I please and do what I like.'

'But women don't have freedom here. They're not allowed to do anything.'

'People in the US don't understand this women-at-home thing. But the women aren't just sitting there, they're doing business. They're selling perfume and fabrics and jewellery. Here in Africa women have it going *on*,' Nadira said. She pointed out that Kano women actually owned most of the achaba motorbikes but let their sons or male relatives ride them and earn money. Kano society wasn't necessarily what it seemed on the surface. But I wondered whether Nadira owed her freedom partly to being American and relatively wealthy. Coming from the diaspora certainly gave me freedom around town – when I arrived at the Emir's Palace in my trousers and T-shirt, announcing myself as a 'journalist from London', the police had bitten back their disapproval of my attire.

The seats around the courtyard down below us were filling up with hundreds of spectators, most of them connected to the royal household in some way. State TV cameras trained their lenses on the crowds. On the edge of the courtyard, groups of rival political party supporters had gathered. One of the parties was protesting the results of the recent local government elections. As the two groups chanted and waved posters and flags at one another, a mounted emir's guardsman separated them with a big stick.

The sound of sirens filled the air as the state governor's convoy screamed across the courtyard, kicking up a self-important plume of dust in its wake.

'Only the African man does that,' the woman behind me chuckled to her companion. 'Can you imagine? Thirty cars, just to bring in this governor!' The politician got out of his car and took his seat by the courtyard.

Finally, groups of horse-mounted warriors entered the courtyard in a long procession. They were divided into regiments, each one belonging to a prince or lesser aristocrat. The warriors wore opulent turbans and magnificently billowing *babanriga* gowns of every colour and pattern under the sun: all-white ones, shiny purple ones, gowns with orange and yellow stripes. These macho peacocks bounced on their horses around the edges of the courtyard, followed by drummers, dancing infantrymen and *kirari* singers. Even the horses had embroidered fabric and chain mail draped over their faces. The infantry guards carried placards inscribed with names, denoting the royal title-holder the guards belonged to. Each title-holder is responsible for organising and funding his regiment's costumes – the richer the title-holder, the bigger the entourage.

Lithe warrior regiments marched along on foot while chanting, banging drums or wielding sticks. Some of them had painted their faces bright blue and engaged in fake sword fights. One warrior tied calabashes around his torso and shook his waist to produce a salsa-style percussion, while a chorus of bagpipe-sounding horns wailed in the background.

The Durbar wasn't organised in straight lines like military processions elsewhere in the world. Like many Nigerian rituals, it had less of the symmetry and aesthetic orderliness that preoccupies other cultures. The substance of such festivities, not their neatness, was what mattered.

I enjoyed watching the Durbar, much more than I used to enjoy

the festivities in my own village where I used to feel mildly threatened by not being fully au fait with Ogoni culture. I remember the
affectionate ridicule I used to face when trying to dance Ogoni-
style. I couldn't bend forward and wiggle my backside while
keeping my torso still. I concluded that certain arts can only be
learned during one's early formative years; there seemed no hope of
acquiring them genetically or through effort.

Within each Durbar regiment, I saw certain individuals wearing
turbans tied above their heads to resemble rabbit ears. These were
the sons of the emir, Nadira explained. There appeared to be a
prince within each of the countless groups that cantered past us, and
they came in all ages, shapes and sizes. There was a prince in his
mid-fifties, another in his forties, several teenagers and twenty-
somethings. All of them trooped past, raising a clenched fist in salute
to their father. A small prince, roughly six years old, struggled to
control his small and hyperactive horse. He was trailed by another
prince of a similar age who rode more confidently and wore aviator sunglasses to complement his shiny outfit.

'Knowing how to ride horses and tame them is viewed by the
Fulanis as a form of intellect,' Nadira informed me. By all appear-
ances, the emir's offspring were taught to ride as soon as they could
walk. A four-year-old trotted by on his own horse, wielding his tiny
fist in the air. His two-year-old brother came at the rear of one
group; he was mounted but was escorted by a man who walked
beside the horse and controlled the reins on the prince's behalf.
Nadira and I laughed when the boy raised a tiny fist shrouded in a
black leather glove.

The princes were getting even younger still. I did a double-take
when a baby filed past, perched on a man's lap. His tiny head was
wrapped in a turban just like his brothers, the dense fabric engulfing
his face almost to the point of oblivion. The toddler sat with phe-
nomenal composure. At that age, my nephews would have have
wriggled like wild animals if anyone tried to wrap their faces with

fabric, but this little boy was a bundle of poise and discipline. The age gap between him and his eldest half-brother must have been at least forty-five years.

'I can't believe how many sons the emir has!' I gasped.

'And that's just the *boys*,' Nadira reminded me.

When perhaps the thirtieth bunny-eared prince rode by, I wondered how much time and energy the emir devoted to this conjugal shift work – many of the princes, perhaps a dozen of them, looked the same age, give or take a year. My museum guide Amadu had told me, perhaps jokingly, that when the princes and princesses are brought in front of the emir he identifies them by asking who – among his several wives and concubines – their mother is.

Loud gunshots punctured the air, suddenly. The shots were announcing the arrival of the emir and his massive entourage. Wearing a wide, ornate hat, he was mounted on a horse and shielded by an embroidered umbrella, which signifies the covenant he keeps with his subjects. The entire audience stood up and raised its fists in solidarity. The emir settled in a corner in preparation for the final part of the Durbar. From the opposite side of the courtyard, each of his noblemen and sons charged on horseback towards him. The horses galloped at full speed, kicking up a miniature sandstorm, before suddenly halting about a metre away from the emir. It was an awesome display of horsemanship. The nobleman then raised his sword in salute.

This sort of traditional rule – the amount of patronage involved, the (governmental) expense of maintaining palaces and emirs' salaries – seems inefficient and outdated in any part of the world. Yet at the same time it would be sad ever to see it disappear in the name of modernisation. All that pomp and ceremony can be wonderfully self-affirming for the people, the only chance for a community to display orderliness, glamour and rectitude in an otherwise shabby and incompetent world.

At the end of the Durbar, a mass of people filed out of the palace and clogged the streets, hawking up phlegm and spitting it randomly. The harmattan haze and the setting sun reduced visibility to only a metre or so. A truck rumbled slowly through the crowd. At the back of it stood a handful of government workers closeted inside a metal cage, throwing sachets of insecticide paper onto the streets, to protect against malaria. The scene descended into a melee as men and boys scrambled to catch the sachets, grabbing and pushing one another in the dusty dusk. I sidestepped their flailing limbs and competed with other bystanders to find an available achaba.

The Durbar was over for another year, and as the sun went down over Kano, I rode away from the city centre, glancing back one last time as it reverted to the chaos and indignity of modern life.

9

Where Are Those Stupid Animals?

Nguru and Yankari

The next morning, I sat clamped within a mass of elbows, thighs and shoulders in a Peugeot 505, en route to Nguru, the most northerly town in Nigeria, close to the Niger border. Trees lined the road, which cut through fields of golden grass. Further north, the road became potholed and the roadside grass grew long and intensely green, a brilliant contrast with the cloudless blue sky.

Nguru was situated near a wetlands conservation project I wanted to visit, but my guidebooks offered little information about where to stay or whom to contact. My stomach churned at the possibility of getting lost. Uncertainty seemed to be my most persistent travelling companion in Nigeria.

The Peugeot broke down 13 kilometres outside Nguru. I flagged down a passing achaba and rode into town, where my achaba man asked passers-by for directions to the conservation project. We were sent to a residential-looking house sprawled quietly beneath the shade of several trees next to an open field. The caretaker was surprised to see me – apart from foreign researchers, no other visitors had graced the area in the past year. She invited me to sit down and wait for the conservation field worker to return. Half an hour later, a Nigerian man called Harry Hudson pulled up on his motorcycle. He had work to do, and he hadn't planned on showing me around for the day, but 'I must be a good host,' he smiled, and urged me to hop onto his bike.

Being this close to the Sahara normally made me feel faintly depressed. I disliked its heat and emptiness and claustrophic distance from the sea. But it was a real treat to speed through the open countryside on a motorbike. We rode along the highway towards the Dagona lake, through arid savannah dotted with acacia trees and doum palms; there was not a house or building in sight. Every so often, a lake appeared, transforming the parched landscape into a quenching patchwork of shiny blue water and green reeds. Harry pointed out the oil drums poking out of the ground, explaining that they are used for apportioning land to nomadic cattle grazers as a way of preventing territorial conflicts.

Suddenly, one of the tyres burst and we came to a stop in the middle of nowhere. I became an anxious speck in this vast semi-desert. But soon after, a man on a motorcycle travelling in the opposite direction stopped next to us. The nearest service station was 16 kilometres behind him, he told us, yet to my amazement, he turned around and rode back to fetch help, trundling towards the horizon without complaint. His altruism seemed motivated not by duty but by innate reflex. No matter how alien my surroundings in Nigeria, I always felt cushioned by this safety net of human decency.

Harry fiddled with the bike's wheel while I sat on the edge of the highway and fanned myself. Harry was a shy, Hausa-speaking Igbo ornithologist; a hygiene freak with a delicate constitution who liked to inspect glasses and cutlery before using them. After several years living in the US, he retained a slight Atlanta accent littered with the stubs of half-suppressed swear words. When Harry returned to Nigeria, he asked the Royal Society for the Protection of Birds in the UK for financial help. It donated twenty-five pairs of binoculars, which Harry took around the schools to kindle children's interest in birdwatching.

'I organised trips for schoolchildren to visit the nature reserve in Lagos. But after one year, the government stopped it.'

'Why?' I asked.

He shrugged his shoulders. 'Someone decided to finish it.'

'Why?'

'Do I know? They gave no reason.'

That's just the way it was. Nothing ever lasts in Nigeria. Harry accepted the situation with disgusted resignation. Nowadays, although still living in Lagos, he spends a few months of the year in Dagona, counting the various specimens and monitoring which bird species are still migrating from Europe.

Twenty minutes after our tyre burst, the man on the motorcycle returned with a fresh one, which Harry fixed to the bike. We continued our journey, soon turning off the highway and entering the Chad Basin National Park, a nature reserve that had few visitors, especially now that its tourist accommodation had lapsed into disuse. At the base camp I was introduced to a guide called Zanna, a round-faced Hausa man. He'd spent the afternoon arresting a Fulani cattle grazer and had locked him in the village chief's office on condition of bail. Grazing cattle in the area is illegal.

'What happens to the cows?' I asked.

'They find their own way back home. Sometimes armed robbers take them.'

Fulani nomadic cow herders wander all around West Africa – an area stretching from Mauritania to Sudan – searching for fresh grazing pasture. Their cows' grazing upsets Dagona's environment by compacting the soil and making it harder for trees to grow. The resulting soil erosion has increased siltation of the lake which, combined with the construction of regional dams, has lowered water levels in the lakes, creating water and fish shortages for the local people.

'We want them to have a sense of ownership and management of the land. It's their forefathers' land,' Zanna said of the local people. 'But the Fulanis think they can do what they like with it. Some of them say, "It is our land."'

Grazing cattle illegally seemed a huge risk, considering how difficult it is to flee with several cows. Weren't the grazers worried about getting caught?

'They don't give a shit,' Harry said. It was worth the financial risk because land for grazing was limited.

It was time to see the lake, but the conservation project's solitary truck had engine problems, and Zanna didn't want to risk using it. Harry decided he'd stay behind and let Zanna take me to the lake on his motorcycle instead. The bike was parked by a tree where a calm patas monkey, which resembled a baboon, was tethered by a rope.

'Be careful,' Zanna warned as I walked towards the animal. 'He hates women.' When I approached the monkey it lunged at me, all teeth, paws and squeaks. Misogyny, even within the animal kingdom, was irritating and alarming. Zanna and I mounted his motorcycle and rode into the bush. We were in one of the most remote parts of Nigeria, at least six hours away from any major town or city. The tall, golden grass and intermittent trees harboured patas monkeys, grey monkeys, jackals and squirrels. We rode past the homes of Hausa villagers, ringed by walls made of weaved raffia. Village boys, all of them tall with dark gangly limbs, played football in a sandy field. Beautiful Fulani women wearing their trademark eyeliner and colourful headscarves sashayed through the grass, carrying calabashes filled with cows' milk.

The path wound its way through a patch of dense foliage. Thorns and branches scratched and lashed us as our motorcycle bounced along. Zanna wasn't bothered by it, but I had to bury my face in his back.

We dismounted at the Dagona bird sanctuary. The lake was a large oxbow formation set in the middle of a huge bowl-shaped grassy field. Tens of thousands of Palaearctic birds (from Eurasia and

North Africa) and inter-African migrant waterbirds from Southern Africa and Europe migrate to the area between November and March, fleeing winter. Zanna and I stood at an unthreatening distance to watch dozens of migrating geese, grey herons, egrets, ruffs and storks skim the lake's polished surface, which refracted the evening sky's deep amber glow. I wasn't used to Nigeria being this unspoilt, beautiful, peaceful, untouched by the relentless land-grabbing of our growing population. Zanna said that the local people are encroaching on the land and depleting firewood at accelerating rates. Chopping trees down reduces the bird habitat, especially that of the grey heron and little egrets, which breed here.

Zanna's enthusiasm for the flora and fauna made a gratifying change to the money-chasers in the cities. The bustle of Kano felt a thousand mornings away. In some ways, this contrast from the city gave the Dagona sanctuary its appeal. Admittedly, it was no Serengeti: there were no pink flamingos, no hippo eyes blinking above the water's surface – Ravi's disinterest in Dagona was understandable – but I was enjoying being there.

'Can you see the cow droppings?' Zanna asked me. 'The Fulanis have been grazing here illegally.'

'Are you the only person patrolling the place?'

'No, there are thirty-two of us for the thirty-two square miles, but many of our people are in Kano for the Durbar.'

Zanna said the government had actually reserved land for the Fulanis to graze their cattle, but the herdsmen weren't satisfied with its quality. They believed the grass by the lake was richer, and that 'one cow will make two' if they graze on it. They weren't wrong: the Hausa villagers living by the lake easily grew tomatoes, peppers, onions and other crops in the highly fertile soil.

We rode back to the base camp. After saying goodbye to Zanna and exchanging hostilities with the patas monkey, I mounted Harry's bike for the return trip to Nguru. Rushing to beat the sunset had become a familiar routine on my travels. It would have been more convenient to stay at the sanctuary overnight, but there was no food or accommodation. Harry and I zipped along the highway, praying we'd get back to Nguru without bursting another tyre. At that point I realised I hadn't eaten since leaving Kano in the morning. Hungry, tired, desperate for the toilet, I shivered in the headwind as the bike cruised through the twilight.

Ahead of us I saw two men crossing the highway with a caravan of ten camels. They wore elegant white djellabas that contrasted with the dusky purple sky and red sun liquidizing on the horizon. Riding on a camel each, the men shepherded the animals gracefully along the savannah, blending into their surroundings so regally. I felt we were imposing rudely on the landscape as we cruised along on our metallic blot of a motorcycle. Bound for the distant markets of Kano, the camels disappeared into the semi-darkness like an apparition, taking my traveller blues with them.

The next morning, Harry and I biked across town to pick up Hasan, another ornithologist who was joining us on a bird-watching excursion on the lake. Along the way, Harry stopped to greet passers-by. The traditional Hausa greeting is a long one, performed with perfunctory speed, as though the participants want to complete it as quickly as possible:

'How are you?'

'Fine.'

'How are the children?'

'Fine.'

'Did they eat well?'

'Yes.' And so on and so forth.

Social interaction required time and patience, things the local Hausa people had plenty of. Harry, who was originally from the south, said they were very fatalistic people, and that they accepted death's certainty without fear, often doing nothing to mitigate against misfortune. On some level, this seemed quite liberating.

'Someone will die in a car crash, but they do not say it was because of speeding,' Harry said. 'They say, "His time has come ... God wants it."' Malaria was a big killer in the wetlands area, and the Hausas' attitude to their high child mortality was of the 'God gives, God takes' variety. 'They don't know when one of their kids will die, so they keep having more,' Harry said. 'I have a friend who has three wives and twenty-four kids!'

Harry and Hasan recruited four villagers to load our small boat onto a cart and then attached it to a pair of oxen, which dragged the cart towards the lake shore while we walked alongside it. Harry, Hasan and I lowered our wobbling backsides onto the seats of the small boat and drifted out onto the water. Its clear blue surface was fringed by tall typha reeds flinching in the chilly breeze.

'Here, you can have these Mungo Park binoculars,' Harry said, handing me a chunky old pair, reminiscent of colonial-era British explorers. We observed the different bird species flying above us, perched on trees or standing in the reeds. Harry and Hasan cooed gently over the ruffs and egrets. I inhaled and meditated on this bed of blue tranquillity. I wasn't used to silence of such magnitude.

We were sailing on the lake a few weeks before high season when hundreds of thousands birds migrate here from Europe, their huge flocks almost obliterating the skies.

'What do the villagers think when they see so many birds in the sky?'

'They think about how to get them in their soup pot!' Harry smiled. People kill the birds using line traps or by putting poison on leaves of trees and bushes. The bigger species, such as ducks and storks, are shot with guns.

There was a second, smaller lake roughly 100 metres away from Lake Nguru. We crossed the railway tracks, oxen and boat in tow, and floated on the lake. The water was clear enough for me to see large catfish and red lily stems coiling like electric wires towards the floor. Hassan fished a lily from the water and handed it to me.

'He's in love with you!' Harry joked before picking a bulbous lily fruit out of the water and putting it in his mouth. 'Fishermen eat these. It suppresses their hunger.'

Having skipped breakfast, I grabbed one and bit into its mainly crunchy white body, flecked with green and purple and full of seeds. It tasted of nothing.

Hassan and Harry docked the boat on the edge of an island in the middle of the lake. After fighting our way through the tall reeds we came across the purple feathers of a swan hen scattered on the ground, near a circle of charcoal. Someone had hunted the bird and cooked it. Disappointed, Harry and Hassan stared at the remains, the latest sign of the fragile ecology around us. Locals had chopped down and burnt a mango tree for firewood, he said. The tree would have died anyway since all the island's trees – mangoes, doum palms and debino – fall victim to regular floods. But the absence of trees allowed typha reeds to colonise the soil instead, threatening the rich deposits of potash, which, along with the fruits from the doum palm, is sold by villagers at market.

Each year, money from an international wetlands conservation treaty called the Ramsar Convention is given to Nigeria's Ministry of Environment to protect the lake and its island. But 'There is no visible evidence that the island is being protected. *No* visible evidence,' Harry said, stabbing the sky with an uncharacteristically angry forefinger. 'This island place is *begging* for attention. The government doesn't do anything for us. Even that RAMSAR signboard on the roadside was made by the Wetlands Conservation Project,' he seethed. '*I* put up that sign.'

Harry's mind brimmed with ideas for the island. He dreamed of tourist chalets with locals working as guides, but as the land is state-owned, only the useless government could build such a thing.

The Wetlands Conservation Project had spent a lot of money creating a development plan. After hiring professionals to produce a feasibility study, the Project was allocated ₦40 million a year from the government. Yet it hadn't seen any of that money.

'Why don't you complain about this?' I asked, outraged.

'*Who* do we complain to?' Harry replied, raising his hands in the air.

'The authorities.'

'They don't give a damn.'

'It doesn't matter. You should complain anyway. At least write to a newspaper so they know that you're unhappy with the situation. You can't let them think you're accepting it.'

Harry shook his head. To me he seemed to be behaving as fatalistically as the Hausas he had spoken of earlier in the day. Government corruption had become as inevitable to him as death, except that he was livid about it. But who was I to demand action? Fighting government corruption was a monumental task few people had the time or money to take on.

We rode the boat back to the shore. On the other side of the lake, a train rattled noisily along the railway tracks. Rail used to be a common form of transport in Nigeria. These days, the only passengers are livestock and the poorest traders who can't afford to transport their goods by bus. The locomotive unburied childhood memories of a Nigerian train trip I once took as part of my father's educational sadism. He ordered Zina, Tedum and me to travel by ourselves from Port Harcourt to Zaria on a train service that, even back in 1989, was a no-no for respectable people of sane mind.

The journey lasted half a week, a sweaty, shit-stained odyssey that we can laugh about in retrospect, but which left us seriously questioning our father's love for us at the time. We and our suitcases were cooped up in a dirty compartment with two bunk beds and a heavy jerry can of water that spilled repeatedly onto the floor. The miniscule bathroom allowed enough space for a sink and non-flushing toilet (Tedum's frequent bowel movements were a major source of anger), and changing into our pyjamas at night involved a lot of claustrophobic fumbling by torchlight. The train wasn't entirely safe, either: when Tedum stepped off for fresh air and found ₦200 on the ground, a man threatened to stone him if he didn't hand it over. At night, the coaches stopped for hours at a time at random points, ending our only source of air conditioning and inviting the mosquitoes inside. It was the longest three days and three nights of my life.

Nowadays, the Port Harcourt–Zaria route 'takes even longer than that', according to Harry. The rolling stock is old and decrepit. The government, with the help of Chinese engineers, is planning to build a high-speed train service from Lagos to Abuja, which would be a fabulous alternative to those long, risky road journeys. But I wouldn't be surprised if those future trains slip into disrepair again. Our politicians aren't interested in maintenance. They often commission construction projects purely to receive kickbacks, and once the projects are built, the rot sets in as inevitably as human ageing.

The parallels with Nguru's environment seemed ominous. Letting our train infrastructure crumble was heinous enough, though at least reversible. But doing the same to Nguru's lake island would be a tragedy. As I took one last look at the gorgeous blue water, I rued the possibility that our government might leave Nigeria with neither natural beauty nor a fully functioning economy: the worst of both worlds.

I was ready to leave the sparseness of the extreme north. I craved more trees, more people, more varied, less arid landscapes. From Nguru I dipped southwards by car to the comforting throngs and slightly greener vegetation of Bauchi, a town on the northern edge of the central highland plateau.

The changing landscape was obliterated by a thick fog that smothered the road, permitting only glimpses of undulating green grassland – and the shock appearance of a lorry's registration plate

3 metres ahead. My driver had to stamp on the brakes to avoid a collision.

Five hours later, the fog cleared to reveal Bauchi itself. The town was pleasingly rubbish-free. Its authorities, Junior had told me, had made a concerted effort to clean up the place. Over its main street arched a modern version of a Kano-style kofar, or gate. It gave some character to the same old urban vista of bland, postcolonial architecture, which housed the usual barbershops, plastic tupper-ware outlets and food stalls, all manned by placid Muslim men, their womenfolk as ever invisible. Bauchi is a 200-year-old medium-sized emirate that was once part of the Islamic Sokoto empire, a Fulani sultanate that ruled large swathes of Northern Nigeria from the mid-eighteenth century. The name Bauchi is a derivation of Baushe, an ancient hunter who advised a commander of Sokoto to found a city here. These days, Bauchi is a calm, unassuming place, and the closest city to Nigeria's most famous safari park, the Yankari Game Reserve.

I was in a slightly panicky mood. For the first time on this trip, I had recently checked my bank balance, and was horrified at how much my daily routine of okada rides, goat stews and Internet browsing was costing me. After rifling through my receipts with overdue diligence, I realised that hotel accommodation had formed the bulk of my spending, a galling discovery considering that none of my hotel rooms had justified their price. For someone obsessed by hygiene, hotel rooms were a challenging experience, and 'shower time' was particularly trying. Non-functioning taps, slow-draining baths and mildewed shower curtains clinging to my body had reg-ularly tested my resolve.

So I arrived at my Bauchi hotel anxiously anticipating a variety of stains and malfunctions. My entrance in the lobby was a lesson in customer disservice. A group of people sat silently on chairs, look-ing too inactive to be staff yet too poised to be guests. Some sat in front of a TV, others leaned against a wall; all of them stared at me wordlessly. I stared back – bags in tow – waiting to be welcomed. I was eyeballed some more. Only when I asked if any of them worked there did a man slowly peel himself away from the wall and amble towards the reception desk, his feet dragging across the floor . . . *ssssh, ssssh, sssssh, ssssh.*

He took my deposit and led me to my room – the 'deluxe suite' or some such fiction. The staff on the upper floor apologised for forgetting to supply towels, toilet paper or soap. They weren't lazy, I hoped, just unpractised at serving guests, and doing it, no doubt, for next to no pay. The toilet was thankfully clean (Nigerian hotels never failed in that area), but the air conditioning didn't work, the television set had lost all its buttons, and I had to use my own batteries for the remote control. A lizard dropping rested beneath my blanket, the walls were bespattered with mashed mosquitoes and dried blood; the glass louvred windows – those tired vestiges of 1970s architecture – wouldn't open or close fully, and the cold tap in the bathroom didn't work. All this for a relatively ritzy ₦6,250 per night.

Throughout my travels around West Africa, I'd noticed that many hotels keep the more expensive rooms spotless while neglecting the cheaper ones, as if impressing richer customers were more important than catering to all clients. I suspect that this was influenced by the system of patronage, in which the big chief distributed wealth to the people. Perhaps some Nigerians still perceive wealth as a centralised resource, with rich people the sole source of income, in the same way that oil is viewed as our country's main source of earnings, or the way the staff at the Lagos National Museum targeted the German tourist as if he were the sole opportunity for a tip.

This pattern of decrepitude was wearing me down after three months on the road. But persistent optimism and curiosity compelled me to continue the trip, despite its annoyances. I wanted more of the pleasant surprises that leaped out of Nigeria's chaos and neglect. Besides, I'd been travelling for long enough to know that good things always came unexpectedly, while anticipated joys often didn't materialise.

That night in my hotel room, I settled down to watch one of two TV channels available in my deluxe suite. The first, a state channel, was broadcasting a fuzzy studio debate. The other channel was a digital one, centrally controlled by the hotel management. I prayed that the nameless, faceless philistine behind the controls would select something decent. But he skipped past the news channels, teased me with half a minute of *E! Entertainment*, then settled on *Smackdown Wrestling* for the rest of the evening. It was dull, but at least had the benefit of sending me to sleep more quickly.

Early the next day, I sat alone in the back of a taxi as it cruised past the giant boulders that dotted Bauchi's grasslands, glistening with beads of morning dew. I was on my way to the Yankari National Park Game Reserve. When I first came here with my father as a twelve-year-old, I was sleepless with excitement. We were going to see lions, he told me, and hippos, elephants, monkeys and crocodiles. But it wasn't to be: on arriving at the park we received the devastating news that heavy rains would prevent us from taking a game drive. Our trip was cut short to just one night, which was spent in a chalet watching gangs of cheeky baboons – the only wildlife we laid eyes on – galloping outside the windows. Twenty years on, I wanted to make up for that disappointment.

At the border of Yankari I jumped on an okada that would take me to the central office, known as Wikki Camp, nestled 40 kilometres inside the reservation. Thirty years ago, trundling through this wildlife safari park by motorcycle might have been risky, but the men at the entrance gate assured me it was no problem. Confronting a lion was as likely as finding fresh towels in my Bauchi hotel room. Yankari's animal stock had depleted over the decades. Established in 1950, the reserve once teemed with more than fifty mammal species, including leopards, hyenas, buffalo and hippos.

The cheetahs, giraffes and gazelles are now extinct as a result of organised poaching and a rinderpest epidemic in the 1970s and 1980s. Several hundred elephants still remain, however, and the lion population has managed to defy depletion.

My okada cruised along Yankari's tarmacked road, past a sign that issued the warning: WILD ANIMALS PRESENT. TAKE CARE. The only wild animal we spotted was a monkey in the forest trees. My okada man, apparently a stranger to wildlife, pointed it out excitedly. At Wikki Camp's main booking office, I bagged the last seat on a big truck ready to depart on a game drive. My vehicle was overtaken by a second truck containing two dozen Indian men, who waved their hands and roared jubilantly as they moved off in a different direction. Several grey patas monkeys scattered from our vehicle as it rumbled into the reserve's misty, deciduous forest.

Our game warden, perched near the truck's bonnet, told me he'd spotted a pride of lions three days before. I bristled with excitement. Almost immediately, we came across three majestic waterbucks munching between some trees and twisting their powerful necks to stare at us. Everyone took obligatory photos before the driver moved on. Waterbucks were all very well but, frankly, lions and elephants were the animals we had come to see.

'Where are these stupid animals?' asked a woman in light-hearted disgust. The woman, Njide, was the mother of the large family sitting around me, and she was speaking our minds. Safari had brought out the eco-philistines in us. Rather than delighting in the everyday flora and fauna of Nigeria's beautiful ecosystem, we dismissed the white-rumped vultures, agama lizards, *Afzelia* trees and butterflies in impatient anticipation of the more dramatic big game. As we scoured the forest for Big Beasts, desperation began to play tricks on our eyes: every leaf looked like a lion's tail; every vertical branch was definitely an elephant's leg.

'Look!' someone cried out from the back. 'On the right!' The truck braked urgently as we peered intensely into the forest.

'It's white tree bark,' the game warden confirmed. Everyone kissed their teeth and sighed in disappointment.

'Come now, let's go,' Njide implored, anxious to sight something more interesting.

Every so often, the warden pointed out mounds of elephant dung, steaming on the ground with tantalising freshness. The herd must have been nearby. Everyone perked up and scrutinised the scenery, beady-eyed and desperate. Suddenly the truck stopped, and the warden pointed his finger. Our eyes trained onto several grey, short-legged birds.

'Guinea fowl,' Njide said, kissing her teeth again. 'We see these all the time. *Where* are the elephants and lions?' We rumbled on through the forest. 'Are they all at a meeting?'

For a long time we saw nothing but guinea fowl. After a while, I didn't even have to lay eyes on these birds to know they were there – Njide indicated their presence with her comical sighs and teeth kissing. She was similarly unimpressed by the baboons playing near a fresh spring. When they spotted us, the apes galloped towards our stationary vehicle as if on the attack, then paused a few metres away and stared.

'We can see baboons anywhere,' Njide grumbled, 'even in town.' She and her husband, a doctor from Enugu, had visited Yankari twenty-odd years previously. They had seen all the big animals, she said. This year they had returned with their teenage children, hoping to repeat the experience, but so far Yankari was concealing its treasures.

Suddenly, through the trees, a crocodile slipped into the gentle ripples of the Gaji River, and we spotted another sunbathing on the riverbank. They were exotic enough to ease our disappointment a little. We moved on, past more piles of fresh elephant dung that inflamed our hopes. Later, two large, tawny-coloured western hartebeests leapt across the dirt track in front of us. They looked stunning among the tall yellowy grasses gleaming in the sunlight.

But they – and Njide's dreaded guinea fowls – were all we managed to see in the game drive's final leg. We rolled into the driveway of the base camp where the Indian tourists, still in an exuberant mood, passed us again on their way to yet another game drive, no doubt dissatisfied with their first one.

The wildlife that we'd seen was a dwindling time capsule, a flash from a past that I couldn't fully imagine but lamented nonetheless. Yankari wasn't our only game reserve, however. Others, such as the Gashaka-Gumti National Park in the south-east, supposedly teem with chimpanzees, giraffes, lions and elephants. But these places are virtually inaccessible to the ordinary tourist unless they can afford their own vehicles, tents and wardens.

Shaking off my disappointment, I disembarked from the truck and ran down some stone steps. At the bottom was the Wikki Springs, a stunning natural thermal spring filled with pure, cobalt-blue water that bubbled at a very agreeable 31°C. I had vague memories of visiting it with my father. Somewhere at home, there's a grainy photograph of Zina and me in our 'wet-look' Jheri-curl hairstyles, posing with Tedum by the water. Then, we were the sole visitors there. The scene couldn't have been more different now. Several Hausa men and boys were swimming in the spring, their dark, glistening bodies dive-bombing from the branches of the tamarind tree arching overhead. They laughed, roared, splashed about and hawked phlegm into the crystal-clear pool while their mothers and sisters sat on the water's edge, restricting themselves to the vicarious pleasure of spectatorship. I sat with them and ate a lunch of jollof rice before leaving Yankari and returning to Bauchi.

For all my excitement about the safari, the most interesting attraction of the day turned out to be near my hotel. I decided to visit the tomb of Tafawa Balewa, Nigeria's first post-independence prime minister, who holds the sadly everlasting distinction of being one of our least corrupt premiers. I remember his avuncular visage on the corner of old banknotes, a white turban wrapped around his head.

Balewa, one of the few northern politicians to be university educated, fought for the rights of Northern Nigeria and played a role
in creating the Organisation of African Unity, a body that promoted
economic and political cooperation across the continent. Unusually
by today's standards, Balewa openly intervened in crises around
Africa: negotiating during the Congo Crisis of 1960–4 and criticising
the South African Sharpeville Massacre in 1960. But his administration was undermined by internal divisions, and in 1966 he was
deposed in a military coup. Six days after being ousted from office,
Balewa's decomposing body was discovered by a road near Lagos;
the cause of death was uncertain. He was given a Muslim burial in
Bauchi, his home town.

Balewa's tomb lay inside a windowless, artistically asymmetrical
building, built in the 1970s, with a wraparound patterned roof. Its
form was designed to tell the story of Nigeria's journey to independence. I followed the guide and his student tour group through
the entrance, along a tall, cavernous corridor that was almost pitch
black, save for a few tiny rays of light streaming through a lattice of
holes in the wall. These shafts of light symbolised the distant dream
of independence during the dark days of colonialism. As we walked
further down the corridor, bigger holes allowed more light to pour
in, indicating the achievement of independence.

The corridor approaching the courtyard contained two sets of
staircases: a deliberately narrow one with short steps (signifying the
ease of life after independence), and a second, wider, staircase with
high steps that represented the difficulty of achieving one's goals in
a colonised Nigeria. The guide instructed everyone to huddle
together and walk pointedly down the narrower independence staircase. One of the students and I couldn't resist taking the bigger, less
congested steps instead. We smiled at one another in tacit understanding; it was a matter of convenience, not a political statement.

The steps led us to a sun-filled open-air courtyard where Tafawa
Balewa's grave lay. The courtyard's high walls were covered in

multicoloured tiles representing Nigeria's myriad ethnic groups. On the grave itself, a mound of pebbles was piled on a rectangular slab of light stone, Balewa's name engraved on its edge. There was no grandeur, no fanfare, just a simple engraving of his name. The space was breezy, elegant and fresh; the grave's simplicity represented everything I imagined about Nigeria of the 1950s and 1960s: a cleaner, less populated, possibly less damaged place.

In the building next door, we were shown a cabinet filled with Balewa's personal effects, including a mini Sony TV gifted to him by Queen Elizabeth II. Beside it was a glass vial containing the very first drops of crude oil pumped by Shell in 1957. The black oil sat in the bottle, looking like a dollop of poison. There weren't many other personal effects, our guide informed us, because Balewa was a simple man, uninterested in consumption. I cynically speculated whether his short tenure in office had prevented him from succumbing to corruption. Still, he was the antithesis of Sani Abacha. After the dictator died suddenly in 1998, the authorities recovered more than $2 billion from his bank accounts, newspapers said. Some of the cash had reportedly been delivered from the central bank to his mansion, where he stored it in mountainous stacks.

Our guide ushered us into a room with a TV monitor. He pushed an ancient-looking videocassette tape into a VCR and played black-and-white footage of Tafawa Balewa making his first speech to the nation as prime minister of a newly independent Nigeria. His voice and face crackled and flickered, as though the footage had been broadcast from a galaxy millions of miles away. His ambitions for Nigeria seemed equally unreachable, leaving me pining nostalgically for a young, forward-looking Nigeria that I never knew.

Back in town, I walked aimlessly along the streets, ignoring the stares my un-Islamic attire attracted. Balewa's tomb had energised me to the extent that when I came across a white arch emblazoned with the words Babangida Square, I didn't feel the usual irritation.

Structures like this, paeans to previous dictators, were everywhere in Nigeria, befouling our towns and cities and street signs like an unwashed bloodstain: Sani Abacha Road, Babangida Drive ... I couldn't understand why they were still there.

I entered Babangida Square, sidestepping the sleeping guardsman at the entrance. The place had become a prairie of grass, so tall and overgrown that I was startled by the sneeze of a goat grazing nearby. A shabby terrace of seats occupied one end of the square, opposite a statue of a nameless soldier. It was a sad, neglected place, and a contrast to Tafawa Balewa's tomb. Our despots don't even look after places named in their honour.

A man passing through the square informed me that the space was used for boy scout parades and similar gatherings.

'Why are there so many street names and parks named after people like Babangida?' I asked the man.

'I don't know,' he replied. 'They put it there when the people are alive, and they leave them like that.'

'It's not because they like these people?'

'No,' he smiled, shaking his head.

So civic neglect keeps the dictators' names up there, rather than pride or solidarity. Which was mildly comforting, I suppose. Inertia is preferable to evil.

10

Hidden Legacies

Jos

With a tense bladder, I sat in the back of a long, ten-seater car. In the seat in front, two female passengers hummed Christian songs to themselves. Ahead of them, a burly, broad-shouldered man in the front passenger seat turned around to grin at the baby sitting with its mother in the row behind him. The infant's giant forehead bulged irresistibly over round glassy eyes and dumpling cheeks. When the man reached out for the baby, the mother handed him to this complete stranger, who stood the tot on his lap and murmured silly nothings to him.

Two hours later, we were in Jos. This former tin-mining town sits on a high plateau in rocky, Wild West scenery filled with dusty grey-brown boulders and beautiful 'hanging rock' formations, which were arranged as though an invisible, playful giant had placed the boulders one on top of the other. Jos was my favourite city as a child. I loved its mosquito-free, high-altitude freshness and the scenery, so fantastically lunar and un-Nigerian.

In my hotel room, I sat on the bed and read the sign pasted on the wall by the hotel management:

CELEBRATIONS FOR WHAT?

What were your personally set goals for this year,
and how much did you achieved?

If you have not achieve at least 50–60% of your goals,
you have no reason to celebrate.

But if you did, then on behalf of the Management
and staff, we wish you a Happy Xmas and more
achievement in the coming year.

This is the time to set the targets.

I'd long ago adopted the British aversion to being patronised, but I was surprisingly comforted by the paternalistic message. It was nice to be in a place where actively promoting such values was acceptable. I needed that kick up the backside sometimes.

I stepped out onto the streets, where rocky hills protruded in the near distance. Jos was filled with people and okadas, despite my memories of its sparseness. Nigerian cities keep growing and growing, it appears. My surroundings conjured up vague fragments of memory, of Jos's cool grey skies, a quiet restaurant serving delicious plantain in a museum, which my father said was the best in the country. Remembering little else about that visit, I headed straight to the museum to jog my memory.

The Jos Museum comprised several parts, including the main exhibition building and the Museum of Traditional Architecture. The latter was certainly the most original. It contained replicas of regional traditional architectural styles around Nigeria. The buildings were constructed in an open-air compound and, according to a sign at the entrance, were situated in geographical order: Igbo buildings in the south-east, Yoruba buildings in the south-west, Tive and Nupe in middle belt, and a replica of the Friday Mosque in Zaria in the north.

The Friday Mosque's interior was beautiful, with arched adobe beams that met at the top to form a dome. Such elegant architecture made from simple materials was an arresting sight, even if the structure looked ripe for demolition. Sunlight streamed through a gaping hole in the mosque's wooden roof, and birds sprang from their nests to swoop past my face. A man sat on an old wooden chair in the centre of the mosque reading a newspaper before tossing it on the floor and sauntering away.

Was this replica the exact size of the original mosque? And when was the original mosque built? I had so many questions, but there were no answers. The museum didn't provide any information. Still, many of the structures were impressive. There were adobe houses with thatched roofs, elegant grooves and cornicing on their walls and floor. The buildings' ethnic origins could only be identified by geography but, with my poor sense of direction, I easily lost track of my compass bearings.

Entering another mystery structure, I encountered a man – the only other visitor at the museum – investigating it too.

'Excuse me, do you know what this building is?' I asked. The short stocky man responded by sarcastically impersonating a know-nothing museum guide.

'As you can see, this is a very, *very* old building,' he deadpanned. 'And this is the entrance,' – he pointed at the door – 'and this is a window.'

Back outside, towards the entrance, a group of men sat under a tree, chatting. I was savvy enough by now to know they were probably museum staff. The silver-haired one stood up and introduced himself as the caretaker.

'Why are the buildings so run-down?' I asked him.

'We renovate the place on a seasonal basis, between September and April because that is the dry season. But we couldn't do it this year because the funds were not forthcoming.'

'Has this happened before?'

'Yes,' he said matter-of-factly.

Grass is always green, rain is always wet, and Nigerian ministry funding is always diverted and misused. The caretaker's de facto job was to sit under a tree and watch the decaying roofs and crumbling buildings. Was there at least some information on these structures that I could look at?

'Some of them have information, but not all,' he said.

I gave up on the architectural exhibits and turned my thoughts to lunch. The museum restaurant was the only firm memory I'd retained from my childhood trip here. Housed in a traditional adobe building, it had served the best fried plantain I had ever eaten, intensifying my lifelong love affair with the food. I *adore* fried plantain's juicy, firm, succulent slices. So far on my journey I'd successfully ordered it at least once every day, only going without if the restaurant had none in stock. My zealousness was worse when I was younger. One summer, staying at our Uncle Letam's house, Zina, Tedum and I ate plantain three times a day every day for two weeks, dismissing our uncle's pleas that we diversify our diet. *Just keep it coming*, we told him, and so he did. We never got bored of the stuff.

That legendary meal at the Jos Museum restaurant took my love of plantain to a new level. They cooked it just right: not too dry and not too soft; moist without losing its firmness. Twenty years on, I was eager for more of the same. But on reaching the restaurant, I was devastated to find that it was temporarily closed. A man directed me, hungry and despondent, to another restaurant inside one of the traditional huts in the middle of 'Chief Ogbwa's compound'. But instead of being a Nigerian eatery in keeping with the museum theme, I was surprised to find a Chinese restaurant with oriental decor and soulful 1980s saxophone music playing on the radio. I sat down at a red-and-white chequered table near two student types who were scrutinising the menu.

'They're not serious,' the boy muttered, aghast at the prices. The pair left without ordering. I found myself alone in the restaurant, eating sweet-and-sour chicken in a breeze that shook the Chinese lanterns hanging from the ceiling beams, and made the paper fans flutter against the walls.

The main building of Jos Museum contains samples of the famous terracotta figurines of the ancient Nok civilisation, a sophisticated society that existed on the Jos Plateau in northern and central Nigeria between 1000 BC and AD 500, and produced some of West Africa's finest and oldest sculptures.

My father had raved about them and stressed their importance, but all efforts to inspire us disappeared down the black hole of our pre-teen incuriosity. At that age we found it impossible to appreciate Nigerian history – our young minds hadn't developed the self-regard and cultural one-upmanship that I think partly nourishes such interests. I value my father's intentions in retrospect, though: I was paying attention now.

For years I had pored over images of the Nok sculptures in books. The large, hollow terracottas are beautiful, haunting, luscious-lipped masterpieces. They depict animals, people or male and female human heads (almost life-size) with highly stylized features, pierced eyes, and elaborate hairstyles and jewellery. Some were moustached dignitaries, some depicted people deformed by disease, others represented people in a variety of poses, including horse riders. Hand-sculpted from clay, then smoothed and polished and fired for several hours, nobody knows what purpose these sculptures – up to a metre high – served. There are theories that they commemorated ancestors or marked graves, or were used as charms to ward off disease, infertility and crop failure.

The Nok terracottas (and the civilisation that made them) were first discovered during tin mining operations in 1928. A mine worker chanced upon a terracotta monkey head buried in the ground near the village of Nok on the Jos Plateau. The artefacts were handed over to a museum in Jos by the English colonel leading the mining operation.

Over the next few decades, thousands more terracotta pieces were plucked from the ground, although most had crumbled in the waterlogged soil. The few figurines to be found intact fetched high prices on the international art market.

In 1943, again near the village of Nok, a tin mining worker found a clay head and took it home to use as a scarecrow. When the director of the mine heard about the finding, he showed it to Bernard Fagg, an archeologist who initiated an official excavation. By the late 1970s, more than 150 figurines had been found on the Jos Plateau. Since then, more figurines have turned up in the Middle Niger valley and the Lower Benue valley, an area of 80,000 square kilometres.

The Nok civilisation flourished at a time when other cultures, such as the early Mayans, were developing too. Stone Age Nigerians had settled and created a complex society that produced this fine artwork. It is thought that perhaps the figurines were produced by a wide range of iron-smelting communities across this part of Nigeria, who may possibly have been precursors to the Yoruba and Benin empires. Whoever the Nok people were, their civilisation disappeared mysteriously around AD 500. Knowledge of them is frustratingly patchy. The region's muddy, acidic soil dissolved every skeleton, temple and home, leaving only an historical enigma that international researchers are still trying to resolve.

When news of the antiquities came to light, it triggered large-scale thievery. Nok sculptures ended up in the homes of rich Western collectors, or locked away in the vaults of European and American museums, never to see the light of day. The Ethnological

Museum in Berlin and the British Museum have several hundred pieces each, while the Louvre in Paris contains some impressive examples. Meanwhile, Jos Museum was bequeathed the sorrier-looking leftovers. The terracottas I saw on display were small and forlorn specimens, the once-haughty refinement of their features now chastened by erosion in the soil. For years Nigerian governments have campaigned for the return of the finest terracottas by Europe and America. But in 2002, Nigeria and France signed an agreement allowing the Nok statues to stay in the Louvre on a twenty-five-year renewable basis – on condition that France acknowledged Nigeria's ownership of the items.

The debate about whether antiquities should remain in their countries of origin simmers on. Some people believe that no country can enjoy automatic claim on ancient artefacts found within their borders because there is no evidence that the people who created the antiquities are direct ancestors of the present-day citizens of the region. Yale professor Kwame Appiah has written: 'We don't know whether Nok sculptures were commissioned by kings or commoners; we don't know whether the people who made them and the people who paid for them thought of them as belonging to the kingdom, to a man, to a lineage, to the gods. One thing we know for sure, however, is that they didn't make them for Nigeria.'

But Appiah went on to say that if an artefact is 'found in a country, and no one can establish an existing claim on it, the government gets to decide what to do with it'. He added that if artefacts such as the Nok terracottas are of high cultural value, 'It would be better to think of them [the government] as trustees for humanity.'

I felt cheated that I should travel all this way to Jos – the source – and find some of the least fine examples of Nok terracottas. But after experiencing the crumbling replica buildings of the Archaeological Museum, a treasonous corner of my mind made peace with the foreign custody of some of our antiquities. At least they're guaranteed better security and maintenance in museums abroad, and will be viewed by a wider audience. Without these artefacts in the West, I think the world might know a little less about Nigerian history.

Walking along the streets of Jos afterwards, I came across the National Film Institute. Curious about its activities, I decided to investigate the premises. After passing through the unmanned entrance, I entered a brightly lit warehouse, its shelves stacked with celluloid negatives of Nigerian life dating back to 1932. The institute had bought many of its films from British archives in London, and its staff in Jos cleaned, restored and preserved the celluloid tapes. I wanted to know if they had any footage of my father that perhaps I hadn't seen before.

The lady in charge asked me what I was looking for.

'I'd like to watch some of these reels.'

'You need to have written permission,' she replied.

'How long will it take?'

'Two or three days. There is a lot of bureaucracy. Once they sign and give permission then we can let you watch the film.'

Disappointingly, it was my last day in Jos. I explained to the woman my reasons for coming here.

'Ken Saro-Wiwa was your father?' asked a visitor, a strapping pale-skinned woman. Her big eyes widened and a gap-toothed smile lit up her face. 'Oh, he was a hero! He made me aware of how important it is to stand up for your rights,' she said. 'Because of your father I decided to make people here aware of their rights. Me, I am Igbo, but I want people here to fight for what is theirs.'

The woman, Ruth, was referring to the Birom people. These Christians are indigenous to the Jos region but these days find themselves competing for jobs and farmland with Hausa and Fulani migrants from the north. Here in Nigeria's middle belt, the Islamic north meets the Christian south, two dissonant communities with a common need for survival. Biroms and Hausas have learnt to live side by side, but the peoples are like two mildly combustible elements that occasionally sputter on contact beneath the city's placid surface. In 2001, those sputters erupted into a full-blown explosion.

It began during the local government election, which was contested between the incumbent People's Democratic Party (PDP) – a mainly Christian party – and the largely Muslim All Nigerian People's Party (ANPP). After losing in a massive landslide, the ANPP accused the PDP of electoral fraud. Scuffles between their rival supporters drew upon old religious tensions, although the fundamental problem was economic.

Nigeria's oil-reliant economy runs on a system of patronage in which the ruling party dishes out jobs and oil contracts to its friends and supporters. Those who are kept out of this largesse must fend for themselves in the tiny, non-oil sectors. To some Nigerians, losing an election is equivalent to facing an economic depression, inspiring panic, profound fear and bitterness. Elections become high-stakes affairs, in which human lives become expendable.

After the election results, mobs of largely unemployed young men grabbed sticks, knives, guns and machetes, and took to the streets. People were stabbed and burned, churches razed, bodies lay unclaimed in mosques. Seven thousand people evacuated their homes. But the episode, like most in Nigeria, only lasted a few days – the seams of our society fray without actually tearing apart. The army restored order, and ordinary life resumed once again in Jos, its inter-ethnic bitterness simmering down to indoor grumbles and jostling for resources.

Ruth, though an ethnic Igbo, had lived in Jos for years, and her loyalties lay firmly with the Christian Birom people.

'These Hausa-Fulanis have taken over,' she complained, highlighting the numerous Muslim-owned businesses in town. 'And the Biroms are working as security men,' she fumed, nodding at the security guard sitting and listening on a table nearby. 'The Birom youths say, "We go to Kaduna . . . the Hausas are there; we come home to Jos and we cannot get job here."'

Ruth was particularly irked by the voting power she claimed Hausas enjoyed as a result of their larger numbers.

'The Hausa man can have four wives and ten children with each wife. The Birom man has just one wife and, let's say, four children. Come election time, who has the most power? There's no border in the north with Niger state. A Hausa man's brother can come down here, vote, and return. You cannot do that sort of thing in the south! These Hausas buy a plot of land with nothing but *goats* on it, then they claim fifty people live there. Oh it *boils* my stomach.'

In matters as fraught as these I couldn't be sure where the truth lay. Nevertheless, I loved Ruth's spirit. It was a gust of fresh air that cleared the cobwebs of female compliance so prevalent (at least on the surface) in these parts.

'Didn't the government hold a national census recently?' I asked.

'That census was rigged as well,' Ruth harrumphed. Something had to be done about it, and she wasn't going to be a mere specta-tor. 'I don't believe in all this "turn the other cheek",' she declared. The security guard grunted in agreement. 'God knew that eighty per cent of human beings are right-handed. If I come and slap you,' – Ruth pretended to slap my left cheek with her right hand – 'you can defend yourself. You can use your right hand to stop me, you see? So you must fight and stand up for your rights.' Her logic confused me slightly, but I was enjoying it nevertheless. I'd never heard such an entertaining argument against the turn-the-other-cheek philosophy.

'When you pray, you must keep one eye *open*,' Ruth said. She bent her head and clasped her hands in prayer while her bulging left eye scanned her surroundings with comic suspicion. The security guy chuckled with me. 'If you do not vote, you cannot complain to God that the election was rigged,' she continued. 'But if you reg-ister, and the election was rigged, you can say, "God, I stand before you,"' – she raised her hand, still clutching her mobile phone – "'I voted for my man but he was denied."'

'I try to encourage women to register to vote. Some will say, "Ay, but my shop . . . I cannot leave my shop." But if she does not vote, how can she complain when the election is rigged? You must stand up and be counted! So I try to create awareness among people, one by one.'

'How do you do that?'

'I speak to people with influence, who can spread the awareness further. I go around and disciple this person, then the next. Your father's struggle touched me.' I glowed with gratitude. 'He created a disciple in me,' she beamed. 'Your father's blood speaks!'

Kingdom of Heaven

Maiduguri and Sukur

The beautiful morning sunshine poured grace onto an inglorious scene. Cars clogged the gas station, more than twenty vehicles lined up in a convoy that snaked out beyond the forecourt and onto the road leading out of town. Our driver was hoping to refuel for our journey to Maiduguri, a city in Nigeria's far north-east. Oil shortages seemed to happen more frequently in Jos than in any other town I'd visited, although none of my fellow passengers knew why.

'I think maybe they are withholding oil because the government will soon raise the oil price,' one man suggested.

Everyone in the car kissed their teeth and mopped their faces with handkerchiefs.

'Sometimes the advertised prices are not the same as the prices at the pump,' complained the man next to me.

I climbed out of the car to stretch my legs. All along the queue, drivers were vacating their cars to speak to the station staff. Sometimes, the conversations resulted in their moving faster up the line. Feeling restless, I peered into the window of the forecourt office.

'Are you looking for something?' asked a man wearing a baseball cap and leaning against a car, a toothpick wedged smarmily between his teeth. 'I am the manager here.'

'I was just looking around,' I said. 'How come there's so little gas?'

'Are you a journalist?'

'No, I just want to understand the situation. I don't live in Nigeria.'

'You know, a Nigerian always answers a question with a question,' he grinned evasively.

Oil shortages are a regular part of Nigerian life, and the cliché about 'selling ice to Eskimos' rings embarrassingly true here. Although we're the twelfth-largest oil producer in the world, we still import billions of dollars worth of refined fuel because our government hasn't built enough refineries. Ordinary Nigerians speculatively grumble that the oil ministers (who have lucrative contracts to import refined oil) deliberately maintain the status quo, in order to make more money. They cause fuel shortages at the forecourts of their privately owned gas stations by selling their oil to black marketeers (at an inflated price) instead of regular car owners. These black market vendors are generally young men who stand on the roadside with cartloads of petrol cans. Every driver heading out of town has to decide whether to wait at the forecourts or take their chances and find fuel along the highway.

'Why are there shortages?' I again asked the gas station manager. Saying nothing, he folded his arms and grinned some more, exuding the arrogance of a man who has benefited from flouting the rules. He tipped his head back and inhaled. But just as he opened his mouth to speak, my driver ordered me back into the car – our tank was full, it was time to go. I marched back to the vehicle, annoyed that he had been let off the hook. Perhaps it was for the best, anyway. I was slamming myself against a brick wall of selfishness, and nothing productive would come of it.

The road east to Maiduguri cut through beautiful yellow grassy plains and large boulders that had been defaced by the names of electoral candidates. Dotting the roadside for miles were baobab trees, with their characteristic upside-down appearance; their thick trunks sprouted skinny branches that resembled roots, reaching towards the sky in petrified supplication. Between my many naps, I glimpsed towering anthills, Hausa cow herders resting their arms on sticks laid across their shoulders, and women on the roadside selling pyramids of purple onions and supernaturally red tomatoes. I wanted to stay on that road forever.

In the afternoon I reached Maiduguri, a hot Islamic city slowly being buried alive by Saharan sands blowing in from the north. Maiduguri once lay less than an hour's drive from the mighty Lake Chad, on Nigeria's north-eastern border. But that distance has stretched to more than two hours. One of the world's most voluminous bodies of freshwater is being sucked dry by irrigation, dwindling rainfall and desertification caused by the felling of trees. The lake, once an expanse of 26,000 square kilometres in the 1960s, now occupies a humbling 1,500 square kilometres.

My guidebook raved about one particular state-run hotel in Maiduguri. Arriving at the unlit lobby, I stood at the reception desk, waiting for someone to attend to me. Several minutes passed. I flopped into an old armchair and stared at an abstract painting on the wall next to the presidential photo.

Eventually, a very cheerful man introducing himself as Columbus trotted limply into the lobby, as if his limbs were controlled by a puppeteer's strings. He looked drunk.

'Saro-Wiwa!' he exclaimed as I filled out the check-in form. 'You are from Rivers State.'

'Yes.'

'I am so happy to see a fellow southerner! I am from Imo.' His round face and bulbous nose came from my neck of the woods, though his apparent inebria cancelled out any sense of affinity.

Columbus led me up a wide staircase to my room, furnished some time in the early 1980s and seemingly untouched since then. The 1970s-style cylinder lampshades, circular tables and squares of

ancient carpeting looked unstained and unworn, as if mummified by
the shroud of dust coating the entire room. The water pump was
broken. In the bathroom, Columbus showed me the buckets of
water I would have to use for bathing and flushing the toilet. I half
wished I'd bought a tent and slept outside. Without running water
or electricity, I felt I was staying in a glorified shack and paying for
some pretty bathroom tiles and carpeting.

'This is your towel,' Columbus told me, patting the towel and
throwing up a swirling cloud of dust.

'Maiduguri is very dusty,' he said. *Or perhaps*, I thought to myself,
the room hasn't been cleaned in a while? He moved around the room
with exaggerated meticulousness, dusting down the tables, chairs
and bed coverings. 'I always like to help my people,' he said. 'I will
give you discount. I don't want no wahala for you.' He reduced the
tariff from an audacious ₦10,000 down to a slap-in-the-face ₦5,000.
I didn't have the strength to argue.

Running low on cash, I took an okada into the town centre,
hoping to find an ATM machine. The paved streets were con-
cealed beneath 5 centimetres of Saharan sand. I trudged along.
None of the banks accepted Visa cards. I'd have to conserve my
money until I reached the next big city. Feeling more anxious than
necessary, I headed to the market to buy a *wrappa* (a traditional
patterned cloth worn around women's waists) to spread over my
dusty hotel bed. The market was a particularly fly-ridden and
dispiriting affair. I fought my way through tightly packed stalls, feeling clobbered by fatigue, the heat and the sand. My surroundings
merged into a nauseating blur: the veiled women, the men's kufi
hats, the mosque minarets, the okadas sliding along the Saharan
streets. Stomach cramps and rapidly depleting funds had unleashed
the misanthropic beast within me and sapped my patience with
everyone and everything. I tutted impatiently whenever people
walked in my path, and my unending quest for small change took
a ruthless turn: after buying a fistful of groundnuts, I waited cold-

heartedly as the vendor rummaged her pockets to find change for my ₦1,000 note.

Unable to face it all, I returned to the hotel. The sight of my dusty, hot room brought on a complete collapse in morale. I spread my wrappa over the bed cover and curled up like a self-pitying foetus.

It was dark when I woke up. Columbus had warned me that NEPA, the state electricity supply, wasn't working, and the hotel generator was broken. I fumbled for the lamp switch. Nothing happened when I turned it on. Outside was pitch black too – without even the beams of light from a streetlamp. I left the room by torchlight and stared into the corridor, a dark, silent vortex hiding all sorts of potential horrors. Was I the only guest in this *entire* hotel? Trying to suppress my fear of the dark, I hurried down the central staircase and into the shadows of the lobby, which was eerily empty too, like the aftermath of an apocalypse. Columbus was nowhere to be found. Perhaps the penultimate person to leave planet Earth had remembered to turn off the lights. I pushed open the main door and walked gingerly into the car park. Several seconds after passing through the door, I heard it slam violently behind me. Before I could let out a scream, I realised that the door had simply bounced open and shut again. A quick scan of the hotel's exterior revealed that not a single candle illuminated any of the windows; I think I really was the only guest.

The distant light of an okada grew larger and quickly lit up the street. 'Can you take me to Mr Biggs?' I asked the driver, feeling hollow with loneliness. Mr Biggs was a relatively new and ubiquitous fast-food chain. I could always rely on its unwholesome, mass-produced Nigerian dishes when I lacked the energy to find a proper eatery. Under a brilliant starry sky, we cruised through the sandy, unlit residential streets. The bike skidded and slid in all directions on the sand, nearly throwing us off several times. I arrived at Mr Biggs and comforted myself with a polystyrene boxful of jollof rice and rubber chicken, eaten under a dim, bluish light and a TV screen broadcasting Nigerian hip-hop videos. The singers were simulating the fabulousness of an American lifestyle using the most economical of props – hotel swimming pools, cheap sunglasses, old cars.

By the time I returned to the hotel, the electricity was flowing. I switched on the TV, although the only transmission available was the local state NTA channel. Three men were solemnly singing traditional Hausa music and shaking percussion instruments in front of the garish swirls of a cheap, computer-generated backdrop. In my eyes, the imagery was Nigeria exemplified: shoddiness without apology. It triggered the deepest dysphoria I'd felt so far. I was fed up with expensive inadequacy, fed up with unpredictability and low standards. Rarely do I feel homesick or isolated while travelling, but on this night, my resilience was punctured, the accumulated tensions of the past few weeks releasing themselves from my body with a deflated whimper. I switched off the TV and the light and fell asleep, dreaming of ATMs and aeroplanes.

The silvery morning sun rose up and lifted my spirits with it. My taxi careened through the pretty Borno State countryside, along tree-lined roads flanked by flat grassland and fields striated with crops. In the distance, the hazy Mandara mountains erupted from the plains. Somewhere at the top of those mountains was my destination – Sukur, a Stone Age mountain kingdom 900 metres above sea level on the Cameroonian border. Sukur is a UNESCO World Heritage Site. Its people still live in stone dwellings and employ Stone Age techniques for smelting iron, and – in a rare combination of land use – their farming terraces double up as burial sites.

At the foot of the Mandara range, we stopped at the local secretariat of Magadali town, where the staff introduced me to Simon, a man from Sukur who would escort me to the top of the mountain.

Getting to Sukur involved a long climb up the mountain, a sweltering ascent along centuries-old granite steps constructed at an ungodly gradient. From further up the mountain I looked down at the valley extended below me, its trees sprinkled over the plain like green peppercorns on a bed of mustard-coloured grass. All was quiet, except for the mooing of the cows wafted by the wind across the vast emptiness.

Thirty minutes into the climb, I stopped at one of the stone benches to catch my breath. The pain drained from my legs but I was too shattered to ask Simon any questions; all I could do was point breathlessly at an animal running across the pathway.

'It's a squirrel,' he said without a puff. By himself, Simon said he could walk to the top of the mountain in forty minutes, wearing only floppy slippers. We continued up the mountain, passing a formidable old woman who shuffled with the aid of a stick while balancing a basket of fruit on her head. She was at least three hours and a million steps from her destination, yet seemed undaunted and unhurried. Time stretched measurelessly ahead of her, without demand. But for me, time was circular; it ruled my life and hemmed me in like a hamster on a treadmill. My climb was a time-consuming means to an end, and I wanted to finish it as quickly as possible.

Soon after the old woman, a teenage schoolboy loped past. Sukur had no school, so all children are taught in Magadali, returning home only on the weekends. Everything the people needed, be it education, jobs or hospital treatment, was obtained in Madagali. As I heaved myself up each stone step, taking in demoralising views of Simon's backside zooming ahead with powerful ease, I concluded that I would gladly live life illiterate, unemployed and sickly if it meant evading this daily torture.

I wondered what sort of event drove the Sukur people to live at such bothersome altitudes. My guidebook informed me that the word 'Sukur' comes from *at sukur*, which means 'feuding' in the local Bura language. The people of Sukur possibly settled here after a battle of some kind. Simon said this wasn't true. His only explanation was that the Sukur – Hausa-speaking Christians – migrated here from Cameroon so that they could 'live more comfortably'.

Towards the top of the mountain, we passed terraced fields where the Sukur people grow millet and groundnut and, uniquely, bury their royalty (the commoners are buried in the village). The area just outside the village entrance was scattered with tamarind trees, and a baobab tree which the Sukurs believe will turn you into a hermaphrodite if you touch it. As if to emphasise the seriousness of the threat, the tree had been cordoned off with tape, which only made me want to touch it even more.

An hour and ten minutes later, Simon and I finally entered the kingdom of Sukur. The tiny town was perched on a hilltop between several mountain peaks covered in scrubby vegetation and boulders sprinkled precariously over the vertiginous slopes. The town's circular stone huts were topped with raffia roofs, thatched in a beautiful criss-cross pattern. Their simplicity and smooth greyness looked beautiful against the blue sky. Apart from the 'kamikaze' horse flies smashing into my face, it was a peaceful, calming place. Young boys gathered around me, grinning inquisitively. Dusty, dry and coarsened through walking on the jagged rocks, their feet looked as though they were made of stone. My pampered, moisturised soles flinched painfully on contact with the rocks, even through my shoes.

The boys showed me around the village. They led me to the 'caves' where royal blacksmiths still make axes and sickles the Stone Age way, using hand-operated bellows in stone furnaces. Several girls (who were tasked with all the work, apparently) were fetching water from a stone well when they caught sight of me. They scattered from my camera lens in fits of giggles, fearful of being photographed. The boys, on the other hand, idled freely and jostled for space in my viewfinder.

Back at the village entrance, Simon gave me a tour of the *xidi*'s (king's) compound. Sukur's royal lineage isn't dynastic – the Sukur people elect their king on a performance-led basis. Only the *dur* (title-holders) can do the choosing, and only a member of their clan can become the xidi. A member of the royal family materialised from the crowd and accompanied us. He removed his shoes and cap before we entered the king's compound, inside which was a complex of rooms made entirely from stone. It was the stuff of my childhood dreams, a *Flintstones* fantasy of stone corridors connecting several rooms, all fashioned from rock and filled with stone furniture. There was a VIP guest room, a watchtower, a meeting area for title-holders, a granary room, a horse stable, and a reception room for visitors awaiting an audience with the xidi. Heavy rains had collapsed the ceiling of the room (now empty) for storing drums, but the king's bathing house was still intact.

The complex contained several narrow gates to the outside, one of which is only ever used for transporting each xidi out of the compound when he dies.

Simon showed me the stone throne where the xidi sits and passes rulings on disputes. Village leaders sit around him on the floor.

We moved on to the stone cattle pen. 'Sukur people are good at fattening bulls,' Simon informed me. The bulls are fed through a hole in the wall separating the pen from the room where the grain is stored. As we walked, a dozen or so boys followed me, crowding into every room I entered, blocking my view and watching me intensely. Under normal circumstances I might have shooed them away impatiently, but they were so smiley and sweet, I bit my tongue and craned my neck for a better view of my surroundings.

'And this is the multipurpose room,' Simon said. We entered a round circular hut with a large tree trunk standing in the centre, as if it had crashed in from the sky. Sukur people used the room for initiations, court cases, conferences and corporal punishment. In the old days, criminals' legs were yanked through a square hole in the

wall and pinned down with a heavy branch while their torso languished on the outside of the building.

'Then you would beat them until they confessed their crime,'
Simon explained. For some reason, he and the boys and I found this
very amusing. Sukur imagination seemed particularly inspired where
punishment was concerned: 200 years ago, the villagers dug a very
deep pit so that they could lob miscreants into it irretrievably. It fell
into disuse once the villagers began taking their disputes to the civil
courts.

After finishing our tour of the royal complex, Simon led me to
the Mini Museum. It lived up to its name, consisting of a hut less
than 2 metres in radius. I liked its bijou cuteness. On display were
examples of Sukur's artefacts, unchanged since the Stone Age and,
in some cases, still in use: a type of grinding stone still used by elderly Sukur women for making grain; cots, containers and raincoats
made out of grass; *dubul* iron bars, the former currency for marriage
dowries; a piece of iron slag; tubular-shaped grass beer filters; traditional trays, also made out of grass; a tall iron spear; a hippo-hide
shield; baskets and old leather slippers.

Simon showed me the sleeping mats, which were also exhibits in
the museum. The men's mats were flat grass ones; the women's
were made of rounded guinea corn sticks, which resembled
bamboo. They seemed designed for maximum discomfort. I'll never
understand why women throughout the world are made to suffer in
such petty ways.

'Why are the women's mats are so uncomfortable?' I asked.

'I don't know,' Simon smiled.

My father once told me that it was customary in our village to
give food to the menfolk first. Even in times of scarcity, male stomachs took priority over those of women and children. In our house
in Port Harcourt, we had a watered-down version of this primacy.
My father would sit at one end of the dining table where his fancy
crockery and cutlery were laid out over a carefully folded tablecloth.

At the other end, we children had to make do with plain crockery and a naked table top.

'Why do *you* get all the fancy stuff?' we asked, indignant but amused.

'Because I'm the man of the house,' he beamed.

Simon introduced me to Sukur's current xidi in the royal compound. His name was Gizik Kinakakau, a pleasant and relaxed eighty-seven-year-old who had outlived his teeth and much of his eyesight. His wrinkled, reddish-brown skin almost matched his brown djellaba and headscarf, which he draped over his kufi hat. A former cattle rearer, he was elected as the xidi in 1983. I asked him questions while Simon translated, his Sukur words and sentences sounding ten times as long as my English ones.

'Why were you chosen?' I asked the xidi.

'I never dreamt I would become king, but since the beginning I never fought with anyone,' Kinakakau said in gentle tones. 'I always helped people and made sacrifices. I am a poor man. I didn't have money to give to anyone to elect me.'

Poverty seems to be the only recipe for maintaining humility in our leaders. I suspected that the xidi's lack of economic power made him far less autocratic and corrupt than the politicians in government. His humble leadership was the very opposite of that of the siren-wailing buffoons occupying the state governorships. He told me that he happily accepts criticism from his people: after the Zoaku festival held every September, the Sukur community holds an annual meeting during which the people are given the chance to wag a finger at their king and find fault with his leadership. The Xidi said he even apologises if he's done something wrong, despite having the power to order a villager to sacrifice their valuable ram or bull when a visitor arrives.

'How many wives do you have?' I asked him.

'I have one wife.'

'Just the one?'

Everyone laughed at my surprise.

'I don't like to have more than one wife,' the Xidi shook his head. 'I once had a second wife but we divorced after two years.'

'What was the problem?'

He smiled. 'If a man has many wives in his house, the problems will be many.' Kinakakau's restrained loins had produced just five children, most of whom lived in Sukur.

His powers were gradually fading. In traditional times, the Xidi had the final word during community disputes. These days the law courts deal with them, but Gizik didn't resent the modern legal system as it deters the cow thieves who used to steal from Sukur with impunity. The kingdom has changed in other ways, too. People once walked all the way to Maiduguri when they needed big-city goods, and herbalists, not hospitals, would minister to people's afflictions. They now make the journey in three hours by car, and get medical treatment there; the kingdom is opening up to the wider world.

Once upon a time, my village bore the same placid simplicity. I found myself envying Sukur's isolation, so high up in the mountains, away from the predation, the oil wells and the armed gangs that stirred so much fever down in the tropics.

'Do you want Sukur to change or stay the same?'

'I am praying for the government to take serious action to bring social amenities,' the Xidi said. 'If that happens I will be very happy.' Sukur needs a secondary school, a hospital, a craft training centre and water 'so the place will be more developed than it is now'. A cable car would be an added bonus for both tourists and the Sukur people. The Xidi turned and pointed towards the top of the mountain. A small crowd of people were shuffling slowly up the slopes, hoisting a teenage girl above their shoulders. She had sprained her ankle, Simon explained. 'You see,' the Xidi said, 'this is the problem people are facing here presently. We need health facilities.'

'Have you been anywhere outside Sukur?' I asked.

'I have visited Borno, Yobe, Gombe, Taraba and Cameroon,' he said. They were all neighbouring states.

'Did you like these places?'

'Since the beginning Sukur has been a blessed land. I learned this from my grandfather. If I stay in Maiduguri I can't be king,' he chuckled. 'So I prefer to stay here in Sukur.'

Although it was time for me to return south again, a part of me wanted to stay here too. From Sukur's splendid elevation, I stared at the distant horizon towards the rest of Nigeria, and for a second I yearned for this country to throw itself back to an Iron Age of sorts. I fancied being in a place where the gap between expectation and reality didn't leave such a frustrating chasm; where I was at the mercy of nature's caprices, not corruption's iron fist; and I was ruled by a leader who, blessed with the miracle of humble introspection, actually listened to my gripes. Relatively speaking, that seemed like heaven.

12

Masquerade Mischief

Calabar

I stepped off the aeroplane into the Calabar evening, and inhaled. The vegetative aroma of moist tropical air steamed through my nostrils, a welcome change from the desiccated sands of the north's Saharan air. I was very happy to be back down south, and especially pleased to be in Calabar.

'You can't miss Calabar,' my uncle Owens had told me over the phone. Calabar, capital of Cross River State in the south-east, is the favourite city of many Nigerians. It's Nigerian good governance made manifest, a city where a little vision and a smidgen of ambition had made it as well groomed as Abuja but without the sterility or manufactured ambience; the one place where Nigeria can exhibit itself to the world without shame. On Calabar's spotless streets, civic pride was shockingly abundant: colourful Christmas ribbons still lay draped across government buildings, across the fire station and even the Mr Fans fast-food place; public bins with PLEASE USE ME signs lined the roads (this, in a country where most cities don't have any refuse bins). Roadside billboards reminded passers-by that AIDS IS REAL, SEX IS RISKY and you should PAY YOUR TAXES. One billboard displayed photos of the 'clean roads' and 'good drainage' that come from paying the taxman.

The local Efik people credited all this to their long-standing culture of cleanliness (sniffily contrasted with the Yorubas in Lagos), and the work of Cross River's ambitious ex-governor Donald Duke, who chose not to suckle at the teat of national oil revenue but to make an asset out of Cross River's natural beauty instead, turning it into Nigeria's tourism capital. I wanted Calabar to be the capital city, too. Deep down, I suspect it likes to think it is. In the town centre, a gargantuan Nigerian flag – visible from miles away – flapped in the river breeze, an emblem of this ambitious usurper of a city.

A bright and enervating sun burned the sky the next morning. I flagged down an okada and was surprised when the heavy-set driver silently handed me a protective helmet. Dismissing his orders, I rested the helmet on my knee, reluctant to dishevel my hair, but the okada man soon spotted my bare head in the wing mirror and applied the brakes.

'You *must* wear the helmet,' he insisted for the second time. 'It's the law.' I looked around and saw other women okada passengers with their helmets perched begrudgingly on top of their braided hairdos. It really was the law. Two months in Nigeria was all it had taken for me to capitulate to the culture of transgression. Throwing plastic bottles into ditches or ignoring my seatbelt had become second nature to me. But here in Calabar I was forced to relearn good citizenship.

We zoomed towards the riverside, down a serpentine road winding through fresh lawns and trees, bound for Calabar's National Museum. The museum was in a yellow, pinewood colonial building with overhanging eaves and verandahs. Raised on stilts, it perched on a hill that overlooked the magnificent, palm-fringed estuary of the Cross River, from where shiploads of slaves were sent to the Americas 500 years ago. The museum was the best in the country, stuffed with Calabari artefacts that detailed how the slave trade transformed the Efiks from fishermen and farmers into Anglophile traders.

The Portuguese navigator Diogo Cão is thought to have first landed ashore in the Calabar region in 1482. By 1505 slaves from the area were being sent abroad. Selection for slavery was a broad, equal-opportunities affair: war criminals, prisoners of war, debtors, insubordinate children or servants, weakened enemies and their families all found themselves shackled and marched onto boats destined for São Tomé or the West Indies. Most slaves were seized during raids (organised by local Efik slave traders) from Igboland, plus the lands of the Ibibio people, the Cameroon highlands, and even as far as the Benue River basin towards central Nigeria.

This manpower was exchanged for European goods: tobacco, rum, brandy, gin, guns, gunpowder, cannon, swords, cloth, furniture, brass basins, beads, mirrors and champagne (not much has changed in the latter respect – Nigeria was the world's biggest importer of champagne during the oil boom of the early 1980s). The Efik chiefs – like many of our rulers of today – didn't bother to learn the technologies that created these foreign products. But they coveted the items, along with the British lifestyle. English-style houses and furniture were imported as symbols of prestige and power designed to impress the chiefs' African and European trading partners. The houses, prefabricated in Liverpool, had wooden floors, chandeliers, cabinets and framed photographs on their walls. In a fabulously ostentatious move, an Efik king called Eyo even laid down a red carpet on the floor of his extra-long royal canoe. In the centre of the boat was a tiny roofed cabin, where King Eyo would sit on plump cushions.

In 1843, Efik chiefs invited teachers and missionaries to use their land in and around Calabar. Decades of contact with Europeans began to influence Efik culture quite heavily. By the end of the nineteenth century, the Efik nobility had Christianised their family names. Surnames such as Effiom became Ephraim, and Okon became Hogan. Other names, including Duke and Henshaw, were also adopted, while fiefdoms such as Atakpa became known as Duke Town.

Calabar's elites discarded the traditional *ofon isin* (waist cloth) and *ofon idem* (top cloth) used during ceremonial occasions, and replaced them with Victorian top hats, brass helmets, medallions and masonry lodge aprons. Efik ladies, paying no heed to the tropical heat, wore flowing Victorian dresses with matching elbow-length gloves. The museum displayed old photographs of these Calabar kings and queens in their European-style crowns, posing with starchy Victorian sombreness while sitting on thrones, appearing regal yet somehow diminished by their imitation. But contact with outsiders brought genuine benefits. Many Efiks became literate, and by the eighteenth century were noting down their trading business in diaries. The early colonial administration relied on them as administrative officers, which led to the Efiks' mid-twentieth-century dominance in Nigeria's civil service.

Donald Duke, a descendant of this elite, became governor of Cross River State in 2000. Considered one of the more proactive politicians, Duke was among the few governors not to be investigated for corruption by the EFCC while in office. Under his stewardship, he cleaned up Calabar, made it more attractive to investors, and Cross River became Nigeria's premier state for tourism.

Calabar's riverside, once witness to the forced export of slaves, was now an entertainment area. Early that evening, I visited the Marina Resort, a new waterfront development further west from the museum. Children squealed on a merry-go-round, and couples strolled along a jetty that protruded into the shimmering Cross River. Fishermen hauled nets beside moored speedboats. An ordinary scene in most other countries, but in Nigeria such a relaxed, man-made environment was worth talking about. And, it seemed, worth dressing up for: one couple clothed their sullen twin boys in black shirts, white suits and black trilby hats perched at raffish angles. They looked like reluctant extras from Michael Jackson's 'Smooth Criminal' video.

Opposite the merry-go-round, the authorities had built a modern waxwork slave museum. The lights weren't working in the first room I entered. Out of the unsettling dimness loomed a wooden slave ship, where the tops of several human heads and several pairs of feet poked out of the vessel's side, startling me. They belonged to the waxwork models of slaves tethered on deck, but in the shadows of the unlit room their heads, and especially their feet, looked terrifyingly lifelike.

Other rooms contained waxwork sets representing various scenarios from the slave trade. There was a slave market, people tending fields of sugar cane, slaves being hung or emancipated. All the waxwork figures had gratifyingly authentic-looking Afro hair on their heads (Western reproductions of Afro hair usually involve an unrealistic woolly fuzz). Background speakers emitted the barks of vicious dogs chasing a runaway slave, or the pained howls of slaves being branded by hot irons for identification. It was harrowing, shudder-inducing stuff, exactly as slavery should be portrayed, without the guilt, the kid gloves, or the dispassion of the slave museum in Badagry. I knew I could rely on Nigerians to present this chapter of history in a raw, indelicate fashion. How I wished we held the cultural monopoly on the portrayal of African history.

Back at the hotel that evening, I ordered dinner at the front desk. Emmanuel, the receptionist, was a very sweet young man who went out of his way to make my stay as comfortable as possible. He was attentive, professional, timely, and took care to caress my ego at every opportunity, bombarding me with a volley of superlatives and compliments. He was everything one could possibly wish for in hotel staff. In a repeat of the night before, I requested rice and goat meat stew. Emmanuel called the kitchen to place my order, diligently setting the phone on loudspeaker to prove that my order was being expedited.

'Do you have goat?' he asked the cook.

'No,' she replied.

Emmanuel: 'Do you have chicken?'

Cook: 'No.'

Emmanuel: 'Do you have rice and stew?'

Cook: 'No, we have no rice.'

Emmanuel: 'Then get some then.'

Cook: 'No. I will not go out this night.'

Emmanuel: 'But I have a guest who desperately needs to eat.' (He kindly added that embellishment.)

Cook: 'I will *not* go out.'

Emmanuel looked up at me: 'Don't worry,' he said, 'we'll get some rice.'

Cook: 'OK.'

Emmanuel: 'No, I'm not talking to you! I was reassuring our guest that she will get some rice.' He angrily dropped the receiver. 'Don't worry, we will bring you your food.' His face was disappointed, and a little embarrassed. I was witnessing the battle of the two Nigerias: the cooperative side that tries to impress and provide, versus the selfish and unprofessional side, holding the other one back.

In the end, professionalism triumphed over inertia, and I went to bed on a very satisfied stomach.

'Africa time,' Ophelia sighed. She and I and her friend were sitting among rows of empty chairs beneath a tarpaulin canopy, and fanning away the brutal heat. It was three o'clock in the afternoon, but their friend's wedding, scheduled for two o'clock, still hadn't started. Luckily for me, I was dressed in a cool T-shirt instead of the long, hot wrappas Ophelia and Jessica were wearing, because I was attending this wedding at short notice.

Ophelia had invited me at the last minute after finding me pottering around the hallway of her house. I hadn't intended to trespass – the house stood on the side of a busy Calabar road, and looked completely unoccupied. Its 1920s English style, assaulted by tropical heat and poor maintenance, had taken on an appealing dilapidation. I'd walked through its gaping front door to investigate, only to find Ophelia walking down the stairs. Unperturbed by my presence in her home, she casually offered me a drink and invited me to her friend's wedding.

And so there we were, sitting in a small residential side street, waiting for all the guests to arrive. We were almost sun-blinded by the sea of white plastic chairs around us. What insanity had compelled us to be punctual?

'Africa time, *nawa-oo*,' Ophelia repeated regretfully. 'They should have said twelve o'clock ... people would take their time to come at two or three. Then we would have started by now.'

'It dey vex me that,' Ophelia's friend lamented.

In the background, the DJ played synthesiser versions of Roberta Flack's 'Killing Me Softly' and Norah Jones's 'Don't Know Why' over and over again on a loop. The songs' sluggish melodies seemed to slow down time itself.

'I beg, let them start,' Ophelia's friend implored, guests or no guests. Somewhere in the vicinity, the bride and groom must have been sitting ready and waiting.

The only distraction came from across the street, where we spotted a tiny fifteen-month-old girl walking with her mother, wearing nothing but a nappy, and carrying a mini jerrycan of water like a responsible adult.

'Just look at her!' Ophelia squealed in delight. 'She wants to help her mother, o!' We had a good laugh at that.

Finally, the guests began to arrive. Women sauntered towards the seats, wearing wrappas of every colour and pattern, their majestic head ties soaring skywards. The men wore the traditional clothing of many south-eastern people (including my own Ogoni): thigh-length, long-sleeved white shirts with round-neck collars, teamed with beaded necklaces, a wrappa from the waist down, plus a walking stick and bowler hat – the accoutrements of ageing Victorian gentlemen. The bowler hat was once the standard head gear, but these days anything goes: ear-flapped caps, Kangol flat caps or cowboy hats. Some people have given cowboy hats the nickname 'Resource Control' hats since they've been adopted by some people in the Niger Delta who are campaigning for more control over the oil wealth. The person responsible for this new trend, so I was told, is Peter Odili, the Stetson-wearing former governor of Rivers State. South-easterners seem unique among Nigerians in the fluidity of our traditional wardrobe – we've been co-opting foreign and modern influences since colonial times.

Ophelia and I had moved to a smaller 'in-law' tent next to the house of the groom's parents. We listened to the MC announcing the names of the various chiefs and their wives attending the event. The band began playing Nigerian highlife music with their electric guitars and trumpets, while women carried drinks on gold trays for the newly-weds' parents and elders, who were sitting inside the house.

In the distance the drumbeats grew louder and louder, and people chanted a song in Efik ('We are bringing the husband!'). The groom arrived with his male entourage, enveloped by a gaggle of women dancers. He and his men shuffled down the street in time with the rhythm, laughing and singing. Dancing beneath a large parasol, they punched the air with their walking sticks and bowler hats, the whole lot bobbing to the drumbeat, a happy mass of limbs inching slowly towards the house.

The groom and his dancing coterie approached the in-law tent to loud cheers and claps from the seated guests. Just before entering the house, he turned to the crowd, raised his arms and wiggled his hips once more. Everyone cheered again, even more loudly and enthusiastically. The groom then disappeared into the house to join his waiting bride for the private part of the wedding ceremony.

While this went on, the guests got ready to eat. I could barely contain my glee when women began distributing pots of jollof rice, goat meat and *moi moi*, a steamed pudding made from black-eyed peas and onions. The party had truly started now. People ate and chatted amongst themselves while the MC cracked jokes on the mike. A boy ferried boxes of wrapped presents into the house. Another child led a bleating goat into the building, a gift for the bride and groom.

'What's happening inside?' I asked Ophelia.

'The parents and elders are talking to the bride and groom,' she explained. 'They ask the husband how he intends to take care of the wife and household. The man and woman are told they must stay together until death. They will tell the husband that he must have *patience*. And the wife must *endure*.'

Endure. That word featured heavily in Ophelia's explanation. She repeated it several times. Still, I found something very appealing about the parents and elders of newly-wed couples giving stern talks about the virtues of patience and endurance. It seemed the antithesis of the fancy-dress 'Las Vegas' approach to marriage.

Traditionally, Calabar women were fattened before marriage. The woman spent weeks in a fattening room where her husband-to-be gave her a small bucket of *gari* (powdered, uncooked cassava mixed with water) twice a day to soften her skin before her body was massaged. Afterwards, the woman would sleep for two or three hours, then stuff her belly with other foods. This gruelling routine of force-feeding and sleeping lasted from one week to three months, depending on how quickly the woman developed the necessary flab. The government has now banned the practice for health reasons, though a defiant few still continue it.

Half an hour later, several of the traditional dancers emerged from inside the house, looking magnificent. Ornate gold combs cascaded down their hair weaves, and their smiling faces glittered with matching gold paint. Their arms and legs were covered with feathered bands and bells, while a kaleidoscope of beads criss-crossed their torsos, colour coordination be damned. After them came the stout newly-weds, dancing out of the house and onto the street. Several guests gathered round to dance alongside them and shower them confetti-style with ₦500 notes or slap the money against their bodies. As the notes floated onto the ground, two designated collectors scooped them up into plastic bags.

If the government has its way, this money-throwing practice will be scrapped. For weeks, I'd seen state TV commercials ordering the nation not to abuse its newly issued banknotes. In the commercials, the police break up a joyful wedding celebration and fine the guests ₦50,000 for violating the notes. At the end, a stern voice says: 'No march am, no squeeze am ... otherwise government go charge you, o!'

This was one Nigerian law I was happy to break. The newly-weds grinned and danced to the music, shuffling their feet and making their way slowly through the crowd. There was no starchy, ritualised dancing, but a freestyle boogie from the soul, laced with humour. People stuck out their bottoms and pouted theatrically. Two men faced one another, twisting and gyrating their hips as they lowered themselves towards the ground. Even the masquerade playfully followed me around (masquerades are costumed men who wear masks representing spirits that possess the human body, making their wearers dance).

A new song started playing, a new rhythm that immediately gripped everyone, infected them, rotated their hips and turned their smiles into frowns of exquisite concentration. Ecstasy was a serious business.

This, I realised, is what Nigeria does best. The weddings, the humour, the music – often too visceral to convey in our tourism brochures – were what made Nigeria special. It was an epiphany for me. The concept of 'Transwonderland' with all its artifice and modernity wasn't our strength right now, but it didn't matter. The alternative was so much better and richer.

The masquerade stood in front of me and wordlessly cocked itself sideways as if asking me something in jest. I waved it goodbye and returned to my hotel, feeling pleased to be a Nigerian.

As the motorised canoe sped through the choppy waters of the Cross River two days later, I crouched to avoid the fountain of sea spray spewing from the side of the boat. Goodbye to smooth hair. I sat with several other passengers behind a mountain of suitcases, big bags of rice, and crates of wine and soft drinks. The boat sliced through the gold-flecked, olive-green water, fringed by glorious mangroves, palm trees, and Calabar's lush hills rising around us. Nestled among this bountiful greenery were oil installations, petrol helipads and, peeping furtively above the foliage, the home of Charles Taylor. The former Liberian president and warlord was granted asylum in Calabar by President Obasanjo in 2003. Taylor was eventually extradited to face war crime charges, but his wife and children still live in Calabar, enjoying these fabulous river views.

We docked at a short jetty in Creek Town, a small settlement further down the river. WELCOME TO THE CENTRE OF BLACK CIVILIZATION, the signboard said. Its message was more aspirational than indicative: we were actually standing close to the very part of the river where hundreds of thousands of slaves were transferred from canoes to ships and taken to the Americas. Many of them were Igbo people, whose stocky, strong physiques made them valuable as slaves, a fellow passenger told me. Creek Town is the heartland of the Efik people who settled here in the fifteenth century before spreading out into Calabar. The town was also one of the first areas of Nigeria to be settled by missionaries.

One of my fellow passengers helped me onto the jetty. Ekpenyong Cobham was in his forties, a tall, quiet version of the American boxer George Foreman. Ekpenyong was the only person I'd met who sweated as much as I did. In awe, I watched as he used his fingers like windshield wipers to slake sheets of sweat off his bald pate before dabbing the re-emergent perspiration beads with a saturated handkerchief. Ekpenyong told me he used to run a traditional dance troupe that performed around Cross River State. One year, a French visitor to Nigeria was so impressed by the troupe he invited them to a festival in Paris.

'How did you find Paris?' I asked.

'It was wonderful,' he replied in his quiet baritone. 'The streets were so clean. I looked at Paris and I realised that we Nigerians like to dupe people.'

'I know. All our politicians want to do is steal. They don't want to build a Paris.'

Ekpenyong agreed. 'In Nigeria, if you are not a thief, you are nowhere.'

I thought he was criticising corruption, but I was wrong. 'I liked Babangida *very* much,' he said, referring to the former military dictator. 'When the national debt was ₦10 billion, Babangida was worth ₦33 billion.' Ekpenyong's eyes flashed with approval.

'But that money should have gone to the rest of the country,' I said incredulously. 'Aren't you angry about that?'

He shook his head. 'I would do *exactly* the same,' he smiled. 'If you go to government and come back with nothing, your people will think you have not used your head *wisely*.'

The former state governor, Donald Duke, came from Creek Town but, judging by its state of decay, he hadn't used his head 'wisely' here. It was a listless place, a rural, goat-strewn backwater, where people made palm wine and counted the hours on their porches. Despite the village atmosphere, it was officially a town, and most houses were made of cement rather than the traditional adobe and thatch. The green lawns fronting each house gave one of the few indications that this was one of the first areas to make contact with the British.

In the tall-grassed cemetery, the headstones of English missionaries who worked in Creek Town from the eighteenth century sprouted at forlorn angles. Their old Presbyterian Church, one of the oldest in Nigeria, had retained its original wooden pews, pulpit and organ, which had been gathering dust in the choir gallery since 1850. The church creaked with a pre-evangelical quaintness.

Back outside, Ekpenyong introduced me to a young relative of his, Benson, a good-looking twenty-two-year-old with a dark angular face disfigured by knife wound scars. Despite not having a university degree, his English was as good as any graduate, and he seemed innately overqualified to be a hotel housekeeper, the job he was hunting for. Benson had done this sort of work in Abuja and Calabar, but quit after an African American tourist falsely promised him employment in the US.

'He said he would get me work in Atlanta,' Benson said. 'He gave me his telephone number and said I should call him. But I never heard from him again. It's not easy to find a new job in Nigeria. If you don't have godfather* you cannot move.'

As Benson and I sauntered along the sandy path we encountered a masquerade. Over the decades, Nigerians have incorporated masquerades into our Christmas celebrations, with bands of masked dancers parading through the streets, sometimes travelling miles away from their home towns or villages.

The Creek Town masquerades were striking. They had smeared themselves with a mixture of palm oil and charcoal to give their bodies a glossy, jet-black hue from head to toe. Their masks were also black with grotesque human features protruding from an opulent raffia mane. The masks were decorated with monkey skulls and topped with a plume of banana leaves. The jerky crouching movements of the masked men jingled the small bells attached to their raffia miniskirts. It was so scarily compelling, I had to take a photograph.

'They want money for the photos,' Benson told me. Reluctantly,

---

* 'Godfather' is usually a political term describing men who have the power to appoint others in political roles.

I paid the masquerade as well as the other three that we encountered on our way back to the jetty.

Ekpenyong was sitting on his motorcycle by the riverbank, waiting to meet a friend who was arriving on the next boat from Calabar. Another masquerade approached us, standing opposite me and shaking his creepy bells. I looked at him but gave no money. Did I need to? I hadn't taken a photograph, and I'd run out of small change anyway.

Suddenly, the masked spirit moved forward and slapped me firmly, but not too painfully, across my face. I was stunned. He slapped me again, smearing my neck with black oil. Ekpenyong rebuked him in their dialect and instructed me to mount his motorbike. As the engine revved up, the masked thug raised the small cane attached to his belt and whipped my arm with it. I was still trying to absorb what had happened when I was whipped a second time. Ekpenyong shouted at him again, but the man challenged him with wordless, defiant lunges accompanied by spooky bell-tinkling. To my dismay, Ekpenyong angrily motioned to him, *dared* him, to attack me once more.

'Let's just go!' I screamed, tapping Ekpenyong's back. The masked man took up Ekpenyong's challenge and flinched forwards. 'Oh God, please, let's *go*!' I begged. Quickly, a young man grabbed the masquerade and restrained him with an arm lock, allowing Ekpenyong and me finally to ride away.

'I'm sorry about what happened to you,' an ebony-faced, silver-haired man consoled me. I was sitting in the courtyard of Ekpenyong's house, letting his wife Ekanem wipe the black oil off my face with a cloth. Both she and the man were extremely embarrassed about the incident.

'It's OK, I'm not angry. I know it's just the one person causing trouble,' I said. 'Is money part of the masquerade tradition?'

'No,' the man replied. 'Things have changed . . . it's the condition of the country.'

Though I don't believe in spirits, masquerades still retain a mildly unsettling power. As a child, the mystique of their masks, their speechlessness and obscured eyes scared me. Now, I was all too aware of the flawed, money-grabbing human beings that occasionally stood beneath those costumes; my childhood fears of masquerades were temporarily supplanted by an adult anxiety of a different kind.

'I have reported him to the local masquerade committee,' Ekpenyong assured me.

Ekanem claimed it was an isolated incident. But Benson later told me he acquired his facial scars after fighting with a masked spirit who had tried to mug two tourists in Calabar on Christmas Day.

After lunch, I strolled with Benson and Ekanem to a bar up the hill. We were joined by Ekpenyong, his American friend Ivor, and an older man called Ekpo, who had just learned about what happened to me.

'I'm so sorry. Why do these people expect money? They do *nothing*,' he said, before performing a disgusted imitation of the masquerade's bell-tinkling stance. 'What is *that*?'

'Those boys are from Akwa Ibom State,' Ekanem emphasised. 'They are Ibibios, they're not from here.'

The six of us sat down at the bar and sipped soft drinks while making idle chit-chat. Suddenly, the dogs scrambled to their feet and began barking aggressively. The same bellicose masquerade had arrived and was approaching three teenage girls. They ran away from him, half laughing, half whimpering in fear.

'They want money,' Ivor the American said. 'They like to target women and girls because it's easier.'

The masquerade sauntered off.

Ivor was an anthropologist doing research on the Efiks' male-only secret society, Ekpe. The society is named after a spirit, for whom the men are said to act as messengers. Traditional Efik society was governed by Ekpe members who – in their role as mediums of the spirit – were consulted by villagers to settle disputes. The Ekpe society set and enforced the community's laws, disciplined wrongdoers and organised masquerades, which appeared during the funerals of chiefs or on special occasions, such as Christmas. The Ekpe society's power was sacred, and even kings had to abide by it. When the Efik people began trading with the Europeans in Calabar, Ekpe evolved to govern the rules of commerce too. These days, modern government has eclipsed Ekpe's power, but some villagers still defer to it as a last resort. The society is now technically open to women, young people and foreigners – anyone who can pay the initiation fees.

'I've joined Ekpe too,' Ivor told me.

'Do they normally allow outsiders to join?'

'Oh yeah, anyone can join. You have to take part in a secret initiation. But a lot of people don't want to join any more. Some Christians are against it.'

Ivor was fascinated by the durability of Ekpe's cultural influence. 'Many of the slaves from here were sent to Cuba,' he said. 'Even today you can still find Ekpe societies over there.'

A short while later, Ivor and I paid a visit to Ekpenyong's elderly father, Muri, at his house close to the jetty. His home was a modest affair with a discernible British influence. Old photos and a framed Certificate of Traditional Chieftaincy hung on the walls. The mantelpiece was a Victoriana-style clutter of figurines, photographs and a 60-centimetre-long model of a royal Efik canoe. This elongated version of a traditional canoe was carpeted and had a roofed enclosure in its centre. Nearby was an old photograph of Muri in his younger days, dressed in traditional garb, sunlight bouncing off his domed skull. The photo was taken during the Isim dance, a dance of regeneration that the children of royalty perform when the *obong* (king) dies.

'Ekpenyong didn't tell me he was royalty!' I remarked.

'He's like that,' Ivor grinned. 'He won't tell you these things.'

Muri's full title was His Royal Highness Muri Cobham. Like many Efiks, his ancestors had adopted an English surname.

'Can you tell me about Creek Town's history?' I asked Benson. He chuckled and looked down at the floor.

'What?'

'I know very little Creek Town history,' he explained. 'I know more about the outside.' In this post-oral Information Age, people's knowledge tended to be skewed towards modern federal history or Western history.

It was left to Muri to give me the facts. At eighty-three, he spoke extremely slowly, much like my paternal grandfather. Between questions, his rheumy eyes stared into the distance.

'There are four villages in Creek Town,' Benson translated for me. 'Adakuko, Mbarakom, Otong, Efut. Before Christianity, Ekpe was the only government. Then a man called Honesty brought the missionaries here . . .'

Muri, although old and listless, was discernibly bored by this conversation. I changed tack:

'What was life like when you were young, and how have things changed since?'

The old man livened up immediately. 'In the old days things were cheap and not difficult. Now, *everything* is a problem or struggle. The masquerade boys are a problem. Ekpe used to run Creek society. But the government has divided us into many local authorities. Each one is governed by a clan. This can cause problems because the head of one clan cannot intervene in the problems of another. Sometimes there is a lack of unity in decision-making. If God wants to put an end to this system then let him come. We are tired.' He wiped his face resignedly.

'If you are against the law of Ekpe you have to pay a penalty,' Muri continued. The Ekpe secret society still had its uses, even though it has been relegated to a ceremonial role. Infighting clans still call upon it as a last resort to mediate in disputes. But for the most part, the authority of Ekpe and elderly folks has been corroded by modern government, especially in relation to the more quotidian aspects of Creek Town life.

'Sunday used to be a rest day,' Muri said. 'You were not allowed to play traditional drums. But now it happens. If the elders challenge it, the youngsters defy you. Government is in the young man's hands. It is no longer in the old man's hands.'

A man of Muri's age must have digested all these social changes with difficulty. Mounted on his wall was a black-and-white photo of a female relative who had been fattened for marriage.

'People used to spend Christmas here,' Benson's grandmother informed me, scratching her short shock of white hair. 'Now they spend it in Calabar. They like the carnival and Christmas Village. Our market used to be so big. Look at it now. Only a few small things they are selling. Everybody wants to go to Calabar Market.'

Creek Town still clings to a few old traditions. People still bang the *nkong*, a metal instrument, to send messages from village to village; a bell is still rung to announce deaths, and the old cannon is fired during regattas, festivals, coronations and for royal deaths. But these were minor stitches in an unravelling tapestry.

Later in the afternoon, as Ivor and I waited to board the boat back to Calabar, we watched two little boys catching fish, using small balls of gari as bait. The aggressive masquerade was now chasing another girl around the jetty. She giggled fearfully and hid behind old man Ekpo who was eyeing the masquerade with calm disapproval. The masked man stared at her as if weighing up the consequences of smacking her. He chose to walk away, perhaps chastened by the chiding he had received from Ekpenyong and the masquerade committee. I resisted an urge to taunt him.

After the final passenger dropped into the boat, it motored away from the jetty back towards Calabar. Ekpenyong waved goodbye from the waterside. The brutish masquerade stood next to him, with his big mask and raffia mane, all hostilities forgotten. The pair of them made a comical sight as they chatted and gesticulated, shrinking gradually into the distance.

Until the early twentieth century, each district of Calabar (including Creek Town) had its own obong (king). Then the districts were merged into one, ruled by a single supreme obong, who was selected by the Traditional Council. This arrangement has created an accession bottleneck in which the *etubom* (prince) from each district is equally eligible to succeed the obong when he dies.

Ivor had invited me to meet his friend, His Royal Highness Etubom Bassey Ekpo Bassey IV, a high-ranking member of the Efik royal family. A former journalist and vocal opponent of past military regimes, Bassey once ran in the Cross River gubernatorial elections. It turned out that he was also acquainted with my father. Ivor led me to his offices on the second floor of a fading 1960s building close to the river.

Bassey, a light-skinned man in his fifties, was watching an English football match at full volume on the TV. He pumped my hand and murmured a distracted hello, unable to break his fixation with the game in which Arsenal, his favourite team, were playing. Nigerians are *obsessed* with football, and support a handful of European teams. I had yet to meet anyone who did not support either Arsenal, Chelsea, Real Madrid or Barcelona.

'I knew your father,' Bassey told me, one eye still on the game. 'He was right about his campaign, but his mistake was that he fought everybody. He should have kept some people on his side, but he criticised everybody ... the Yorubas, the Igbos, the Hausas. He made too many enemies.' My father was definitely an idealist, not a politician. I used to accompany him to the offices and homes of people similar to Bassey, where they would loudly bemoan Nigeria's ills while my siblings and I sipped Fanta under the crossfire of angry analysis.

'Why don't Nigerians go on strikes and agitate as much as we used to?' I asked Bassey.

'There is a lack of leadership,' Bassey replied. 'The leaders don't want to commit class suicide. They want their comforts. They saw the example of your father and they know that if they fight they could die.

'Hunger is what weighed the universities down. Babangida's reforms made living very, very expensive. That destroyed the leftist movements on campuses and made it difficult for people to find time for intellectual pursuits. The intellectual activity on campus simply disappeared. I think the last generation who know the difference between right and wrong are on their way out.'

Bassey's focus had also switched away from that sort of politics. He was an ardent enthusiast of pre-Christian traditions, and his ambitions to become the next obong were being obstructed by rival pro-Christian princes. The previous obong, himself a Soldier of Christ, had dedicated his throne to God and banned all libations at his meetings, allowing Christian prayers only. But Bassey was fighting for a return to indigenous, animist rituals and ceremonies. On this particular evening, however, Arsenal versus Blackburn Rovers was the only duel that interested him; my attempts at serious conversation were futile. But I didn't mind. I had arrived unannounced and, frankly, the football was hijacking my attention, too.

'Is the Calabar royal family under threat?' I asked.

Taking his eyes off the television for a just a second, Bassey handed me a sheet of paper. 'This is a speech I made the other day,' he said. I took the sheet of paper, grateful for some – any – information, then said my goodbyes and left the building.

Sitting on my hotel bed, I read the piece of paper. Bassey's speech, addressed to the heads of Efik royal houses on New Year's Eve, reprehended people who wanted to 'demonise' traditional rulers. Bassey criticised rulers who had become Muslims or Christians and 'abolished the performance of traditional rites', converting their prayer houses to mosques and churches.

The etubom wasn't against modern religions but he wanted to continue traditional libations which, he said, were done

> to invoke and honour our fathers and mothers who lived here; very much in the manner that Christians relate with their saints, long dead.
>
> Europeans who brought Christianity to us do not joke with their tradition. They brought Easter, a pagan feast into Christian worship; they avoid the number 13 in public buildings; and will break a bottle of wine on a new ship at commissioning. All Saints Day is for going to the gravesides of their ancestors (and in the Catholic countries of Latin America, people go with food and drink to spend days with their ancestors). All these are godly because their practitioners are not black; ours are satanic because we are black.
>
> Out of their strong inferiority complex, our refugee traditional rulers call out to Abraham, Isaac and Jacob (who, incidentally, did not worship the god of Christians), but are too embarrassed to call out to their own fathers who might have lived better lives than those ancestors of the Jews.
>
> Today, I ask these refugees to stand aside while we formalise the Etubom Traditional Council once more.

I found myself endorsing Prince Bassey's cause (at least notionally – who knows what machinations underscore these political conflicts). It was pleasing to see someone challenging evangelism's eclipsing of old customs, which were the only unique things about Nigeria's culture and aesthetics. I hadn't cared about these things before – my family's Christianity and my foreign urban upbringing had bred an indifference to animism. But now I was starting to acquire a taste for the indigenous. Where would Nigeria be without those exciting weddings and (non-aggressive) masquerades and libations? They had been the best part of my journey so far, the things that made this country worth visiting. Relinquishing our traditional heritage might be worthwhile if we could replace it with a modern, developed society, but at the moment we're stumbling into a crack between the two worlds.

That night in my hotel room, I became engrossed in a Nollywood film about a woman who takes a job as a government minister. Intoxicated by her newfound power, she begins treating her daughters atrociously. She beats them, criticises their dress sense and dishes out domestic tasks as if they were her slaves. The actress portraying the mother inhabited her role very naturally. Every order she hissed, every smug pout or bug-eyed glare made me despise her even more. Transfixed with hate, I followed each scene, waiting for the woman to receive retribution (which, being Nollywood, would be reliably brutal and severe). I could barely tear myself away to answer the knock on my door from room service.

But two hours later, I woke up to see the credits rolling. I had nodded off during the film, and I had no idea whether that nasty woman kept her job or not. This happened almost every time I watched these interminable Nollywood films. Yet I sought out these movies most evenings, and as time went on, I found myself caring more and more about the outcomes of the plots. I even surprised myself by recognising the names of the more famous actors, my eyes lighting up at Clem Ohameze's name in the opening credits. What was happening to me?

Being rich in a country that produces nothing but oil isn't easy: upgrading the accoutrements of wealth or obtaining spare parts for one's jet skis or Aston Martin involves much to-ing and fro-ing across the oceans. British Airways runs a lucrative line in ferrying Nigeria's wealthy to Europe to conduct their shopping trips. Sensing an opportunity, Calabar's government decided to build a massive, duty-free shopping complex aimed at keeping some of this spending activity within Nigeria's borders.

The Tinapa retail development, built just outside Calabar, is the jewel in the city's development crown, a business/leisure complex and retail emporium where Lagos and Abuja millionaires can buy their jewels and Tommy Hilfiger casual wear without schlepping to Dubai or London. I'd seen the CNN commercials: aerial views of a modern concrete complex bursting with clothing stores, restaurants and cinemas – the latest manifestation of Calabar's vision of itself as Nigeria's premier city. I was looking forward to visiting.

'There's nothing at Tinapa,' Ivor the American had told me. At the time, I assumed he was speaking figuratively. *He's American*, I thought dismissively; his definition of a shopping mall was probably stricter than the Nigerian one. Here, even the shabbiest, most thinly stocked outlet proudly described itself as a 'shopping complex'. Surely no retail centre in Nigeria would measure up to Ivor's American notions?

Assuming I could grab a pizza in Tinapa, I skipped lunch and took an okada towards the outskirts of town. We turned off the highway and down an empty, freshly tarmacked road, flanked by very high concrete walls and brand new streetlights. But as the entrance gate neared, my driver turned away from the road, and trundled through a cluster of trees and decrepit houses.

'Where are we going?' I asked him.

'We are going to Tinapa, now,' he answered. 'Okadas cannot enter the gate, so we must go through here.'

Clothes hung from washing lines and chickens lurched and scratched in the littered soil. Outside a mud-brick house, a barefoot toddler played, wearing nothing except her underpants and a curly wig. The place resembled a rural village. My driver parked at a wall where a policeman stood guard.

'Enter through here,' my driver said, pointing to a gap in the wall.

I walked through it and scrambled down a very steep grassy bank, ending up in a vast and mostly empty car park. Assuming the action must be somewhere further away, I walked towards the main building, a modern design surrounded by water features and stone benches. Vacant shop fronts bordered the walkways, save for a few companies that had staked their claim and erected signs and logos. Behind the closed doors of one clothing store, two women were filling the window display with fabrics.

'Where's the restaurant?' I asked a security guard, who kept vigil over the deserted space.

'It's there.' The man pointed to some steps rising to an elevated set of buildings. I clambered up and scoured the emptiness around me.

'I can't see any restaurant,' I hollered down to him.

'It has not opened.'

Why didn't he tell me that *before*? He smiled up at me politely, probably thinking he was talking to a mad woman. The reality of the situation finally dawned on me. Flashbacks of those CNN commercials came to mind as I assembled the pieces of the jigsaw. The TV voiceover had spoken about Tinapa in the present tense, not the future. As far as I can remember, it gave no indication that the development – 7,000 square metres of it – was tenantless. And no one in Calabar had told me I was wasting my time when I'd asked them how to get here. They'd simply given me directions and sent me on my deluded way, presumably assuming that I was knowingly visiting a work in progress.

My stomach was angrier than I was. It grumbled and squealed as I approached the top of another flight of steps, which culminated at the crest of a hill. From the top of the stairs, the river shimmered in the distance. Looming in the foreground was a building with a huge golden dome and a King Kong gorilla perched on top of it, holding a NOLLYWOOD sign. This was Tinapa's entertainment complex. Muddled cultural referencing aside, it looked exciting. A sign

outside the building listed its intended uses: post-production, editing and sound studios, screening theatre, office, café, movie sets
workshop, pre-production suites. The intention was grand, but I
couldn't envisage Lagos-based Nollywood directors dropping their
laptops and flying to Calabar to edit their shaky-cam productions in
Tinapa's state-of-the art editing suites.

The movie theme park was situated behind the post-production
suites. *Jurassic Park* dinosaurs manned its entrance. I walked through
the gate, past a soldier lying almost supine in his chair. Springing
upright, he demanded to know where I was going, and reprimanded
me for 'marching in' without his permission. I had to apologise
before he let me through.

In the theme park, an outdoor amphitheatre was dotted with
waxwork statues, a wonderland of cowboys and Indians, a knight in
shining armour, the detective Dick Tracy, Disney-like gnomes and
giant plastic flowers, which bloomed amid the din of construction
work. A European foreman barked impatiently at his Nigerian
workers. Jabbing an angry forefinger at the blueprints, he instructed
his employees as though they were recalcitrant children. Before my
indignation spilled over, I reminded myself that Nigerian foremen
treat their staff the same way.

The men were working for a German construction group. Work
was due to have finished in 2006, and it had cost the government
and investors nearly $350 million so far. Three million visitors were
supposed to be traipsing through here each year eventually, parking
their SUVs, staying at the hotel, and generating $2.5 billion in rev-
enue. It was hard to imagine it all. Harder still was envisaging those
notoriously corrupt customs officers tolerating the idea of duty-free
trading.

A young man, one of the few other visitors at Tinapa, was standing nearby. I asked him what he thought of Tinapa. With a sceptical
shake of the head, he branded the project a scam. 'You cannot carry
money from government like that,' he said. 'You must put it

through something first.' The ex-governor Donald Duke, for all his virtues, was as corrupt as the others, the man claimed. Tinapa was his Big White Elephant, an excuse to build a project and collect kickbacks.

This top-down approach to boosting Calabar's economy seemed hollow. I'd heard Nigerian politicians' endless talk about theme parks, tourist resorts, shopping malls and their 'trickle down' effects on the economy. But there's no such thing as 'trickle down' in Nigeria – money trickles upwards or evaporates on contact with air. I couldn't see how Tinapa's tax-free retail would stop six-year-old kids selling bananas on a weekday instead of attending school, or stop toddlers like the girl in the village next door to Tinapa playing barefoot and unclothed among chickens.

I had forgotten to ask the okada man who brought me here to return and pick me up, and there was no other public transport. A few hundred metres away, a taxi deposited someone and drove off slowly but I didn't have the strength or speed to catch it. Almost crazed with hunger, I dragged my feet through Tinapa's concrete wilderness, past the unblemished road signs and strips of grass lining the dirt-free sidewalk. The afternoon sun bounced off the new tarmac and blinded my eyes. I was close to fainting.

Forty minutes later, on the road leading out of the development, a lone okada materialised in the distance, on the lookout for a cus-tomer. His beady eyes spotted me and we beckoned to one another. I exhaled with relief as he rumbled towards me, the buzz of his engine filling the air like music.

'Mr Biggs,' I instructed him. He whisked me back to Calabar.

13

Spoiling Nature's Spoils

Cross River State

Sonny was my father's driver for over twenty years. He was the one who had chauffeured us around Nigeria on that big trip of 1988. I had last seen him in 1990, on my final summer holiday in Nigeria. An Ogoni from the same village as my family, Sonny was an opinionated and forthright autodidact who always seemed over-qualified for his station in life. He picked me up the next morning in the family's car. Now approaching his mid-fifties, Sonny still looked the same – slim build, slight overbite and a fantastically chiselled face. But his hair glinted with silver and, in my father's absence, he took on a more avuncular and authoritative role with me, which made for an awkward dynamic since I was now a grown adult paying for the petrol and dictating the itinerary.

We were driving to Ikom, a town north of Calabar where archaeologists at the turn of the century had found ancient stone monoliths carved with hieroglyphics. As there were no signs directing us to the monoliths, we stopped on the roadside and asked a policeman.

'Good afternoon, chief,' the officer greeted Sonny. People often assumed Sonny was a 'chief' because he drove an SUV, although it was actually a borrowed car. Money, power and respect were so tightly interwoven, it was amusing to see how simply driving the right car could elevate one's perceived status and compel others to kowtow.

In the late afternoon, we arrived at Alok, a village just north of Ikom, set in flat, sparsely wooded grassland. Three scruffy kids led us to a house where we would find the man in charge of the monoliths. I stepped onto the verandah and knocked on the door. A rotund man in his fifties wearing a pink towel around his impressive girth opened the door and greeted me warmly.

'Hello, I'm looking to see the stone monoliths,' I said, feeling guilty for arriving unannounced.

'Wait.' The man stepped out and called out a boy's name . . . no response. He called out for him again, and again, but the boy wasn't answering.

'*Where* is that boy? He's the one who keeps the key for the gate.' The big man pointed at a cluster of monoliths sequestered inside a compound near his house. 'What is this nonsense,' he muttered to himself in embarrassment. 'If he knows he cannot be here, he should give the key to someone else. Sorry,' – he turned to me – ' . . . I'm coming.'

A minute later, he emerged fully dressed and introduced himself as Chief Sylvanus Ekoh Akong, higher technical officer for the Commission for Museums and Monuments. Sylvanus was in charge of antiquities in the area, but without the keys he couldn't show us the main monolith site. He led us to another site a mile away in a grassy field where, aside from a small fire crackling unthreateningly in a clump of bushes, the tall grass swayed silently in the golden evening breeze.

The monoliths stood scattered around a 2,000-square-metre field with no protective fencing. They were fat phallic-shaped basaltic rocks, around 1.2 metres high, keeling helplessly towards the ground. They had stylised human features – with gaping mouths and eyes, slightly reminiscent of Mayan carvings, and rows of dots arched across their brows. The monoliths were arranged in circles, possibly in the centre of an ancient village, archaeologists have suggested. By some estimates, they date as far back as 2000 BC. Sylvanus said that around 450 of these circles lay scattered around the region. Two monolith sites have been fully excavated, while another twenty-five need to be fully unearthed. I was intrigued by what other secrets the soil might be harbouring.

Each rock (known as an *akwanshi*) contains a unique set of geometric carvings called *insibidi*. No one knows exactly what these hieroglyphics signify, but they're thought to convey specific information – rules and regulations, perhaps. Chief Sylvanus pointed to a figure-of-eight symbol, saying that it represented a staff of office for senior villagers.

'This is a person with a hunchback problem,' he said, showing me a monolith with a bulge at the back of it. 'You see this cross?' Sylvanus pointed to the front of the rock. 'It means "human beings coming together". It is the same cross that we Christians use as a symbol of Christ.'

Sylvanus also believed the crosses were used as mathematical symbols. There was also a Y-shape carving, symbolising the Benue–Niger river confluence, which represents the centre of the earth, or the biblical Garden of Eden. The stones, Sylvanus claimed, were inspired by the pyramids of Egypt. He pointed to a rock with swirls on it.

'They depict the woman who started giving birth to all of us,' he said. '*Agbor shi she* means the "founding mother" or Eve.' The equivalent phrase in Hebrew is *shi shi*, Sylvanus said. He and some Nigerian researchers believed that the similarity proves a link between Alok and Jesus and the Holy Land. Evangelism's strong arm was influencing Nigerian historical research too, it seemed.

Back at the main, fenced-off monolith site, Sylvanus, Sonny and I peeped through the wrought-iron railings and looked at the circle of monoliths nestled among the trees and long grass. The spirals on each stone signified weather. Anti-clockwise meant good weather, clockwise meant bad weather. 'Today, they use these spirals in modern meteorology,' Sylvanus claimed, referring to the shorthand swirls and arrows denoting rain and wind on weather maps.

I was a little sceptical of these interpretations, with one eye on the Bible and the West, as if our identity were tethered to these parts of the world. Whatever the carvings really mean, they've been adopted by contemporary Nigerian culture. The patterns are reproduced in regional hairstyles for certain occasions, such as marriage, and also appear on the cloths used to make costumes for members of Ekpe.

'These marks here . . .', Chief Sylvanus pointed at some swirls on the stones. 'In Benue state, the Tiv, Igala and Nupe peoples have the same marks on their faces. It is the tribal marks that you take to know who is who. But they are not allowing anyone to put tribal marks any more. They say they are disfiguring their faces.'

Africa has a reputation as a place where change rarely happens. But its people and cultures are constantly shifting, disappearing; buried beneath the sands of time and governmental indifference to history. Our ancestors' enigmatic traces are interpreted and misinterpreted by everyone and anyone. I guess we'll only discover the truth when our universities receive proper funding and start producing world-class historians and archaeologists again. Apart from thinly funded work by home-grown and overseas academics, Nigeria seems a poorly researched country, a half-empty page readily soiled by anyone with a racial, religious or economic agenda, be they evangelicals looking for links to Israel, or foreign racists wanting to deny African history altogether. I left Ikom feeling teased by its secrets, and all the more ravenous for knowledge about the past.

Nothing is more beautiful than a rainforest in the morning mist. The sunlight shot through the towering trees, giving their greenness a dewy, sparkling translucence, which hinted at the possibility that spirits truly existed in the forest. Sonny and I were cruising north from Ikom the next morning, negotiating a narrow, bumpy road cleaved open by gorges of soil erosion. The other vehicles on the road did not fare as well as our 4 x 4. With their minimal suspension, they clattered along the road, windows rattling, the cars' lifespans shortening with every expensive jolt. Capitalism is an odd thing: the parts of the world with the best roads also have cars with the best suspension, whereas countries like Nigeria with the worst soil erosion and the worst roads tend to have poor-suspension vehicles. If only economics mirrored the natural world's propensity to adapt.

We turned off the highway and into the forest, along a narrow, red soil path that was even rougher than the main road. The looming forest, now enveloping us on all sides, seemed less enchanting and slightly more intimidating. The bugs, the heat, the unknown fauna lurking in the darkness – I would be walking within it soon. We entered the Afi Mountain Wildlife Sanctuary, an area of protected rainforest holding its ground against encroaching humanity. South-eastern Nigeria is blessed with some of the most biodiverse land on the planet. Gorillas, chimpanzees and drill monkeys live here, as well as civet cats, parrots, eagles and other monkey species.

If someone told me all of this as a child, I clearly wasn't paying attention. I used to stare from the balcony of our Port Harcourt home and dream of roaming exotic places, oblivious to the rainforest that lay two hours behind me, as virginal as anywhere in the Amazon or Congo. Rainforests weren't something I associated with Nigeria. Our acres of palm trees and farmland and urban sprawl were far more familiar to me.

The Afi Drill Ranch on the edge of the rainforest was dedicated to protecting drill monkeys and chimpanzees. Only about 300 Cross River gorillas are left in the wild, and the chimpanzees are threatened by poachers and hunters. The ranch protects the drill monkeys and chimpanzees, but lets the gorillas roam freely. It was established and run by Liza Gadsby, a formidable blonde American in her late forties, who slightly resembles the model Lauren Hutton. Liza first arrived in Nigeria in the 1980s while overlanding in West Africa with her boyfriend (now her husband). They had stopped in Ibadan to get parts for their Land Rover, back in the days when the town still had an assembly plant. There they met a friend who was involved in animal conservation in Cameroon. Eventually, the American pair settled in Cross River State and created a primate protection programme.

Afi's base camp was nestled in a clearing surrounded by beautiful folds of dense forest. Nearby were heaps of bush mangoes stockpiled for feeding the monkeys and apes, and in the distance, the Afi mountain itself soared upwards through the foliage. In her tent, Liza was making herself porridge for breakfast, next to a shelf lined with American novels.

'The gorillas live up there,' she said, pointing at the massif. Sighting this reclusive species was next to impossible. Liza said three British men had stayed at Afi Ranch on their friend's pre-wedding stag week, and spent seven days hiking up the steep mountain, searching for gorillas. They found a trail of faeces only.

'On the index of diversity, Nigeria's primates make it the third most biodiverse country in Africa,' Liza informed me. The country has a bounty of fauna, but we're losing it. She blamed it on the 'Nigerian government and the Nigerian people. We used to have giraffe in Borno State, and rhino. But they're all gone.'

'What happened to them?'

'Poached for their meat. People like their bush meat. Animal husbandry has never really been a part of the way of life here,' she said, referring to Buanchor, the village near Afi Ranch. 'They let their goats wander around – they don't eat them. Do you know what the main meat source for people here is?'

'No.'

'Frozen fish from Europe.'

'*What?*'

'There aren't any fish left in the rivers because they put chemicals in the river to kill the fish and catch them.' Sonny nodded in confirmation.

I didn't know giraffes were even edible. There seems to be a place in Nigerian cooking pots for anything that moves. I adore meat but limit my intake for health reasons; but I had found eating vegetarian in some hotels and restaurants next to impossible. Waiters and waitresses stared at me as if I were insane. I remember one very nice staff worker at my Ibadan hotel being particularly resistant to my request for jollof rice without goat:

'Why?' she frowned in disbelief.

'I don't feel like it tonight.'

'But you must have meat.'

'I don't want any.'

'Is there something wrong with it?'

'Yes,' I said, pouncing on the opportunity to lie. 'It's . . . it's too tough.'

'We will make it tender.'

'No, please, I just don't want to have any meat.'

'You will like it.'

'No, I really don't want any.'

'You will *like* it.'

' . . . OK.'

In many parts of Nigeria, eating a meal without meat was a pointless, flavourless endeavour that needed urgent rectifying. Quite often, my request was simply disregarded, and my rice would arrive with hunks of goat or chicken defiantly embedded in it.

In the rainforest of Cross River State, monkeys have been hunted close to extinction. Afi Drill Ranch protects the drill monkeys and chimpanzees by keeping them in enclosures. One of the ranch keepers, a man called James, led Sonny and me to the spacious ape enclosures, fenced with electric wiring. The first enclosure contained several galloping drill monkeys. Despite their name, drill monkeys resemble baboons, except that their fur is silver and their backsides are covered in phenomenally bright pink and blue fur. Ninety per cent of the world's wild drill monkeys come from this part of Nigeria.

'Can't they climb up the trees and jump over the fence?' I asked James.

'No, drills can climb high, but they don't move from tree to tree,' he said. The animals were depleting the foliage, however, so the ranch was making plans to move them to a new enclosure.

We walked through the trees towards the area where the chimps were kept. The forest hummed with life, and large multi-coloured butterflies bounced incessantly off our faces. En route, James pointed out the mahogany, ebony, *okasi* and iroko trees stretching towards the sky.

'You no go see tree like this in Rivers State,' Sonny said in amazement. Our village, Bane, is highly deforested. Most of the trees were chopped down for farming and oil, or to make canoes, doors and furniture. I was hard for me to imagine that Bane was once like Afi, with a canopy blocking out the sunlight, the forest floor teeming with natural medicines, bush meat, mangoes, avocados, pawpaw, wood – all the necessary ingredients for subsistence living. No wonder Afi's local population had outgrown its natural surroundings.

'A bag of small seed like this will cost ₦1,000 in Port Harcourt!' Sonny picked up a cedar seed. Cedar wood bark is used to treat malaria. The bark is peeled, mixed with a hot drink or soaked in water for a day. Also abundant were the coin-shaped seeds of the *achi* tree, used in cooking. One cup fetches ₦160 in the markets these days, its high price the result of diminishing supplies. But in Afi, the seeds virtually carpeted the ground.

At the chimpanzee enclosure, a chimp beat her chest and stretched out her arm to us, demanding food. She threw banana peel at me, but showed Sonny more respect by doing a press-up in front of him.

'She's greeting you,' James explained to Sonny. He told us that the vulval swelling of the chimp's backside signified that she was in heat and therefore receptive to males. In another part of the enclosure I watched a long-limbed, long-faced chimp with silvery-white fur enjoying his own company. Unlike the others, he was a lowland chimp, native to Equatorial Guinea and Central Africa. He reclined on his back and gazed into my camera lens, a poseur on a photo shoot. A few feet away, a baby lay on top of his mother. She fondled his toes while he pulled savagely at her eyelids and scraped out flecks of dirt.

For the first time, I noticed how closely the soles of the chimpanzees' feet resemble human feet. The texture – the leathery, faint brown swirls – were identical to mine. Seeing it kindled in me an intense affinity with these animals, stronger than I'd ever felt before. The possibility that they may become extinct within a century or two was too catastrophic an outcome to contemplate, the near-equivalent of losing an entire race of humanity. Liza said that roughly 200,000 chimps are left in the African wilderness. Numerically, this was no disaster but, she reminded me, most of the apes live in disparate, isolated teams with no chance of mixing their genes with other groups; each gene pool was tiny.

'We don't want a brother and sister to be sexing, but what can you do?' James shrugged.

After looking at the enclosures, James's colleague Peter took Sonny and me on a walk though the canopy. We filed along a narrow, elevated steel bridge that swung 20 metres or so above the forest floor. It was 450 metres long. Peter strolled along it, walking incredibly quickly without breaking a sweat, but Sonny wasn't so nimble. When we reached one of the viewing platforms built around a tree trunk, he asked to take a break.

'Go ahead, I'll wait here,' he said, dabbing his forehead with a handkerchief. Anxiety lined his forehead. He hadn't told anyone he was afraid of heights. Unfortunately for Sonny, the canopy walk was a one-way system, meaning he had no choice but to shuffle behind me and Peter, not knowing where to look.

'My hand dey shake, o,' he stammered. 'I don't look down . . . It will turn my brain.'

Peter smiled. This wasn't the first time he'd escorted someone who was scared of heights. He once took the governor and his entourage on a walk along the canopy bridge during a state visit. 'It took them *hours*, not minutes!' he grinned, imitating the governor's jittery, mincing steps.

Back at the base camp, I excitedly told Liza about my deepened love for chimpanzees. She lamented that the state showed little interest in the animals. 'We don't get any money from the government,' she said. All her cash was raised during her annual three-month returns to the US. Nigerian zoo curators were corrupt and indifferent towards the animals' survival. In 2002, the woman in charge of Ibadan University's zoo was sacked after illegally selling four endangered western lowland gorillas to a zoo in Malaysia and pocketing $1 million.

'Nigerians have been cowed into submission,' Liza said from her wooden cabin office overlooking the mountain face. 'They prefer to do nothing and live under this "contractocracy". People like you should come back here and help this country.' I gave her a donation for the ranch before saying goodbye. Walking back to the car, I was simultaneously buoyed with inspiration and freighted by obligation.

Sonny and I continued on the highway north towards the Obudu Cattle Ranch, close to the Cameroonian border. I was looking forward to this portion of the trip. The cattle ranch was the jewel among Nigeria's few tourist resorts, an upscale hotel set in the rarified heights of the Cameroon Mountain range. Spending a night here would be my one concession to luxury on this trip.

Towards the foot of the mountain, the road became less

congested and was obsequiously surfaced with better tarmac for the Obudu Ranch guests who travel along it. Other guests prefer to skip the road and arrive by helicopter. Sonny and I wound higher and higher up the mountain, into white mists that clung to the grassy slopes, rising around us like sleeping green giants. Palm trees gave way to a scattering of temperate trees covered in beautiful red leaves. We were leaving behind the heat, humidity and mosquitoes of the tropical lowlands and ascending to heaven. I immediately felt invigorated by the drop in temperature. No longer was I bullied or suffocated by tropical heat; there was space to take stock and think.

The ranch started life as a colonial farm established by Scots in the early 1950s. It then expanded to become a retreat where ruddy-faced expats could escape the heat. Now it was a getaway for well-off Nigerians.

At the main hotel, I offloaded my bags, said goodbye to Sonny and checked into my room. I did a quick tour, ecstatic at the power shower, the patterned wallpaper, the soft clean carpet, the TV and the remote control with – praise be – functioning batteries!

Lunch was a solitary affair in the emptyish dining room. The silence was surreal, and so was the decor – three haystacks with wine bottles perched decoratively on top of them, and a large model cow standing beside them. The menu was limited in its range but not in the audacity of its prices. I had to take a deep breath when I saw that the main course cost ₦5,000.

After lunch, I took a walk outside, past the tennis courts, down a sloping path and into a bucolic picture book. The green hills and valleys were reminiscent of the English Yorkshire Dales. Fresian cows munched on the yellowing grass; horses grazed by fields of potato, cabbage, lettuce and carrots. Feeling serene, I walked down a path to a leafy grotto where a small bridge arched over a river that bubbled beneath a 3-metre waterfall. Behind me, a golf course undulated into the distance, its trees looking fresh and ghostly in the mist. It was glorious, almost unreal.

A chilly late-afternoon wind picked up and sprinkled goose bumps over my arms. I hurried back to my room and listened in a vegetative state to the hectoring yap of CNN reporters. After dinner, back on my firm bed and staring at the carpeted, wood-carved comforts around me, I felt faintly uneasy. Wasn't all this quiet, cleanliness and cool air what I'd been craving these last few months? Solitude was partly to blame, but there was more to it. Dare I say it, I think I was missing the chaos, the *jagga jagga* of Nigerian life. The term jagga jagga, slang for 'messed up', was made famous by hip-hop artist Eedris Abdulkareem in his song of the same name, which criticised contemporary Nigerian society. I half longed for the infuriating but amusing lack of protocol I'd experienced on my journey so far: room service staff lingering in the doorway for conversation; the receptionist asking for my telephone number; hotel cleaners arguing with one another along the corridors ('Don't talk to me as if I am your boyfriend. I have not requested a co-wife, so stop bothering me.'). At Obudu, everyone was perfectly compliant and dull. The place felt too clean and quiet. It reminded me of Ewell in England, where I grew up. Nothing ever happened there: no dramas, serious crime, water shortages, robberies, glamour, excitement, flavour – nothing that might affect one's equilibrium. Its dullness was the trade-off for material comfort and stability, and so was Obudu's.

After breakfast the next morning, I strolled in the dewy morning greyness and exchanged greetings with a passing old couple, who were one of the few pairs of guests at the ranch during this post-Christmas period. At the top of a hill I sat on a bench and watched cows chewing the cud on the grassy slopes, and the sweetest kid goat bleating forlornly for its mother. Within minutes, the mist rolled in amazingly quickly, erasing the hills, cows and trees, and wrapping me in a sea of white oblivion. I strolled down to the ranch's Beehive Natural Reserve, a wedge of forest at the bottom of a hill with a tropical microclimate all of its own. In a matter of minutes I went from the Yorkshire Dales to a humid rainforest rustling with dewy, hundred-year-old ferns.

The afternoon sun vaporised the mist, allowing me to take a ride on the cable car, the 'longest in Africa'. The car floated above the hills and cows grazing next to a precipice I hadn't realised was there. As I moved above and past it, the ground plunged into a valley hundreds of feet deep, giving the impression that the cable car was taking off vertically. Yellow-grassed mountain peaks jutted in every direction, interspersed with red-leafed trees. And it was deathly quiet, the cable car moving along as if propelled on silent wings.

Three maintenance workers passed me in the opposite direction and waved hello, nonchalantly reclining in a shallow metal crate and looking perfectly at ease with the frightening altitude. Suddenly, my cable car stopped. Perhaps the electricity had cut out. My car hung noiselessly, suspended in mid-air. Fighting an urge to throw my notebook out of the window, I eyed the valley floor through the glass floor. For three minutes I sat back and daydreamed in the cool, tranquil air. Stillness of this kind was hard to come by in urban Nigeria; I inhaled deeply, savouring every moment, amazed at the restorative power of a few minutes of dead air. My mind was made up: this is what I ultimately needed, to be away from the commotion of people and okadas, and away from the oppressive sterility of quiet hotels – hanging in the middle of absolutely nowhere, in a mist of white nothingness. Sometimes, changing altitude, not latitude, was the best way to find peace.

The following morning I faced the logistical puzzle of leaving the ranch without my own 4 x 4 or helicopter. High-end Nigerian tourism doesn't cater for the middle-income traveller relying on public transport. The ranch staff tried finding transport to take me to Obudu town, 30 kilometres or so beyond the foot of the mountain. No luck.

'Do you want to take okada?' a man asked, straddling his motor-cycle. I hadn't considered this as an option, not with my heavy suitcase and bulky shoulder bag. Could he seriously fit them – and me – onto a bike and then ride down a steep mountain?

The man nodded as if I'd asked a stupid question, then picked up my suitcase and balanced it on the handlebars of his motorbike. Tautening his back so that he could see the road over my luggage, he urged me to sit down behind him. Slowly we moved off, cautiously winding down the beautiful, sunny mountain, back down to earth, back to the jagga jagga of Nigerian life. I must have been the only guest in Obudu's history to check out in so spectacularly unstylish a fashion. But it didn't matter. I swallowed my pride and enjoyed the ride.

14

Behind the Mask

Benin

My journey took a haphazard swing westwards. I wanted to visit the city of Benin before heading to my home region. Groggy and puffy-eyed, I clambered on board a minibus and promptly fell asleep against the window. During the journey, I lolled in and out of consciousness, my eyes briefly widening to take in bridge after bridge, stretching over luminous green rivers and a thick, domed canopy of palm trees. The Niger River Delta is vast.

We arrived in the market area of the ancient city of Benin. Sunlight bounced off oranges, bananas, batik-dyed cloths and okada wing mirrors, blinding me momentarily as the minibus crawled through the hustling mob of traders and pedestrians. Was the market encroaching on the road or was the traffic driving through the market? I couldn't tell.

Half a millenium ago, finesse, excellence and orderliness ruled here under the magnificent Benin empire, one of West Africa's most influential kingdoms. The empire flourished for 500 years and ruled over an ambitious stretch of Nigeria's southern region. I'd become fascinated with Benin's history after visiting the modern-day Republic of Benin, Nigeria's next-door neighbour, some years before. Great empires didn't feature strongly in the Nigeria I knew from childhood, and most African diasporans I'd met seemed to fixate on caramel-complexioned Nubian princesses and Ethiopian emperors, while overlooking the civilisations of West Africa.

The Benin empire particularly impressed me because it developed without the influence of Islam or Europe. Headed by an oba, it was a highly centralised kingdom that experienced minimal infighting. During its glory days between the fifteenth and seventeenth centuries, the empire expanded through military campaigns, particularly under Oba Ewuare (1440–73) and Oba Esigie (1504–50), and held dominion over large chunks of Southern Nigeria, including Yorubaland and Igboland (as far east as Onitsha), and as far west as Ghana, where the Ga peoples still claim Benin ancestry. The empire's well-disciplined army (estimated by historians to be 20,000 strong) was divided into the oba's specially selected regiment of warriors, a metropolitan regiment, a queen's regiment, and various village regiments, which formed the biggest contingent of the army. The armies adopted a strategy of encircling their enemies and weakening them by cutting off their supplies. Highly organised on the water, they skilfully navigated the labyrinthine creeks and rivers of the Niger Delta to expand their empire eastwards.

Organised administration was another defining characteristic of the Benin regime. Only men with a strong knowledge of the state, its customs and traditions were appointed as prime ministers. And even the oba's succession, though hereditary, had to be confirmed by two senior officials.

I'd seen the Benin empire's famously elegant fifteenth-century bronze castings and masks in museums around Europe. Their intricate carvings depict animals, battle scenes and life at the royal court. The skill involved in producing these was world class. The craftsmen lived and worked in specific districts of the city, alongside woodcarvers, ivory carvers, bead makers, leather makers and blacksmiths who fashioned military swords and spearheads. The kingdom's geometric grid of wide, straight roads was lined with houses, some of which were made of wood and fronted with porches.

Flanking the enormous gate of the oba's palace were two towers, each topped with 15-metre-long bronze pythons. The palace interior was festooned with ornate ivory and bronze sculptures, wooden bas-relief plaques and wooden pillars covered in copper carvings. The kingdom was protected by a wall 9 metres thick and 100 kilometres in circumference. The wall and the oba's palace were partly built by prisoners of war, who also helped to construct the inner city wall and build a 15-metre-deep moat around it.

Benin's wealth and power attracted foreign attention, mainly from the Portuguese, who were the first Europeans to make contact in the 1480s. By the sixteenth century, Benin played host to Christian missionaries, sent its own ambassador to Lisbon and began trading with the British after they visited Benin in 1553.

The British provided guns, textiles and other European goods in exchange for pepper, ivory, palm oil and slaves. The Europeans fomented war between African tribes in order to produce prisoners of war who could become slaves. Although the Benin obas weren't under serious economic pressure to sell slaves, the presence of European firearms made it imperative for them to do so: if they didn't sell slaves, they wouldn't have firearms to defend against their armed enemies. It was a vicious circle.

During the eighteenth century, the Benin empire began to decline. It was the only kingdom on the Nigerian coastline that wasn't under British control, preferring to trade independently and refusing to join the British protectorate. The British Consul General wrote to the oba, stating his intention to visit the kingdom for talks. But the oba asked him to delay his mission because he was performing customary rituals from which foreigners were barred. The Consul General, dismissing the oba's wishes, sent several British officials and traders to Benin anyway.

En route, the men were ambushed outside the city and seven of them were killed. The British responded by launching a punitive expedition against Benin in 1897. Troops ransacked the place, stole the oba's palace artwork and razed the kingdom to the ground before sending the oba into exile. The British justified their actions on the grounds that they were defending themselves against barbarism and the despotic rule of a fetish-priest who indulged in human sacrifices. The artwork they stole was kept by officers or sold to the US and Germany to cover some of the costs of the military action. A few pieces were destroyed during the Second World War.

Benin was a different city now, a witchcraft hotspot (by Aunty Janice's reckoning), with a reputation for armed robberies and modern-day people trafficking. In true Nigerian fashion, the city assiduously downplayed its former illustriousness; one would never guess that one of Africa's greatest empires once preceded the open drains, low-tech Internet cafés and nondescript 1970s architecture laid out before me. Bas-reliefs are still part of the city's cultural aesthetic – I saw a few on shopfronts and residential gates here and there, although the depicted images were now Christian angels with African faces – but Benin's past splendour felt very far away, almost folkloric.

Benin's former glories had now retreated behind the four walls of its museum. Reaching the place felt like a life-threatening challenge, seemingly designed to test one's commitment to its antiquities. The museum was sequestered within the confines of a busy roundabout that forced visitors to sprint across four lanes of ruthless traffic to reach it.

'You run very well!' an okada man shouted after I narrowly avoided being mown down by him. Mildly shaken, I walked across a tatty compound to the museum door. An eighteen-month-old girl in a white party dress waddled towards my legs, wrapped her arms around my knees and grinned up at me.

'Does she know you?' a woman asked with friendly curiosity.

I was equally bemused. 'No.'

The woman was the museum's caretaker and mother of the toddler. I paid her the entrance fee and began examining the artefacts on display. Every object, no matter how minor its function, was designed exquisitely: the sixteenth-century bronze kola nut container shaped like a fish; the bronze cock that was once displayed on altars dedicated to dead queen mothers; the leopard-shaped container for storing water used during the oba's ritual hand washing. I had to restrain myself from stroking the carved ivory armlets, ivory flutes and gorgeous carved elephant tusks.

Since the British invasion of 1897, many of Benin's finest artefacts have been scattered and hoarded around the world, including in the British Museum, the Louvre in Paris and the Ethnological Museum in Berlin. Still, the Benin City National Museum had plenty of wonders on display. My favourites were a gorgeous bronze bust sculpture of a queen mother from the early sixteenth century and a divine pair of stools sent by an oba to a king of Portugal some time in the same century (the museum was vague with the facts). The bases of the stools were decorated with frog and monkey bas-reliefs, the stems had been carved into the form of coiled pythons, and the rounded seats on top had intricate carvings lining their perimeters.

Beneath some beautiful bronze plaques layered with bas-relief carvings, the museum caretaker sat and breastfed her youngest child while chatting to a man who exhibited an in-depth knowledge of the heritage sector.

'The state of Nigerian museums is terrible ... terrible,' the man said. 'In the sixties and seventies Ghanaians used to come to Nigerian museums for training. Now they have overtaken us.' His name was Maurice Archibong, and he turned out to be a travel writer for one of the national newspapers. We exchanged numbers and agreed to continue the conversation in Lagos in a month's time.

Across town, I searched for Chief Ogiamien's house, the only imperial building not razed to the ground by the British. The geriatric building stood next to a noisy motorbike repair garage, the latter overshadowing the former with its modern vigour. Ogiamien's house was made of red earth with the characteristic horizontal grooves running along its exterior walls, and bas-relief carvings decorating one of the doors. There was nothing, no plaque or sign, to celebrate this sole remnant of empire. Metal chairs and low tables cluttered its courtyard.

At the back of the house, among the complex of rooms, a smiley elderly woman sat in an alleyway. I hoped she could tell me more about the house, but she didn't understand English. As I took photos, she gestured to me, speaking in Bini. Unintelligible as her words were, the international language of begging was easy to decipher. I dashed her ₦40 and left.

The oba lineage still continues in Benin, although these days the oba's palace is fighting for supremacy in a world where money and political power wield far more influence than traditional titles. In 2007, the oba of Benin banished the *esama* – a non-hereditary title-holder – from the royal palace after the esama was accused of acting as if he were the oba himself. He certainly enjoyed a lot of power. The esama is the father of the wealthy ex-governor of Edo state, a man who was under investigation for corruption. In an audacious move, the esama ignored the oba's traditional New Year ceremony at the palace, and instead invited several high chiefs to a ceremony of his own.

Catching wind of this, the enraged oba suspended the esama from the palace for flouting palace protocol (an 'abominable act'), and barred him and the naughty chiefs from wearing palace paraphernalia or partaking in palace activities.

This wasn't the first time the oba and the esama had clashed. The esama – ranked sixth in the palace but number one in wealth – was accused of acting above his station when he decorated a visiting Jamaican ex-prime minister with royal beads, a ritual traditionally performed by the oba. The 'upstart' esama also received Ghanaian and Yoruba royalty at the airport in a sumptuous parade before inviting his guests to *his* palace, not the oba's. The esama's son defended his father's behaviour, saying that the esama ought to use his wealth and influence to 'protect' the royal traditions. But the oba considered it an erosion of his status.

Age and seniority used to matter a lot more in Nigerian society. As a child, my older relatives would conclude arguments with me by deploying that most infuriating of non-sequiturs, 'I am your senior!'; any chocolate disputes with Zina, my twin, were routinely settled in her favour because she entered the world ten minutes before me. Age was a prime criterion for competency, respect and authority, and it still imbues certain old men with the belief that they are omniscient demigods beyond reproach. When, for example, President Obasanjo's son accused the then vice-president of corruption, the VP's spokesman issued this response in a national newspaper: 'The VP does not belong to a culture in which children trade words with elders ... Young men who attack men old enough to be their father are dismissed as rude and uncultured. This boy will not be glorified with a response.' The 'boy' in question was a grown man with a PhD.

I'm convinced that gerontocracy stifles individual creativity and innovation. But returning to Nigeria made me realise how much the country's poverty is undermining this old system, anyway: my relative wealth gave me a lot of leverage for a person of my age – gerontocracy is gradually being replaced by corrupt plutocracy.

'We do not talk of his name,' a staff worker at the oba's palace said, wagging her finger sternly. In asking for her opinion on the esama, I had committed a major faux pas.

'But—'

'I said we do *not* talk of him here.' She raised her palm in the air. 'You are a foreigner here, so you didn't know ... but we do not talk of him.' She blinked and shifted huffily in her seat.

I was visiting the palace, or *eguae*, set in a sprawling, modernised compound in the middle of Benin City. The palace hummed with activity. Flags flew everywhere, police strolled about, and royal title-holders donned traditional robes and beads, hurrying from one place to the next. The oba spends most of his time inside the palace, emerging only for festivals and other royal functions. The place retained a certain mystique and was the subject of constant rumours, including whispers that the oba's many wives walk in permanent silence, prohibited from uttering a word.

Could I get a tour of the palace? I asked the oba's staff. They said no. Instead, they offered me a booklet about the history and rules of the palace. One page read:

SOME OF THE QUALIFICATIONS WHICH ENABLE A CITIZEN TO QUALIFY FOR INITIATION INTO EGUAE OBA N'EDO (PALACE):

1) He must be sane.
2) He should be free of infectious diseases, contagious diseases, any deadly diseases.
3) He should not be a descendant of any of the families forbidden to enter the palace or move freely with the free citizens.
4) He must not be an enemy of the oba.
5) A naturalised Bini.

As I read the book, a portly palace staff member called Veronica sat me down at her desk by the palace courtyard. She was a brisk, stocky, short-haired woman whose eyes were windows to a very tenacious soul.

'Where are you from?' she asked.

'Port Harcourt.'

'But you tok like Ingleesh pessin.' I immediately sensed she wasn't asking out of innocent curiosity.

'That's because I went to university in London.'

'Where did you attend secondary school?'

'In Nigeria,' I lied, trying to blink casually at her.

'Which secondary school?' Veronica demanded. She was shaking me down for information, taking detailed inventory of my answers and my life. I searched the sky for a response but gave up when my hesitation lasted too long.

'I went to school in England,' I conceded. The confession would cost me, I knew. Veronica turned to her colleague and said something in their Bini dialect. She mentioned 'London' a couple of times, in tones of restrained glee, as if she'd just won a mini lottery. In her eyes, I had attended secondary school in England, therefore I was rich. I was ready to leave the palace, especially now that they wouldn't give me a tour of the place. But Veronica kept me in my seat. She wanted me to buy a book about Benin and a DVD of the oba's coronation.

'₦3,000,' she said in a freshly adopted salesman's pitch. 'It's a good price . . . good price.' Zealously, she tapped her fingers on the table and eyeballed me. I bargained downwards but didn't have the skill or patience to lower the price to a reasonable level. Eventually I paid an excessive ₦1,200 for the merchandise.

'Won't you dash me something small?' Veronica grinned as she pocketed the cash.

'I don't have money.'

'Yes you do, you are from London,' she replied sharply. Her steely smile and fidgety fingers bullied me into submission. I watched my foolish hands reach into my bag and rummage for small change. As Veronica's eyes bored into my wallet, I wanted to tell her she was wrong to think that I was rich, and that life in England is a never-ending payment of mortgages and bills; liquidity and disposable cash were an illusion. But she would never accept this truth. I sourly gave her ₦100 and said goodbye.

*

By now, Benin's dereliction of its heritage had become a compelling attraction in itself. I went around town, examining the pitiful remnants of the defensive moat that once ringed the ancient kingdom. They were scattered at various points around the city centre, the water now replaced by tall grasses. Signs had been erected reading: YOU ARE CROSSING THE BENIN MOAT, THE GREAT PERIMETER OF ANCIENT BENIN KINGDOM, ONE OF NIGERIA'S GREATEST LANDMARKS. Further on, I saw a smaller sticker that said: 'Benin City walls and moats. Our cultural heritage, our national monuments. Protect them. Do not destroy, do not excavate, do not dump refuse.' The sign was surrounded by a mutinous mountain of banana skins, plastic bottles and wrappers floating in bubbly green sewage slime.

'Aren't people proud of Benin history?' I asked Michael, my okada man. He'd brought me to the widest section of the moat.

'We are,' he replied.

'So why is there so much rubbish here?'

'People are not supposed to build their houses very close. But there is no people to enforce the law, so they can just do whatever they like. You see the rubbish inside the moat? The government is supposed to provide rubbish bin.'

We rode to a large section of moat that was about 9 metres wide and still 6 metres deep, even though vegetation and rubbish clogged its base.

'It's not the people's fault,' Michael said. 'It's the government. You can see how they have tied the rubbish,' he pointed at the tied-up plastic bags. 'They bring it here because there is nowhere else to put it.'

'The moat is much bigger than I thought,' I remarked.

'They dug with shovels, no machinery, just wood that they carve into shovels. They were thick men.' Michael flexed his biceps.

If only the moat's litter were as biodegradable as our history. Perhaps it was wrong of me to expect anyone to take serious interest in the moat's remains. It was historically significant, but its function as a defence against invaders was now obsolete, so why should the people of twenty-first-century Benin care? They had other things to worry about.

Besides, I'd been in the country long enough to take less proprietary pride in the Benin empire than I did when in London. I felt more Ogoni than ever, and Benin's history didn't seem part of my own any more. My ethnic minority status in Nigeria had grown almost as strong as my identity as a racial minority in England. My people, the Ogonis, had been bit-players in the drama of Nigerian history in which the Binis, Yorubas, Hausas and Igbos played a leading role. Mocked as simpletons and cannibals, Ogonis were barely known outside the Delta region until my father made our presence felt.

'Even your Aunty Janice was surprised when I told her we have over 110 villages in Ogoni!' my mother told me. Janice was an Edo from Benin state.

Neighbouring ethnic groups mockingly twisted Ogoni words: *pia pia* (meaning 'people') became *pior pior*, which means 'bad'. According to my mother, Ogonis are characteristically passive and accommodating, to the extent that we became tenants in our own towns. The economic and numerical dominance of the Igbo people engulfed us, their commercially savvy tentacles spreading as far as Bori, the tiny Ogoni town where my father was born. By the start of the Biafran civil war, Igbos owned about 80 per cent of Bori's businesses, my mother told me. Only when the Biafran Republic was declared did most of them vacate the town to join their new republic.

These ethnic disparities were significant at national level. But in a global context, what were the differences between us now? From a foreigner's point of view, the Bini, Yoruba, Ogoni, Igbo and Hausa are all the same; we're all Nigerians, demoted by modern-day corruption – that great equaliser – to bit-players wading in a sea of rubbish and dereliction.

*

On a sunny morning, I boarded a car destined for Ilorin, a town three hours north of Ibadan. The car waited for passengers in the eye of the honking, rumbling swirl of street life. A vendor thrust a book in my face, written by a Nigerian doctor, called *How to Gain Weight*. A song by the singer Asa boomed from a nearby stereo: '*There is fire on the mountain, and nobody seems to be on the run, oh there is fire on the mountain top and no one is running.*'

I paid for two seats at the back of the car to give my thighs breathing space. The gangly man sitting next to me used the extra space to spread his legs as widely as possible, leaving me squeezed once again against the window. I was livid. Months of travelling cheek-by-jowl in cars had instilled in me a new-found loathing of men's legs, which, like air, seem constantly to expand to fill the space available. I'm amazed they're not all buried in Y-shaped coffins.

After so many weeks of travelling in disagreeable conditions, staying positive about Nigeria was difficult when economic success constantly taunted us from the horizon. With oil now costing $140 (₦21,000) a barrel, politicians' complacency over the economy had only deepened, and people were still suffering in the Niger Delta. I tried to envision Ogoniland as an oil-free economy in which we modernised the farming that's sustained us so well for centuries. Fleetingly, I fantasised about a California-style food industry, free from oil spills, with me as a modern farmer exporting fruit and palm oil to foreign markets. My paternal grandfather would be proud.

'When I came to England I saw people tending to their little farms,' he once observed while giving me a lecture about the virtues of toil. 'They were working *hard*.' Bemused, I wondered how he could mistake a front garden for a farm. But in Nigeria, the two can resemble one another. Our farming is largely a small-scale affair with no machinery or fertilizer, just women bent over and sowing, planting and reaping. Whenever my grandmother or aunt said that they were 'going to the farm', I would visualise these diminutive women in their wrappas and headscarves, whistling behind the wheel of a tractor. It was very confusing. I didn't realise that they and the women bending over by the roadside were growing crops – they always looked like they were doing a spot of gardening.

Small-scale farmers like my aunty don't grow enough crops to feed Nigeria's population, which means the country has to import nearly $750 million worth of food. To alleviate the situation, the western state of Kwara plans on mechanising its farms. When Zimbabwe's government declared that it would appropriate farms belonging to white Zimbabweans in 2004, the Kwara State government saw an opportunity and invited thirteen landless Zimbabweans to set up a mechanised agriculture business in Kwara on a twenty-five-year lease. The farmers settled near the town of Ilorin on the Tsonga farms, an area cultivated by the Muslim Nupe people. Some of the Nupe were paid to move off their farms so that the Zimbabweans could start producing soya beans, rice, cassava and dairy products.

For the first six months, while their houses were being built, the Zimbabweans lived like pioneers in makeshift tents. Now, their newly constructed homes were surrounded by verdant lawns, swimming pools and the obligatory dogs maintaining hostilities at the gate. I loved the way these farmers could transfer their know-how to other parts of the world and create oases of high living. Knowledge is such a beautiful, powerful thing.

Initially, some of the Nupe people weren't happy about handing over their land to the Zimbabweans. They believed their farms were being unfairly seized. The Emir of Tsonga was accused of knowingly persuading village leaders (some of whom were illiterate) to sign away their land. In protest, several villagers invaded the emir's palace on his daughter's wedding day to deliver their complaints in person. This new system was too confusing and daunting, they grumbled: complex legalities, new agricultural practices, alien crops. Over time, however, the Nupe broadly accepted the situation, after being mollified by the government's offer of re-allocated land, seeds, equipment, chemicals and cash.

My driver dropped me off outside a milk factory. Shouting above the din of construction work, I asked if I could speak to the farmer in charge. A Nupe man led me to a black Zimbabwean called Onias, who was sitting in an office with his white boss. Dan Swaart was an ex-tobacco farmer, a big man with bright blue eyes, leathery brown arms buried beneath a forest of blond hairs, and a cheery disposition that belied the trauma of being jailed by Mugabe and losing his home. Counting stacks of ₦500 notes piled up on the table near some machinery, Dan paused to give me a friendly handshake.

'Is farming very different in Nigeria?' I asked.

'You have to adapt to the climate and the soil,' he said. 'They've been using this soil for years without fertiliser, so we had to get the right nutrients into it.'

'How does working with Nigerians compare with working with Zimbabweans?'

'They haven't been trained,' Dan said. 'Zimbabweans are disciplined, but here there's no discipline, so you have to bring discipline and teach them to work. They're used to lying under a mango tree for eight hours a day and working for two hours of the day,' Dan laughed. 'So that's a mindset you have to change. But they're good people.'

'How do you communicate with them?'

'We've got supervisors and they speak English. But you know, you speak English to them and they can't understand your English. They talk this pidgin English. They really don't understand,' he beamed. 'When you first get here – especially on the telephone – they're difficult to understand. But once you get the gist, then you're in.'

Dan's aim was to 'pass the knowledge' on to the Nigerians, set up the machinery, get it working and train the people. The

Zimbabweans are teaching the Nupe all the other aspects of mech-anised farming, including how to clear their lands properly and plant with planters.

'You can see them starting to clear their land and starting to think about fertiliser, spacing the planting of your crop properly rather than scattering it like chicken feed,' Dan grinned. 'There's never really been mechanised agriculture in this country. You import sugar, you import rice. They are very sticky on agriculture, but we have changed the mindset. As time goes on you'll start seeing all the businesses getting loans. At first the banks really didn't want to know about agriculture. But now they're giving us money. When we first started, the most anybody could get was ₦10 million. We've pushed that to ₦600 million. It's an enormous difference.'

Their project wasn't without hindrances. During the first two seasons, the Zimbabweans' harvest of imported corn, soya bean and cowpea was not successful, and only 300 of the 13,000 hectares of land had been cultivated. But these problems were caused by financ-ing hiccups, Dan said. Things were improving now.

This was not the first time that foreigners had tried commercial farming in the area. The British, eyeing the region's heavy rainfall and fertile soil, planted imported soya beans, corn and cotton during the first half of the twentieth century. But the crops failed, disrupt-ing a millennium of local agriculture and forcing the colonial authorities to revert to growing groundnuts, cashews and locust beans. This time round, the farmers hope to use a new breed of fer-tilisers to avoid a repeat of the problem.

'How are you finding life in Nigeria?' I asked Dan.

'There's not much of a social life. You don't have theatre, you don't have cinemas, you don't have decent restaurants. Lagos is all right, but we live here. It's a different life to what we had in Zimbabwe. Nigeria is not as bad as people make out. You know, it's a great place. You cannot believe the opportunities for any busi-nessman here. Nigeria is a huge, huge market, and if people just changed their mindset they would reap the benefits like you cannot *believe*. It's a rich country with huge potential. Just bring the technology and you're away.'

'I'm so glad you're bringing fresh milk here,' I told him. 'I can never have the kind of breakfast I want because there's never proper milk! Do you think Nigerians will like pasteurised milk?'

'You know, Nigerians say they don't like fresh milk, but once the people taste it, they'll drink it.'

I let Dan get on with his work. Onias offered to show me around the milk factory currently under construction: milk cooling tanks, pasteurisation tanks and homogenisers, even a machine for packaging long-life milk. Their aim is to pump 45,000 litres a day.

Onias pointed at a map of Africa on the wall and ran his finger along the northern borders of Angola, Zambia and Tanzania. 'There are 120 million people here,' he said, circling Southern Africa. 'And there are 150 million here,' he pointed at Nigeria. 'Amazing! I think Nigeria has got more opportunities than Zimbabwe. It's one of the richest countries in the world. We are going where you are coming from, and you are going where we are coming from!'

Onias radiated enthusiasm and professionalism, always greeting the local people by removing his baseball cap and bowing. He lacked that swagger of the businessman who has grown wealthy through government corruption. A self-described 'heathen' (the only one I encountered in Nigeria), Onias was a professional milkman, born and bred into a cattle-rearing community in Zimbabwe where he learnt to milk cows at the age of four. He became the managing director of the biggest dairy in Zimbabwe before moving to Nigeria with Dan Swaart as the only black man among the Zimbabweans.

'I feel we blacks have a moral obligation to help Dan and the others with the project,' Onias said quietly.

'Why? You didn't take away their farms.'

Onias shrugged his shoulders.

'How are you finding life in Nigeria?' I asked.

'I try to enjoy Nigerian music, and sometimes I eat the food.'

'Have you tried gari?'

'Yes. It was . . . nice,' he stammered diplomatically. 'It's similar to our sadza . . . it's a starch.'

Onias said Nigerian attitudes to farming were very different to Zimbabwe's.

'My two Nigerian friends, they are doctors, they came here to see the farm. They could not believe I was working here on a farm like this! Nigerians don't want to come near cows. They see it as inferior. Only the Fulanis like cows.'

We climbed into his 4 x 4 and toured the Tsonga farms, through flat stretches of soya fields, rice fields and colossal anthills. The Zimbabweans were planning on building chicken abattoirs and an ethanol plant too. All in all, they employed 600 full-time Nupe workers, for whom mechanised farming represented a big cultural shift.

'In the factory we have a big problem on Fridays. They just disappear,' Onias said. 'I said to one guy, "How can I make you a machine operator if you leave it while it's still running?"'

'Why do they disappear like that?'

'I think there's something in Islam that says people can't announce when they're going to pray. I'll go away for a few minutes, come back and find the workers praying on the factory floor! I had to get one husband and wife to job-share because the husband would not work on Fridays, so the wife comes in during those days.'

'Would people work more if you docked their wages?'

'You just have to let them pray,' Onias said. 'If people realise that you don't respect what they respect, they don't like you. The best way is to allow them to express themselves. Then they will agree to work overtime without fuss. They are hard-working, but their faith is powerful.'

Even the leader of the Zimbabwean farmers, Allan Jack – a man described by Onias as a 'pushy' taskmaster – was forced to concede that Friday was a day off. 'That made me laugh,' Onias chuckled.

Life had visibly improved for the Nupe people. As we drove through their villages, dozens of men scooted around on motorcycles provided by the government. Few of them had owned motorbikes a year earlier. And the villages' infrastructure was transforming: the government had built 76 kilometres of new roads, a new borehole to draw potable water, and a GSM mobile phone network. Young Nupe kids can now earn extra cash by selling phone cards. When the farms are fully operational, the government plans to have electricity flowing unblinkingly throughout the villages, and the schoolchildren will be taught how to farm commercially.

Onias and I stopped off at the house of one of the Zimbabweans so that Onias could fetch something. The owner of the house, Paul, was out of the country for a week, and had left his home (with its cable TV and other modern appliances) unlocked.

'How can he leave the house unlocked like this?' I asked.

'It's OK,' Onias assured me. 'Nobody will take anything. Nigerians don't steal.'

He was right in some respects. There were armed highway robberies and museum thefts, certainly, but pettier theft wasn't as prevalent as I feared. On my travels, I'd had no qualms about leaving my bags unattended in a minibus on intercity journeys. I and my fellow passengers would disembark the vehicle, its windows left open, and eat lunch. Nobody stole our things, not even the *alma-jari* street kids who swarm around vehicles in northern towns to beg for food and money.

Interestingly, cheating was more common in economic transactions. Onias said he was shocked when the mother of a farm worker – a woman he knew well – deliberately overcharged him for some eggs, almost doubling the price from the week before. It's as

if our corrupt politics have normalised dishonest financial oppor-
tunism while leaving the rest of our integrity reasonably intact.

Onias drove us through lightly forested land. 'Look at this land,'
he said, pointing at the side of the road. 'It's unutilised. There's only
one guy using it ... growing groundnut. So much of your land is
idle.'

We continued across the grassy floodplains of the river.
Concentrating very little on his driving, Onias kept stretching his
neck to eye the dozens of slim, bony-backed cows grazing on the
land.

'I'm excited when I see that,' he grinned. 'I like cows!' His fetish
for the animals was real. He counted them obsessively, cooing over
them and murmuring his appreciation as we drove along. 'There
must be about two thousand of them!'

The cows belonged to the nomadic Fulani cow herders who live
in the area for part of the year. Their animals, rather lean Bunaji
breeds, eat grass and yield 4 litres of relatively non-nutritious milk
a day, a meagre amount when compared with the 20–25 litres a day
pumped out by commercial, silage-fed Jersey cows. The
Zimbabweans are going to import the Jerseys from South Africa to
interbreed with the heifers. The plan is to mechanise milk collection for Fulani herders around the area. The Fulanis will attach their
cows to milk-pumping machines, then sell the milk at the collection point. It would be a significant culture change for these
nomadic herders, who live in settlements on the swampy floodplains
of the river until the rains flood the area, at which point they move
on.

A quintet of Fulani ladies, carrying loads on their heads, walked
past our car. They were slim, demure and elegant, with pigtail plaits
cascading from colourful headscarves.

'Beautiful ... look at that,' Onias cooed. He loved these women
almost as much as he loved cows. He jokingly pondered how many
cows he could sell in order to buy a Fulani wife. 'Their menfolk

would never give them up,' he chuckled. 'You can never go near the women. The men won't allow it!'

We parked by the banks of the river, under a cluster of big mango trees. Onias pointed out an old, disused water pump by the river. The Tsonga dairy was also going to build an irrigation system for the farms, he informed me. He stared at the river and shook his head, unable to comprehend Nigeria's abundance of fruit, water and animals. All around him lay a vista of squandered opportunities.

'Why isn't anyone *selling* this?' he said, prodding a dangling baby mango. 'You could make nice fruit juice, canned fruit ...' His voice tapered into speculative silence. 'Because of your oil you don't think about the small things. All you need is five or six governors with vision, and this country will really start to develop. This is the *best* country. It is richer than South Africa in national resources, but you have nothing to show for it.'

Before returning to Ilorin, my driver dropped me off in Esie, a dozy village where hundreds of mysterious, ancient soapstone sculptures were excavated in the 1930s. The site of the discovery was now a museum, a plain adobe building set in a tranquil garden where bright red flowers bloomed on low hedges, and the breeze shook the citrus trees.

The museum door, covered in bas-relief carvings, opened into a simple, sunny room filled with the stunning sculptures. Organised in terraced rows, dozens of beautiful, ornate stone effigies lined the four walls. Each sculpted head or figurine was made from pale steatite stone and stood between 14 and 120 centimetres high. Every image had unique, individual facial features and elaborate hairstyles and poses: one covered its mouth in exclamation; another played what looked like a string instrument; one was pregnant.

Intriguingly, the sculptures appeared to be images of people from ethnic groups from all over Nigeria. Some figurines had the striped face markings of the Jos region; a female figure held a bottle of

alligator pepper (Yoruba spiritual medicine); the numerous bead
necklaces on one sculpture were reminiscent of Ibibio culture from
the south-east. One of the largest figurines depicted a female Nupe
warrior wielding a dagger. Other female warriors carried bows and
arrows. Some images had conical or fez-style hats, suggesting a
Fulani link, as did the triple-bunch hairstyles on some female heads.
Other coiffures bore similarities to those of Nok women. The three
parallel lines between the eyes and ears on some sculptures looked
like Nupe face markings. Certain sculptures shared a similarity to the
ancient soapstone carvings of Ife, the Yoruba capital, while the con-
centric circles on cheeks seemingly drew inspiration from Benin
bronzes. Whoever made these sculptures had knowledge of
Nigeria's many ethnic groups. I was fascinated by the idea that a cos-
mopolitan civilization once existed, or that a forward-thinking
explorer once travelled across Nigeria and recorded what he or she
saw.

The sculptures were brought to international attention when an
English missionary, H. G. Ramshaw, excavated many of them in
1933. Researchers at Oxford University carbon-dated these figurines
to 11 AD, but it's still unclear who made them or why. One academic suggested that the sculptures are the work of the Asebu
people who claim to have migrated to the coastal region in the fifteenth century from the desert north of Nigeria. The current
inhabitants of Esie, the Igbomina, didn't build the sculptures –
they're a subgroup of the Yoruba, believed to have migrated to Esie
in the sixteenth century from Oyo, the ancient capital of the Yoruba
empire. The Igbomina believe that the soapstone figurines, known
as *ere*, aren't man-made objects but humans who have been turned
into stone.

Oral explanations for the sculptures vary from village to village.
One legend tells of foreign visitors who arrive in the area and ask the
chief to wait at home in order to receive them. But the chief goes
to farm and bathes in the stream instead. While in the water, he sees

his visitors filing past on their way to his home. Realising his faux pas, the chief rushes home where he finds his visitors impatiently waiting to be received. The chief pretends he's been busy preparing them a meal, but they know that he's lying. Angry, they leave in a huff and curse him. However, the Yoruba gods consider the curse to be an overreaction, so they punish the visitors' excess by turning them into stone.

The museum guide, a rather literal-minded man, didn't believe the turned-to-stone theory. He showed me a figurine of a woman with an unfeasibly elongated neck. 'You see?' he said. 'This shows their ancestors cannot have been turned to stone.'

The museum guide led me outside to a mango tree where the figurines – arranged in semi-circle formation around the *oba ere* (king) – were first discovered before being moved into the museum exhibition gallery. The statue of the king now sits in a shrine by the mango tree. He's flanked by his wife and his *ibari*, the person whose role is to commit suicide when the king dies, accompanying him on his journey to the next life. In front of the oba sculptures sits the figurine of a palace guide, clutching a goblet from which the oba drinks palm wine.

The figurines are regarded as custodians of the land, responsible for bringing fertility, rain, and the occasional act of evil. Their visual power was strong enough to make me empathise with the concept of idol worship, though their current arrangement in the museum's exhibition gallery wasn't quite as striking as their original positions must have been: seven or eight hundred years ago, the thousand-odd sculptures illuminated the clearing in the trees, a stunning sight to visitors emerging from a narrow forest path.

When the effigies were excavated in the 1930s, many of them had been deliberately dismembered, possibly during Islamic raids in the eighteenth century. The figurines also suffered from the 'missionary attitude' of locals who, having converted to Christianity, ignored, destroyed or sold their pagan relics on an international

market hungry for African art. Of the 1,500 sculptures that were
dug up in Esie, 500 were lost or stolen, partly due to the museum's
inadequate security. Maurice Archibong, the travel writer I met in
Benin, told me that thieves once looted Esie's museum after
befriending the security guards and offering them food laced with
a sleep-inducing drug. Maurice also said that the museum's official car, the defunct VW Beetle parked outside, hadn't left the
grounds in twenty years. When the curator needs to transport
these valuable artefacts, he loads them into boxes and hops onto
an okada.

It was quintessentially Nigerian that such impressive artefacts
should be hidden in this adobe hut in a quiet village, like a jewel
furtively tucked away in a fat woman's bosom. Only 200 visitors
passed through the museum gates in an average month. Esie provided the ultimate confirmation, if any were needed, that even the
most illustrious parts of Nigerian history seem to be relentlessly
buried under time and indifference.

Once again, I was disappointed to see another tourist attraction
go so unloved. This ennui repeated itself throughout my travels: the
Osun-Osogbo Sacred Grove, Benin City, Lagos Museum, the
architectural museum in Jos, Lake Nguru. What condition would
they all be in, twenty years from now? A small part of me considered the possibility of working in Nigerian tourism to try to stem
the decline. But that spark of inspiration immediately fizzled at the
prospect of misallocated funds, apathy and dealing with the feck-
lessness of state bureaucracy. By the end, my thoughts degenerated
into a kidnap fantasy in which I abduct Esie's entire collection, like
a social worker removing children from their neglectful parents. I
would keep the sculptures in my backyard and lavish them with the
love and attention they deserved, my conscience cleared by the con-
viction that I was taking better care of them than our government
ever will.

*

Late that evening in my hotel room, I was sucked into another riveting Nollywood film involving a jealous wife in an Igbo chief's polygamous household (give me infidelity, polygamy or jealousy in any storyline, and I'm hooked). The jealous first wife despised the younger and more attractive third wife, who inflamed her envy by giving birth to a long-awaited male heir. The first wife tried to kill the baby prince, but she failed. Without condoning the first wife's behaviour, I empathised with her rage and insecurity, and I rather hoped she would avoid an ugly fate. But, as usual, the story's outcome became a hazy blur that merged into a nonsensical dream. I floated into a deep sleep and missed out on the film's ending yet again.

15

Tending the Backyard

Port Harcourt

At the end of a sleepy bus journey, I arrived in Port Harcourt (or 'Potakot' as it is pronounced). I was born in this city in the mid-1970s, when its nickname of the 'Garden City' seemed less of a misnomer. Now my home town was an uninviting metropolis, its grey flyovers soaring above a vista of banal concrete buildings, isolated palm trees and the tarpaulined labyrinth of the central market. Established as a coal-exporting port in 1912, Port Harcourt has barely transcended its industrial roots. Money, oil, family ties and an absence of alternatives are the main things yoking people to this dystopia, I think.

Sonny drove me back to the family house at the edge of town, along a road where soldiers stopped cars and made officious requests to see 'your papers'. The tensions of old came flooding back. Roadblocks like these, once common in the 1980s, no longer existed elsewhere in the country now that the military dictatorship had ended. But Port Harcourt is a tense oil city with its finger still hovering over the trigger. It's constantly expanding as its wealth sucks poor people from the countryside every year. New buildings and churches jostle for space on roadsides that were once silent. I saw more churches here than in any other part of the country. There were so many of them they'd seemingly run out of traditional

names: FRESH OIL CATHEDRAL and CHRISTIAN RESTORATION AND
REPAIRS MINISTRIES placards sprouted like weeds from the roadside,
the tangible signs of all manner of desperation.

We turned off the expressway and into the Igbo neighbourhood
where our family home sits. The streets were flanked by high walls
and iron gates, over which I caught glimpses of the rectilinear 1970s
houses, painted in pale pastels or leached white, with red-headed
lizards scaling their walls and corrugated iron rooftops. Verandahs
looked out onto driveways planted with banana and mango trees
and white lady-of-the-night flowers that wait until sundown before
unleashing their fragrance into the air. I could still hear a mysterious, invisible bird that sings freakishly human-sounding melodies
from the trees.

Our house used to stand on the very edge of town on a silent,
middle-class street next to the bush. Behind our garden wall loomed
a mysterious forest of palm trees where we would throw our banana
and mango skins. Wildlife thrived there, including the infamous
green snake that once shimmied into the kitchen and brushed
against Zina's unsuspecting foot (her screams could be heard in
Cameroon). Nowadays, we've acquired several neighbours, and
sunlight streams over the wall, liberated from the dark forest canopy.
Our noiseless street has developed into a little superhighway, with
lorries and okadas constantly rumbling past the fruits stalls, mini
supermarkets, hairdressers and countless church placards.

The house itself was more or less the same, a modest three-bed-
room residence that was always too small to fit the whole family.
The same portraits still hung on the walls, including the large one
of my father posing imperiously with a pipe between his lips. The
blue 1970s mosaic tiles in the hallway and staircase – old enough to
have survived two fashion cycles – gave the house an echoey, cavernous ambience. My father's interior decor tastes weren't brilliant.
He was a discerning aesthete in many respects, judging by the quality and composition of his photography, but when it came to decor

or colour scheming he seemed to lose his vision completely (my mother had no say in these matters). I once had an argument with my father after he insisted – to my undying mystification – that a man's socks should always be the same colour as his shoes. Nonsensical as his sartorial reasoning might have been, I rather wished he'd applied it to the interior of the house; at least then we might have had curtains that matched the red-orange paisley carpet, not the geometric, black-and-white drapes he chose instead.

My father's only concession to good taste was the glamorous portrait of my mother, painted on their tenth wedding anniversary in 1976. From the time I was about ten, my mother stopped joining us on our two-month holidays in Nigeria in order to continue working in England. Zina and I would often stare at that portrait, wishing she were there to neutralise our father's influence and undo his decisions.

Junior had since inherited the house and had installed flooring that matched the curtains. But being boss still didn't allow him to stamp his full imprimatur on the decor: when he hired a team of men to pave the driveway in pale stone, they seized the initiative and laid down a few red slabs that spelled out the word 'LOVE'. Junior could only shrug at the infuriating but endearing gesture.

The living-room walls displayed photographs of us as children. Most of them were taken in England, our large-toothed faces foregrounding the lawns of Surrey and Derbyshire prep schools. The sight of it yanked me back in time and space, and confusingly oriented my mind away from this house and this country. Upstairs, my father's tiny study was the one room that felt inhabited. It was here that he typed his manuscripts and raged by telephone about Ogoni injustices, his anger interspersed with loud belly laughs. His untouched bookshelves revealed a range of surprising interests (*Jews & Arabs*; a Jackie Onassis biography) that had long since been submerged by concerns over oil spills. In these books I found common ground with him, and for the first time I regretfully

imagined the kind of adult relationship we might have had if
circumstances had been different. He was the type of father you
adored until the age of eight, but once you grew a mind of your
own, the attrition began. He could tell great children's stories, and
he could talk on an adult level. But he wasn't so good during those
intermediary teenage years when you had outgrown your cuteness
and malleability, and his flaws materialised like a rash, and you
strayed from the path of greatness he had mapped out for you. But
in my twenties, I noticed our interests converging, particularly
around travel. I once rifled through his old passports and was
surprised to see visa stamps from countries such as Ethiopia and
Suriname. Why did he go? What did he make of these places? I'll
never know the full story.

After completing my tour of the house, I sat in the living room
and pondered what to do with myself. This was the first time I had
stayed here alone. Back in the day, our father would leave us at
home all day most days while he went to work. We never did very
much in Port Harcourt. During those hours of TV-less boredom,
we survived on sibling companionship and Hollywood films, sub-
sisting on the same two or three movies recorded off British TV on
our Betamax VCR. Our tolerance for repetition was high: *Coming
to America* and *Tootsie* were watched at least once every day, to the
point that we knew the dialogue inside out. By summer's end we'd
learnt to swear like Eddie Murphy and speak in a Southern falsetto,
Dustin Hoffman-style.

Twenty years on, I needed a similar distraction. I felt a little
lonely and abandoned, and more aware of the void left by my
brother and father's deaths. The emptiness of the house accentuated
that sense of family depletion. In my childhood, my parents' strained
marriage – already cleaved by geography – left me and my siblings
feeling as if we were on the margins of the extended family. We
were a separate appendage on the family tree, the 'London' ones
who never knew our cousins as well as they knew each other. My

father had his own life in Nigeria, away from ours. And so this lizard-strewn shell of a house, our supposed 'home', offered me little sense of homecoming or belonging; only a few shards of memory. But I was glad of it. Port Harcourt had become an undesirable place to live, and I had the option of evacuating without leaving a piece of myself behind.

My mother's predicament was rather different. She desperately wanted to live in Port Harcourt but had been obliged to raise her children in England on my father's wishes. After she had retired and self-determination, that elusive beast, was finally won, her plans to retire in Port Harcourt were tainted by the threat of violence and instability.

I felt thoroughly immobilised in this house, too. Sonny was away for the weekend, so I had no driver. The idea of travelling around by my beloved okadas suddenly seemed too strange and adventurous since my past experiences of Port Harcourt involved being driven around town to the houses of various relatives and family friends. I wanted more of the same. Home towns have a way of infantilising you like that. The elderly nightwatchman only encouraged that regression when he warned me to 'No take okada.' Too dangerous, he said. And so I stood in my bedroom, clutching at the wrought-iron bars across the window like a child prisoner.

The bars had been installed to protect us from robbers, although they failed spectacularly. I still shudder at the memory of the night, sometime around 1984, when thieves attacked our house. Emboldened by their faith in police inaction, they hammered shamelessly at the metal bars, slowly prising them open, disregarding my mother's screamed insults from behind the gates at the top of the staircase. They bashed and banged without haste, squeezed through the window and helped themselves to our electronic goods. I'll never forget the chilling sound of the TV plug being wrenched from its socket.

Yet, compared with today, Port Harcourt was safe back then. Armed militant gangs claiming to fight for their indigenous right to oil wealth had turned my home town into a semi war zone the previous year, the skies reverberating with the crackle of gunfire. And kidnapping foreign oil workers and wealthy Nigerians has become big business. Abduction syndicates infiltrate all sectors of society, including the airports. Apparently, the staff at airline offices give alerts when plane tickets are purchased, then their co-conspirators, workers at the airports, track which car the kidnap target enters. One of my mother's friends was kidnapped this way. Somewhere along the road, she was asked (with surprising gentleness) to step out of her car and into armed captivity, where she briefly remained until a ransom was paid.

The tangle of corruption is woven tightly in Port Harcourt. Police are known to sell arms to kidnappers, and the navy sometimes colludes with gangs in stealing oil and shipping it. Traditional commerce no longer provides quite the same sustenance, either. Many rental properties, once tenanted by expat oil workers, lie empty, considered unsafe.

The sun was now setting and shunting me closer to the dreaded prospect of spending my first night here alone. Deebom the cook told me that the electricity had cut out for several days. If I wanted relief from the humidity I would have to buy fuel (or 'fwell', as everyone pronounces it) to power the house generator. The price – ₦3,000 for 25 litres – nearly floored me. After pointlessly protesting to him about the cost, I handed him the money to buy it on the main street.

'You must off the generator after eleven o'clock,' Deebom advised when he returned.

'Why?'

'The fwell will finish if you leave it on all night.'

I didn't want to believe him. The thought of sleeping in that heat without an air con was unbearable, so I kept the generator switched

on until the early hours, regardless of the consequences. When, pre-
dictably, it stopped working early the next evening, I was still
shocked, shocked at the perversity that so much money was needed
to sustain a few hours of basic comfort. When the state supply fails,
I realised, buying one's own power is not a cheap option, even for
the middle classes; only the very rich can do it. If it cost this much
to run a household, I dreaded to think how this expense devoured
the profit margins of small businesses. Nigeria can never develop
under such circumstances.

Dodgy electricity supplies took the predictability out of everyday
life: drying one's hair at a salon was fraught with risk, and power
cuts sometimes plunged supermarket aisles into darkness, immobil-
ising shoppers and tempting thieves. In the nightclub beneath my
hotel room in Ibadan, I remember hearing a hip-hop tune thump-
ing through the building. When it suddenly stopped mid-song, I
mentally pictured the scene: clubbers grinding and flirting to the
rhythm one minute, then left in embarrassing limbo when the electricity snatched away the music and lights.

For decades, the government has done nothing to fix this situation. The previous administration sank $13.2 billion dollars into
restoring our power network, but there's nothing to show for it. No
one knows where the money went; the nation has literally been left
in the dark over the issue. Yet certain politicians still like to think
they can develop the economy without fixing this fundamental
spanner in our daily works. They even produced a fanciful document called 'Vision 2020' detailing how Nigeria plans to become a
leading economy within twelve years. The concept induced wry
cackles among Nigerians. How, they asked, can we build an aero-
nautics programme when we can't power a light bulb for more than
five hours a day?

Two mornings later, with corruption very much on our minds,
Sonny and I drove along the traffic-logged expressway leading out

of Port Harcourt. Sticking out of the tall roadside grass was a billboard with a government message that said: DON'T BADMOUTH NIGERIA! THINGS ARE CHANGING.

We were on our way to Ndoni, a small town about 200 kilometres from Port Harcourt, the home town of Rivers State's former governor, Peter Odili. Sonny and I were on a mission to see how politicians spend their pilfered monies. I'd recently read in the newspaper that one of the worst of them, the ex-president Ibrahim Babangida, was itching to run for president again. As we waited in a long line at a gas station, I asked Sonny why the former dictator wanted to re-enter politics. Had his billions run out?

'He just wants power,' Sonny said.

'Why does he need more power?'

'Because when he goes to London, nobody knows who he is any more. When he was president he went to the US ... people over there received him ... he went to the White House. When he came to Port Harcourt they would announce it on the TV and radio the night before. He would come here with his big entourage of cars. That is it, now ... they want power. They like it.'

Sonny's theory was that the process of enriching oneself through politics naturally creates enemies. Therefore the politician in question needs protection, which in itself requires money, which requires more power. They don't want to go the way of the assassinated former president Murtala Mohammed, Sonny believed.

Sonny said that people were particularly disgusted with Odili, a man said to have used the billions he allegedly stole in office to set up Arik Airlines, a domestic carrier. Sonny repeated speculation that Odili greenlighted the construction of three gas turbines in Port Harcourt just to receive kickbacks. The government received a big budget, built the turbines with shoddy, cheap haste, then pocketed the difference. Now the turbines have stopped working, only a few years after being built.

On the highway towards Ndoni, a minibus had parked at the side of the road, its passengers milling about and motioning for us to keep driving.

'Armed robbery,' Sonny explained. The passengers reassured us that it was safe to proceed: we had missed the robbery by ten minutes. Earlier that morning Sonny had scolded me for always being late, but I suspected he was now secretly grateful for my tardiness. Further ahead of the robbed minibus, a police patrol vehicle had parked haphazardly on the roadside, its doors flung open in haste, its body perforated with bullet holes. Three officers were wading frantically into the thick bush, pushing aside tall grasses with one hand and clutching rifles with the other, chasing the armed robbers who had fled into the forest. Minutes later, a radio news bulletin reported the kidnapping of two foreigners in Port Harcourt. The dangers of life in the Niger Delta suddenly seemed all too tangible and real.

Odili was said to be partly responsible for the lawlessness. During the 2003 elections, as he ran for the governorship of Rivers State, the ruling People's Democratic Party distributed weapons to gangs in order to intimidate voters. Two gangs – the Niger Delta People's Volunteer Force (NDPVF) and the Icelanders – were hired by Odili to ensure a 'positive' outcome in the elections. But soon after the polls, the leader of the NDPVF fell out with the Rivers State government, which reacted by urging the Icelanders to destroy the NDPVF. The result was low-intensity warfare, conducted freely on the streets of Port Harcourt. Ordinary streets, bars and restaurants were caught in a crossfire of explosives and automatic weapons. I read newspaper reports of gangsters operating with impunity, robbing banks, gunning down policemen, hacking at the city's stability with machetes and knives. Fortunately, no one in my family was affected, but many other blameless people died.

In 2004, President Obasanjo brokered a truce between the gang leaders. The gangs, however, never disarmed. Angered by the politicians' false promises of jobs and financial security, they continued robbing banks, and practising kidnapping and extortion. Since 2006, more than 200 expat oil workers have been abducted for large ransoms under the political pretext of 'resource control'.

By the summer of 2007, a faction of the Icelanders had broken away and formed a more powerful splinter group called the Outlaws, led by George Soboma. Again, the ruling party called on their services during the 2007 elections. The gangsters were seen handing out money at polling stations, becoming de facto chiefs of security in the city. Since 2003, dozens of similar gangs flourished. Again, many of them were disappointed by the government's unfulfilled promises of jobs and money. They eyed Soboma's position with envy. In time, a coalition of gangs (including the Icelanders) began fighting Soboma and his Outlaws for a bigger slice of government largesse. More havoc was visited on Port Harcourt. My brother Junior had been inside our father's former office on Aggrey Road when he heard the snap of gunfire and the screech of vehicle tyres. For a few apprehensive minutes, the street's small businesses and art shops became the backdrop to gang warfare. I felt slightly violated by it all, even from the safety of London. Though I'd had no intention of living in Port Harcourt, those months of violence made me less of an émigré and more an exile in mourning for my home town.

In the summer of 2007, the federal government sent in a military task force to control the violence. Order was restored but the leaders of the biggest gangs, having outgrown government control, were never captured. In contrast to its rhetoric, the government did nothing to punish the politicians or arrest most of the gang members. And Odili, the former governor who allegedly funded these gangs in the 2003 elections, enjoys immunity from prosecution.

Because Nigeria's oil deposits are concentrated in the Niger Delta, political power in this region (and subsequent control of oil money) is highly prized and ruthlessly fought over. Half a century of corrupt rule has done nothing to build the economy of a region that's earned more than $300 billion since petroleum was discovered. The federal government takes about half of oil revenues and distributes it among the country's thirty-six states. Little of this money benefits ordinary people, least of all Niger Delta people, who have fallen victim to government corruption and the carelessness of the oil industry. Countless oil spills and ceaseless flaring of gas poisons the soil and depletes the rivers of their fish stocks. Age-old farming practices have been disrupted, swelling the numbers of frustrated unemployed men.

My father tried to address this problem non-violently through his Movement for the Survival of the Ogoni People (MOSOP), which campaigned to improve the environment and ensure Delta ethnic groups received our fair share of the oil wealth. Since my father's death in 1995, several militant groups, mainly ethnic Ijaws, have adopted a similar political platform, but achieve their aims by abducting oil workers, sabotaging oil pipelines and forcing oil companies to pay 'protection' money. Their actions have reduced crude oil production by a third since 2006. Gangs such as the Niger Delta Vigilantes attack oil installations to extort money or force the oil companies to create local development projects, which has placated a few people.

These gangs, including the NDPVF, are embedded in a muddy, interchangeable world of criminality and politics. One minute they're fighting the government for 'resource control', the next they're cooperating with corrupt politicians and policemen to set up arms deals and oil bunkering ventures (oil bunkering involves tapping pipelines and selling the oil on the local and foreign black market).

On the road to Ndoni, Rivers State felt like a feral place. The violence had leapt from the newspaper pages and was playing out in front of me. Sleeping was the only way for me to escape the anxiety.

The road branching off the highway to Odili's home town was freshly tarmacked, and sturdy new bridges carried us across the

numerous rivers and creeks of the Niger River Delta. We turned off
the highway and into a sleepy village situated by the steep sandy
banks of a magnificently blue river. The tidy streets, paved with
interlocking stone slabs, contained only a handful of pedestrians,
including a woman strolling contentedly beneath a blue parasol. A
bus station under construction nearby was fronted by a sign pro-
claiming it an ULTRA-MODERN MOTOR PARK.

'How many vehicles are coming here?' Sonny snorted. 'This was
just swamp before.' He pointed at a clump of trees across the street.
Building a motor park seemed an unnecessary expense, considering
the size of the village. Like voyeurs, we cruised around, taking
inventory of the diverted oil wealth surrounding us.

'Look at it,' Sonny murmured, 'look at our money. Odili has
turned the village into a town!' Street lights – only 4.5 metres apart –
lined the roads. One or two of them were even switched on despite
the midday sun, as if smugly emphasising Ndoni's constant power
supply. Electricity seemed more a status symbol here than a basic
requirement for the functioning of daily life.

Odili's mansion was unmissable: a big white colonnaded structure with a red tiled roof, a satellite dish and several air con units
barnacling its exterior. Almost as a statement of virtue, the house
stood next to a Catholic church, a fancy red-and-white building,
fenced off by an ornate metal gate. Other alleged beneficiaries of
Odili's governorship had built mansions in the vicinity. They had
two-storey, glass-fronted atriums, with the owner's names – Onyema
Hall or Oshinili Villa – emblazoned hubristically across them.

'These houses look empty,' I commented.

'That's because they are staying in Port Harcourt – where there's
no light.' Sonny sneered at the irony. People spent most of their
time in the big city. Nearby was a plot of land scattered with palm
trees that had been felled to make way for the construction of more
houses. Sonny and I rolled slowly along the streets, past a huge
house with a thatched rotunda in the garden, which Sonny

suspected belonged to Peter Odili's older brother. Odili liked to spread his wealth. He is renowned for dashing people money – ₦20 million here, ₦50 million there.

'You cannot get close to him and come back empty-handed,' Sonny said. But what good had Odili really done for Ndoni? The town was still a quiet backwater: messy-haired women still sold fruit and groundnuts on the side of the spotless streets; the school building was a shabby confection of peeling yellow paint, and the pupils ran around in tatty uniforms. How typical that the church should be in better shape than the primary school.

'When you are in power you bring development to your village,' Sonny insisted, to my surprise.

'But they should be bringing development to *everyone*. Can you imagine British prime ministers developing their home towns in England and no one else's? They don't do that.'

'But you cannot be in government for eight years and your village is still bush,' Sonny countered. He told me that when he and my brother Ken attended the funeral of a politician's mother at their village, he was taken aback by the scruffiness of the village. 'If you are in government you must develop your village and your people. Otherwise what will they take for remember you?'

I had assumed Sonny was against Ndoni's development. In fact, he was simply annoyed that no Ogoni person had had the chance to occupy high political office and develop our villages similarly. He didn't support corruption the way Ekpenyong in Calabar did, but he was still in favour of allocating funds along ethnic lines.

'*Nobody* from the south has become a minister in Abuja,' Sonny fumed. 'When I was in Abuja with your father and he saw the way they were building the place, he always be angry. *Twenty-four hours a day, he was angry.*'

I remember that rage. My father would grumble at the gleaming skyscrapers, venting livid clouds of tobacco smoke through his nostrils as he complained about oil money developing the north but not the south. However, he didn't believe in politicians diverting public funds to help their own village at the expense of others. He was too high-minded to delve too much into Nigerian politics, the rottenness of which I now fully appreciated. In the upper echelons of government, it isn't easy to keep one's head down and do a good job. Having principles is considered a sign of weakness by many politicians, who will punish those who try to uphold any morals. If a governor or senator doesn't help his or her friends and kinsmen, not only do they face the wrath of their nearest and dearest, but their political enemies will see feebleness in their honesty and begin sharpening the knives. In a system like this, politicians of a dishonest bent will gladly swim with the corrupt tide rather than get washed up alone on the penniless banks of virtue.

The next day, at my mother's suggestion, I visited my aunty at her shop on the other side of Port Harcourt. Known to all as Big Mama (real name Elizabeth), she's my mother's eldest sister, a large, frank, gregarious septuagenarian who once celebrated my puberty by playfully poking my breasts and cackling long and hard. Her ribaldry couldn't be more different from my mother's prim reserve, yet their faces are almost exactly alike; seeing my mother in Big Mama's every smile or frown brought on pangs of homesickness after four months on the road.

I met Big Mama at her small fabric shop across town, next to the law office of her son, Tom. I hadn't seen Tom since he was a good-looking, spirited university student. Nowadays, his handsome face was plumper and fringed with slightly greying hair. The last fourteen years had taken their toll. His father, an Ogoni activist, was murdered with three other men in 1994. The Abacha regime exploited their deaths and falsely accused my father and eight of his colleagues of inciting the murders, although on that day none of them had been allowed to enter Ogoniland where the murders took place.

It created a fissure in the family that had taken more than a decade to close. Time had passed and wounds were healing; we didn't dwell on these issues. In such family matters I still felt like a child somehow, and I naturally excluded myself from these 'adult' concerns. Besides, Port Harcourt's violence seem to occupy Big Mama's thoughts these days.

'It's so dangerous now,' she complained. Almost every week the streets flinched in the crossfire of gang bullets.

Tom asked me why I was in Nigeria. I told him I was travelling around the country and writing a book about my experiences.

'Why are you writing?' he said. 'Junior was the one to do that sort of thing. I thought you and Zina would become doctors or lawyers.'

Our cultural differences ran deep. 'I don't want to be a doctor or lawyer. I'm doing things that I find interesting. I can't pursue a career just because I'm expected to.'

'You should come back to Nigeria.'

'I can't just come back here.'

'Why not?'

'I don't know the country well enough ... That's partly what my trip is about. I'm getting to know the place.' My dislike for the country was softening into a wavering ambiguity.

'You're like one of those 1950s British women who never leave England and don't want to try new things,' Tom declared.

'No, I'm not!' I retorted, irked by his inaccuracy, and a little threatened by the suggestion. 'You can't just move to a country you don't know very well. I need to understand how it works. And I've left England plenty of times. I've been all over West Africa too.'

'Oh,' Tom said, 'I didn't realise.'

To bolster my case, I mentioned how expensive it was to travel around Nigeria.

'Junior could buy you a first-class ticket to Abuja if you want him to,' Tom said. 'He works in government.'

'No, he couldn't, he doesn't have money to spend on me. And even if he did, I wouldn't expect him to.'

'But you can ask him.'

'Why would I? He's not my father. He should spend his money on his sons. If I want my own ticket I'll buy it myself.'

'You think like a British person,' Tom jibed with a smile. My family like to confront, prod, dissect and disparage with the kindest of intentions – but it rubbed raw against my diasporan sensibilities, which were more used to British-style individualism and all the ginger diplomacy that comes with it.

Changing the subject, I asked Big Mama whether her Catholic church was becoming more evangelical in the style of its services.

'Oh yes!' she said, raising her hand in approval. 'We even have *prayer warriors* in our church!' By 'prayer warriors' she meant worshippers who commit their lives to praying for others. 'Do you go to church?' she asked.

'No,' I stammered, half considering lying.

Big Mama's face crumpled into a mortified frown. Tom, who'd become a devout Christian over the years, was equally shocked. After quizzing me about the Bible and exposing every hole in my knowledge, he devoted the rest of our chat to Saving me.

He was wasting his energy. For years my mother, God bless her, tried unsuccessfully to drag me to church. Born a Catholic, she would take Zina, Tedum and me to mass every Sunday to instil the devoutness that our father – not so religious a man – strove to minimise. But a childhood spent marinating in stolid, European-style worship was enough to permanently kill my enthusiasm for church-going.

Not even the evangelical Pentecostal services that my mother converted to could sway me. When we were around twelve, she took Zina and me to an evening service, our first taste of evangelical worship. We obeyed the pastor's call to stand up and introduce ourselves to the beaming congregation. Then we watched in bewilderment as the pastor roared down the mike, touching people's foreheads and blessing them before they collapsed in spent heaps in the arms of fellow worshippers. Zina and I were soon ushered onstage to receive blessings. The pastor placed a gentle palm on our foreheads while belting praises to Jeezos. Naive to the protocol, we resisted the growing pressure of his palm with tautened necks and heavy feet, waiting for a divine force to knock us out. But as the pastor's palm grew more and more insistent, we realised it was best to give in and launch ourselves backwards. The congregation went wild.

Amateur dramatics aside, the service was very uplifting. Had I been raised in that church from the start, things might have been different, but by age twelve I was stuck in my lapsed ways and nothing could make me attend church regularly. My mother sadly resigned herself to the situation.

My father wasn't troubled by this. He disliked excessive fixation on religion if it distracted people from their work or education. I discovered this on a Sunday afternoon in Port Harcourt when I was about nine years old. A cousin of mine, Patience, had visited our house while my father was at the office. Patience – an extremely devout teenager who didn't want to go to university – suggested that Zina, Tedum and I cut up several pieces of paper and inscribe them with phrases such as 'Jesus Loves Me' and 'God Lives'. For us youngsters, it was a fun exercise, a chance to whip out our felt-tip pens and express ourselves artistically. We pasted the colourful signs high up on our bedroom wall and admired the results. But when our father returned home, the sight of our handiwork detonated a rage we'd never seen in him before.

'Take this off the wall!' he boomed. 'Take it off *now!*' He jumped up and ripped off bits of paper himself. We scurried around the room removing the slogans, while he fumed and ranted, ordering us to speed it up. Apoplectic, he turned to a sobbingly defiant Patience and urged her – ordered her – to concentrate on her studies, not on twenty-four-hour prayer. Then he directed his wrath towards me and my siblings. We were *not* to get hooked on this 'opiate of the masses', he warned. I was quaking and confused, too young to understand his anger, which appeared to be mixed with an uncharacteristic panic. My father was a proactive man who believed in action, self-sufficiency, progress. He wanted Ogonis to get educated, to become doctors and lawyers, or geologists with knowledge of the oil industry. Although, according to my brother Junior, our father became more spiritual and devoted to prayer towards the end of his life, at this point he was an agnostic who sought to fix problems, not pray for them to go away. With Nigeria in the grip of a military dictatorship, he feared that people like Patience were slipping into a religious coma.

More than twenty years on, I sympathised with my father, yet I was on the receiving end of cousin Tom and Big Mama's reverse outrage at my church absences. Tom, intent on laying all seven shades of Jesus on me, was now referring to our planned weekend get-together as an 'appointment'. Stiffened with a sudden rectitude, he addressed me in church-pastor tones; all jibes and grins had gone.

I sat and listened like a petrified nine-year-old, surprised at my own silence. I was unable to defend my non-attendance at church. In the face of this muscular faith, the religious defiance I displayed at Janice's house at the start of my trip had gradually peeled away after a few months in Nigeria. Tom had exposed an inner cowardice that had lain dormant and unchallenged after a lifetime in England. Up until now, I'd assumed that my father was a thousand times braver than I was. Now I realised he was a *million* times more so. He had faced up to a ruthless political and commercial system that willingly killed anyone who challenged it. I, meanwhile, was rattled by the harmless reprimands of my Born Again relatives. This certainly wasn't the voyage of discovery I'd had in mind when starting this trip.

The episode distanced me slightly from my relatives. In the years since I last saw them they seemed possessed, literally, floating away from me on a path of Righteousness. What happened to the irreverent buoyancy of the old days? Perhaps I overestimated the extent of change – children don't register adults' burdens – but there was a perceptible difference in my aunt and cousin's spirits that alienated me. I had been warming to Nigeria over the last few weeks, but now the chill had crept in again.

The best part of the next morning was spent procrastinating in bed and staring at the ceiling. I was due to go to Bane, my family's village, to which every year during our childhood summer holidays my father banished me, Zina and Tedum for a few days. In our mother's absence, the three of us were at the mercy of our father's itinerary. My mosquito-bitten experiences instilled a lifelong unease about Bane (or rural life anywhere in the world, for that matter). I always left the village with the euphoric feeling that I'd been given another chance at life.

For once, I was making this trip voluntarily. I had the power to come and go as I pleased, yet I still felt a reflexive dread, as if I were being marched towards purgatory. The morning's grey, saturated clouds bulged above us as Sonny and I climbed into the car. On the road to Bane, the abundance of buildings and church signs diminished, eventually giving way to acres of flat, tree-less farmland. In the 1980s, my fetish for perfectly shaped palm trees kept me alert on this road. I kept a constant vigil for the shapeliest specimens, with their thick round fronds and pencil-straight trunks. But now I would have been glad to see *any* tree, no matter how wretched. Farming had cleared many of them, and the fumes from oil production, coupled with the burning of fields by farmers, were choking the trees and turning some of them brown.

We passed through the tiny town of Bori, where my father was born, and where he sold palm wine on the streets as a ten-year-old boy. Bori, though growing bigger by the year, still felt like a small hamlet, a slender collection of iron-roofed buildings on either side of the road, jammed with people and okadas, mini food markets and a rainbow of plastic ware. Through the window I heard snippets of conversation in our dialect, Khana, swirling around me at unusually amplified levels, like a strange dream. In my everyday life, Khana was restricted to telephone conversations between my mother and her friends or family; it was a minority language barely heard in Nigeria, let alone England. But here in Bori, it was the dominant language. Having spent four months travelling around as an ethnic foreigner, being in a place where Khana was widely spoken carried a new and deep significance. These were *my* people – not sharp-nosed Hausas, or Efiks, Biroms or Yorubas – but Ogonis.

Most special of all, I was in a place where everyone could say my name properly. Having the name Noo (pronounced 'gnaw') is a heavy cross to bear. Not only is it the same word for 'crude oil' in Khana – the most unpoetic of injustices – but the specific tonality of the name makes it impossible for foreigners and most Nigerians to pronounce correctly. Barely a day goes by when I'm not explaining my name to a new acquaintance, repeating it, spelling it, repeating it again, then resignedly accepting their mispronunciation. Finally, I was in the one place on Earth where everyone gets it right straight away.

Sonny returned from a market stall and drove on towards Bane. Above the flat stretches of green acres, the sky's ashen murk became dotted with bright orange oil flares. We were nearing Bane village. My father used to point out the flares in disgust, bemoaning their environmental impact, while I would nod blankly, too young to understand the implications. The oil companies burn off excess gas, which is a by-product of oil extraction. With the correct (though very expensive) infrastructure, the gas could be captured and exported at huge profit, but instead it's burned away to pollute the skies; our wealth going up in flames.

The road leading to the village was smooth and tarmacked, an improvement on the old days when heavy rain and giant potholes – Mother Nature's speed bumps – made the last 5 kilometres of the journey take twice as long as the preceding 110 kilometres. On entering Bane, we rolled past adobe thatched-roof houses nestled between palm trees, waddling goats and small, balloon-bellied children who stared drop-jawed as our car rolled past. Bane still lacks running water or a permanent supply of electricity, but modern houses are springing up all the time. We passed one house that had a gold lion carving on the front door and the words LION OF JUDAH etched above it. Sonny, too, owns a cute red-brick and mustard bungalow. As more people build houses, the village is gradually looking less rustic.

Deeper into the village, the tarmac stopped and the road became sandy. The heat bludgeoned me as I climbed out of the car outside my father's white bungalow. It stood close to the unpainted, window-less church on the edge of his parents' compound. My grandfather's two-storey house towered above the surrounding bungalows belonging to some of his six wives, including my grandmother. All of them are dead now. Their graves filled up the compound, converting it into a graveyard of sorts. That's the tradition: we bury our dead next to their homes.

My father, however, is buried in a public field in the village as a tribute to his struggle. His body had been dumped unceremoniously in a grave after he and his eight colleagues were murdered by Sani Abacha's regime. It had taken some years to retrieve the remains: we had to wait for democratic elections, then ask the government to locate the grave, and finally the bones had to be identified through forensic tests.

In 2005, my brother Junior, sister Zina, half-sister Singto, Uncle Owens and I prepared the remains for burial. As Junior brought out the large bag containing our father's dissembled skeleton, Zina cried out loud on the far edge of the room. Singto watched silently through her tears. I decided that the situation was only as macabre as my mind would allow, so I forced myself to lift out a long bone wrapped in newspaper. Uncle Owens, a medical doctor, helped us to identify and arrange each femur, fibula, metacarpal and rib, settling our minds into a more industrious mood as we assembled the skeleton.

Before long, everyone was helping out. It was hard to conceive that these coarse brown objects we held in our hands were our father, a once energetic man with dark, stocky flesh. In vain, I searched for his face in the skull now resting at one end of the coffin. The two front teeth were missing. How and why, I didn't know. But when Junior placed a pipe between the upper and lower jaws, his teeth metamorphosed into that familiar smile.

My father was always the one who made the decisions in the family, but now we were taking charge of him, deciding the fate of his remains. When I think of the day he showed me the architectural drawings of the bungalow twenty-odd years ago ('. . . this is the lounge, that's the living room, that'll be your bedroom . . . we'll spend summer holidays in this house . . .'), I doubt he ever imagined we would be using one of the rooms as a temporary morgue. It had now made the house uninhabitable in my view, and I certainly wasn't going to spend the night there by myself.

'You fear your father's spirit will worry you?' Sonny asked.

'Sort of . . . not really. I just don't like all these graves being right outside everyone's houses. We should have a cemetery.'

'You cannot have a cemetery . . . the place will grow into bush,' Sonny explained. Cemeteries were a wholly unsuitable idea, he believed. 'My brother is buried next to my mother outside her house.'

'Yeah, well, I don't like it. Having a grave next to the house is like putting a bed inside the bathroom. There's an appropriate place for everything.'

Sonny laughed.

My grandparents' compound was silent and empty except for the odd goat and sporadic children's game. I was used to visiting Bane with one or both of my parents, in the days when the machinery of hospitality seemed to grind into action of its own accord. But now that I was on my own, and my grandparents were all dead, there was no one to greet me or feed me. As I pottered about, examining the graves, I recalled my cousin Ketiwe once telling me that she felt little reason to visit Bane now that our grandparents were gone.

In their absence, our grandparents aroused a curiosity in me about who they were as people, the nooks and crannies of their personalities. I wondered what characteristics, aside perhaps from my sporting ability, they had passed on to me, and which parts of my character had been nurtured in England. Was my fastidiousness genetic, or the product of eight years in a dirty boarding school? Was my short temper sown in my DNA, or fashioned in the rush-hour carriages of London underground trains? Which of my ancestors was musical? I had never considered the finer details of their personalities. And this empty village wouldn't provide the answers. I chastised myself for not asking these questions when they were alive.

Sonny and I drove to the house of my maternal grandmother Daada, half a kilometre away down a sandy path. My mother and her sisters had helped to build Daada's house when they were young. It was a simple adobe structure, fitted with glass windows, wooden padlocked doors and wiring set up in endless anticipation of electricity. Daada's grave lies near the house, along with the graves of her husband and her youngest daughter, my Aunty Rose. My cousin Barisi still lived in the compound with her mother Aunty Naayira, a darker, more sinewy version of my mother. She had just finished a day of planting cassava at the farm and squealed with delight when she saw me.

They cooked me gari and soup. Its aroma triggered memories of the dilemma we faced when both my grandmothers cooked lunch for us kids. Because we always stayed in our paternal compound, we generally ate there first, meaning we were never hungry enough to accept Daada's meals at her house. The social mores underpinning the offering of food were lost on us. Turning down Daada's lunch was simply our logical response to having a full stomach, but she took it as an incomprehensible snub, which we had to rectify by stuffing ourselves in a gut-busting encore.

This time, I ate with leisurely ease. My cousin Barisi sat with me. In our younger days, she, Zina and I would tease each other and banter freely. Now she was all grown up with a husband and four beautiful kids, her natural buoyancy weighed down by money worries and other unspoken woes. Because of her new job at the local government office, she'd had to move back to Bane with her children while her husband stayed in a nearby town.

Conversation with Barisi and Aunty Naayira revolved around updates on family members ('What of Zina? What of Gian? What of Junior? What of Nene? How are your nephews?'). Then Barisi and her mother were joined by Dorcas, a neighbour. The three of them began chatting in Khana while I ate my gari and tried not to let another bead of sweat plop from my forehead into my soup. Silently I watched them. They were physically elegant women, yet hardy and blessed with practical skills like cooking, house-building and farming. My proficiencies were confined to my fingertips: tapping keyboards and flicking switches; cerebral know-how that contributed nothing to the workings of everyday village life.

Barisi and Aunty Naayira mentioned mine and Zina's names between giggles.

'What are you talking about?' I asked.

'Nothing,' Barisi absent-mindedly replied, keen to continue the conversation with the others. Sensing that they were reminiscing about us, I wanted in on the chat but I was being firewalled by language. My Khana isn't fluent. The everyday basic vocabulary is buried deep in my mental hard drive, but without practice I can't hold my own in conversation. My childhood indifference towards this non-fluency gradually strengthened into embarrassment, then intense resentment. My parents spoke to Zina and me primarily in English, expecting that we would learn Khana when we were older, in the same way that they had acquired English as a second language. They mistakenly assumed that Khana could wade against the cultural tsunami of the Anglophone world. But Khana was too small a language to compete with English, which holds all the vocal tools for modern life: no Ogoni person can have a worldly conversation without importing chunks of English. So the latter became my mother tongue.

And now it made me feel small here in my relatives' house, and I was reluctant to utter even the few words I knew. I think I inherited this linguistic awkwardness from my paternal grandmother, 'Mama', who I always assumed couldn't speak English until my father told me she actually knew a little bit but was 'too embarrassed' to practise it on us. Hindsight makes it all clearer: Zina, Tedum and I probably came across as self-centred, toy-focused brats, subconsciously exuding a very Western disregard for their elders, which Mama possibly found alienating. Daada didn't speak English either. Our relationship with both grandmothers was a warm but generally conversation-less affair, and now, just like Mama, I preferred to stay mute than speak Khana like an inarticulate toddler. I sat back and enjoyed snippets of their nattering. Anyhow, there was little about my life that I could tell them: property ladders, career choices, publishers – they were meaningless details in this context. Births, deaths, marriages were the only news worth sharing.

As Barisi, Dorcas and Aunty Naayira chatted away, I took a walk to the river nearby, smiling wordlessly at the half-naked, hernia-bellied children whose dark, lean faces stared at mine as I ambled past. If we share fairly recent ancestors, then the lineage has most definitely forked; their poverty and my relative wealth separated not just our lives but our morphologies too, it seemed.

The river was beautiful, flowing at a lower altitude to the village, and fringed with green vegetation and mangrove swamps. We knew only vaguely of its presence when we were children, since most of our days in Bane were spent perspiring in our grandparents' houses. When Zina and I came across it again in 2005, we were in awe of its beauty, like tourists. No one else quite understood our excitement. The village boys drew little aesthetic pleasure from this place where they routinely bathed and caught fish, *bari*. Zina had asked some boys to unlock one of the fishing canoes and let us ride in it. They obeyed, bemused as to why we wanted to drift aimlessly along the water.

I returned to Daada's house and perused Barisi's photo album, feeling increasingly weakened by the sweltering air, and waiting subconsciously for permission to leave. Then I gleefully remembered that I was on my own schedule.

I decided to get going.

Returning to Bane as an adult hadn't changed my feelings about the place. There was no cathartic awakening or joyful homecoming. No matter how much my dislike of the village had diminished and my respect for my relatives had grown, any new, romanticised perspectives quickly evaporated in the steaming humidity. Besides, living in the countryside seemed pointless if one wasn't getting one's knees dirty on the farm. Urban-style idleness isn't much fun without urban amusements. But perhaps one day in the future, a new world order, global oil shortages or British pension poverty might force me to live in Bane. I wouldn't be bored into complete stupefaction – the village has a large enough population to support what I like to call the 'gossip threshold': enough people to sustain juicy gossip on a regular basis. I knew from past experience that talking about other people is the only entertainment when there aren't any new books to read, films to watch or web pages to surf. Life here would be tolerable in that respect. But I would have to learn Khana. And the heat – my God, it was too much.

Now I understood why my father never once spent the night here during our childhood stays. He luxuriated in the air-conditioned solitude of his Port Harcourt study while dispatching us to the village. As much as he loved Bane, his attachment to the place was an emotional one that didn't require his physical presence.

As Sonny drove me back to Port Harcourt, I wondered how Bane would evolve in the future. Only the old and the very young stayed here these days; migration to the cities has been draining it, and every other Nigerian village, for years. I wondered whether it would remain a quiet village, sprouting new graves and modern, fleetingly inhabited brick houses. Or would it evolve to become a town, like many villages in England? I couldn't imagine it. Urbanisation requires industrialisation and an influx of people and capital from around the country, but outsiders rarely settle in Nigerian rural areas. The land usually remains the preserve of its indigenous ethnic group. Whatever happens, Bane is the one place on earth that feels like mine, whether I want to stay here or not. I need no title deeds to this place; and found comfort in the thought that my genes alone grant me an undisputed claim to the land.

16

Truth and Reconciliation

Lagos

'This will kill all your worms,' the salesman bellowed to us on the danfo. 'You feel hungry after you have eaten . . . it go "fut, fut, fut" when you go to toilet . . . there was a man and woman, when they were kissing, and the worm—'

I blocked my ears and sang to myself, to the amusement of the passengers next to me. It still wasn't enough to drown out the merchant's anecdote, which he delivered – in all its unspeakable detail – loudly enough to penetrate my 'la-la-la's.

I was back in the 'Centre of Excellence', back to the hard sell and noise, although I had now become inured to Lagos's incomprehensibilities and chaos. The doctor's sign advertising MONEY WONDERFUL FOWL SOUP no longer aroused my curiosity.

'God will punish you!' a male passenger shouted out to the driver as the danfo pulled into a gas station. 'You should refuel *before* you collect passengers.' As the bus queued up for fuel, the humidity resumed its damp grip, prompting everyone to fan themselves with religious pamphlets amid a chorus of teeth kissing.

I was on my way to the National Museum to have lunch with Maurice Archibong, the travel journalist I had met in Benin. Maurice was a smart, skinny, mild-mannered man in his forties with delicate dietary requirements thanks to a stomach ulcer. He asked for no pepper in his stew, but the waitress insisted it would be too bland.

'You see what I mean when I tell you that Nigerians are unnecessarily inhospitable?' Maurice said, tasting his stew. 'I *told* her no pepper.'

Maurice was a one-man chronicler of Nigeria's cultural heritage. He travelled all around the country writing about cultural and historical sites. Studies on Nigeria were sparse, he told me. The Historical Association of Nigeria ('It should be called the Association of Nigerian Historians') has thousands of professors as members but little work gets done.

'I don't know if it's for want of funding. Nobody is interested because there isn't money to chase, so I just go by myself and document everything. Nigeria is a vast place. Very vast place.'

'I had no idea how rich it is,' I told him. 'We have *ten* times what Ghana and Côte d'Ivoire have in culture and artefacts.'

'If not more so.'

Both of us had visited the Ashanti palace in Kumasi, Ghana, and were impressed by its museum. Ghanaians took real care of their exhibits.

'That's because they don't have oil,' Maurice said, 'so they must use their heads. Here we have been pampered by nature. Every time I go to the museum, I try to see how we're losing out. Because we're not able to put things in their proper places. And lots of looting goes on in our museums. Even the top officials are partaking in theft.'

The 800-year-old soapstone figurines at Esie sprang to mind.

'I'm so impressed by them,' I gushed. 'Do you think the figurines come from the twelfth century or later?'

'I think there was carbon dating. But bear in mind that the dating was not done in Nigeria. It was taken to Europe. And sometimes the specimens are taken there and never come back. I'm sure they don't involve Nigerian scientists in the dating process. So we are at the mercy of what the Europeans tell us.'

'But twelfth-century is pretty flattering,' I said, not quite sharing Maurice's distrust of Western scientists.

'Flattering enough, but they could be older. You must be accurate. How do you know? The researchers didn't take it elsewhere for confirmation, you understand. If it were a bipolar world and you dated something in the West, you would take it to the East for "control" dating.'

'I love those figurines so much, I wanted to steal one.'

Maurice tipped his head back and laughed loudly. 'Where would you keep it?'

'In my bedroom. I'd just want to look at it when I wake up.'

'Ah, but you need to make sure the things do not have powers. Some persons have stolen those things and had to return them. There's a story ... I can't prove it empirically, but somebody went to a shrine in his village and stole some objects, which he sold to some German guy. The German took it home, but every evening there would be some cries in the room where the artefact was kept. He didn't know where the sound was coming from but he suspected it was from that object. When the sounds kept coming from that part of the room he knew it must be the artefact. So he went to the trouble of flying all the way back to Nigeria to return it!'

In the taxi on our return to the mainland, Maurice regaled me with the stories he had covered during his days as a news reporter. The occasional headless bodies discovered around town; the boy who gouged his girlfriend's eyes out in order to sell them to marabouts for black magic purposes. Along with most Lagosians, Maurice was disgusted by it all, but almost as confounded by European society, where 'people don't believe in *anything*'.

Maurice's openness to the supernatural was unexpected, and made me feel more isolated than ever. Four and a half months in Nigeria hadn't made it any easier for me to digest the widespread enthusiasm for the paranormal. I was still reeling from a newspaper opinion article I'd recently read in which the columnist, complaining about speeding drivers on our roads, called upon 'those who administer prayers to exorcise the demons that possess these drivers'. Government initiatives hadn't been factored into his solution to the problem.

When I mentioned this article to Aunty Janice later that evening, it quickly led to another religious quarrel.

'We can't rely on prayer to solve this problem,' I carped. 'How can demons make people speed on the roads? We have to create practical solutions to our problems!'

'How?' Aunty Janice angrily asked. 'What can the child on the street selling groundnut do to change things? The child's parents must go around and beg for money to send her to school ... she graduates but she is not paid well and must stay with her parents because she cannot afford her own home. *What* is she to do?'

Aunty Janice had misunderstood me. She thought I was criticising individual Nigerians for not escaping poverty, but my worries actually lay with a broader mindset, which saw a link between living standards and the spiritual.

'I'm not saying it's easy, but if a large part of the country believes in practical solutions, then eventually a few individuals like my father will emerge, and they'll try to change things!'

'People don't want to fight the government like your father. They have families. They don't want to die!'

'Well, Europe became what it is today because people took matters into their own hands. They realised they had control of their own destiny.'

'Europeans are wealthy because they *prayed*,' Aunty responded.

'But they don't pray now, and they're even better off than they were four hundred years ago!'

'Their ancestors prayed and this has helped their descendants. But now that they're not praying things will go bad again in the future.'

Things might very well go downhill, but not, I believed, due to

a lack of prayer. I was a little annoyed that future events (oil shortages, superbugs, elderly populations) might accidentally validate
Aunty Janice's theory.

'It's a pity that Africans who grow up in Europe are becoming
godless,' she lamented reproachfully.

I was too drained to explain that I was suggesting more pragmatism, not godlessness. Aunty Janice saw me as a hedonistic *oyibo*,
submitting mindlessly to Western values without proper consider-
ation. I didn't want to be seen that way, but fighting her perceptions
was pointless.

We ate dinner silently, in the flickering gloom of the candlelight.

For the next two days, I hung around Victoria Island and Ikoyi to
enjoy the lovelier side of Lagos. I was hit by the traveller's para-
doxical urge to spend money at the penniless end of the journey,
and the desire to purge myself of Nigeria's shabbiness; a reaction to
the strain of the last four months.

And so I drank wine at a Mexican restaurant on Victoria
Island, where the ethnic Lebanese owners smoked cigarettes and
sat back in their chairs with an enviably proprietary air. I perused
the books at the glorious Jazzhole bookstore. At a Thai restaurant,
I overheard fellow diners discussing business ideas in uncharacteristically muted voices, and women with long, opulent weaves,
tight jeans and high heels chatting with their music industry
boyfriends.

While searching a supermarket cake aisle for a present for Mabel,
I fell into conversation with a woman called Marie who turned out
to be my father's contemporary at Ibadan University.

'You'd better control yourself,' Marie joked as I eyed a Black
Forest gateau.

'What are you getting?' I asked.

'Croissants for an old couple. I'm buying five to avoid arguments.'

'Five? How does buying an uneven number avoid arguments?'

'If I buy four the husband won't like it. You know what African men are like . . . the man always has to have more!'

Marie worked for an NGO in Washington, DC. She was the face of Nigeria's lost opportunities: confident, educated, articulate, a rare specimen who wasn't cloying or trying to extract money from me. In fact, she cut the conversation short and went on her sprightly way, as fleeting and elusive as Nigerian success.

Later, I knocked back vodka and Coke at a bar with giant windows looking out onto the lagoon. 'The Girl from Ipanema' wafted into the air-conditioned room. Through the huge windows I watched three European expats on jet skis overtaking a pair of fishermen as they cast a net from their canoe. The green waters of the lagoon sparkled salubriously, yet bobbing against the restaurant walls were plastic bottles, sucked oranges, and sachets of pure water floating like lilies on the surface.

Throughout town I saw glimpses of how handsome Lagos could have been: a few swaying palms lining the seafront like Miami, or the Third Mainland Bridge, an engineering wonder, snaking across the blue lagoon during sunset. I savoured these scenes and tried to block out the waterside stilt-house shanty towns or the partially collapsed skyscraper on Lagos Island, standing erect like a sarcastic standard bearer of our Excellence.

Now that I was ending my journey, though, I realised that Lagos is in fact one of Nigeria's greatest success stories. It's an achievement when 15 million people across 250 ethnic groups can live together relatively harmoniously in an unstructured, dirty metropolis seemingly governed by no one. Lagos is an anthropological case study in how humans interact with one another when confined in tight, ungoverned spaces; proof, as one NGO director once said, that the theory of free competition as a social regulator doesn't work. When two cars inevitably end up locked in a perpendicular stand-off, each party roars at the other for denying him right of way, as if an outrageous breach of protocol has taken place. Every hour some kind of altercation takes place, and as I watched yet another motorcyclist trying to squeeze between two cars, getting stuck and losing a wing mirror, I marvelled at the fact that such incidents generally ended so placidly (and that so many of London's ham-fisted traffic wardens originate from this bedlam).

At CMS, I flung myself across the traffic and jumped into a minibus. London in the old days was once as chaotic as this, its residents having to run for their lives when crossing the torrent of cars and horse buggies. The attitudes and behaviour of British drivers eventually changed, though. Nigeria just needs to catch up. But maybe Lagos isn't a laggard on the bottom rung of urban evolution. Perhaps the city is more futuristic than we care to realise. Isn't its low-tech overcrowding and pollution what our planet is heading towards, after all? As Albert Einstein said, 'I know not with what weapons World War III will be fought, but World War IV will be fought with sticks and stones.' Oil will run out one day. I was saddened by the prospect, but relieved by it, too – Nigeria might be better off, anyway; the country seems innately prepared for a simple, back-to-basics future. It's as if our government has eschewed a fully industrialised economy in favour of the fundamentals of life that will outlive civilisation: growing crops, maintaining extended family networks, worshipping deities.

There were many glimpses of hope: the mechanised farms, Cross River State's tourism, and Lagos's fancy new bus transit system, which I noticed as my minibus cruised along the mainland expressway. The system had been built in the few months since I was last in the city, with its own separate lane. Things were improving. But beneath it all lurked the belief in witchcraft, the oil dependency, the politicians' constant acceptance of low standards, all of it waiting to negate our achievements in an instant. I wasn't sure I had the patience.

'You'll get used to it,' people kept telling me. Knowing my temperament, I would only get used to it and stop being angry if I either had nothing to lose or something to gain from the status quo. I was in neither of those positions. For me, getting used to the situation meant capitulating to it, which required an unhealthy shift in mentality. It's not right to stop being angry about the state of Nigeria, but anger is only useful if one is willing to risk one's life changing the system. Was I brave enough? My cowardice – the extent of it – was one of several revelations for me on this trip. The strength of society's religious fervour had flattened me. I was the cowardly lion, no longer willing to roar my disagreement with my cousin Tom and Big Mama. The Nigerian reliance on God to change material circumstances will ultimately hold our country back even more than corruption, I suspect, but even if I had the strength to challenge excessive religiosity, it would be an enormous task, like extinguishing a forest fire with spittle.

But over time, I had come to love many things about Nigeria: our indigenous heritage, the dances, the masks, the music, the baobab trees and the drill monkeys. I, the progressive urbanite, had become a lover of nature and pre-colonial, animist ceremony; the mirage of a Transwonderland-style holiday wasn't worth chasing. Yet Nigeria, for all its sapphire rivers and weddings and apes, couldn't seduce me fully when all roads snaked back to corruption, the rottenness my father fought against and the cause he died for. At least my journey had cured my emotional fear of the country. It was a far scarier place for those who have to live here, for whom flight was not an option. They had to fight their way through life in a way that I didn't have to, and for that I wanted to hug my father's knees in thanks for raising me abroad and expanding my life choices.

So all was forgiven: the unspeakable train rides, the itchy tropical nights in the village, the enforced essay-writing in hotel rooms. For years they had turned me off Nigeria, but all of it, I now realised, was a necessary induction, a way of 'breadcrumbing' the trail between my village and my life as an émigré. My mistake as a child was to assume that my summers there were a rehearsal for an adult life filled with pounded yam breakfasts and sweaty water-fetching. But my parents had never expected me to live in Nigeria permanently. I could maintain a relationship with it from my chosen home, much as my father engaged with Ogoniland from his air-conditioned office in Port Harcourt.

Of course, returning to Nigeria on my *own* initiative was crucial to the epiphany. Travelling here as an adult helped me to finally wipe away the negative associations and start a new relationship with the country, in which I was prepared to embrace the irritations with tentative arms, and invest some of myself.

Epilogue

For my last three days in Nigeria I stayed with my cousin Loveday and his wife Helen at their modest, second-floor apartment on a quiet street in the Ippu-Ileju neighbourhood, near the airport. Most of my time was spent playing with the eldest of their two daughters, Donu, a precocious three-year-old with an eye for detail: 'Where is your second phone?' she asked me after I finished making a call (Nigerians often have more than one cell phone in case of robbery, or in case a power outage prevents them from recharging). The girl pestered me constantly for pens, paper and alphabet lessons. But above all, she wanted to use my colourful raffia fan, the only thing standing between me and death by dehydration.

'Donu, I need this fan,' I begged her. 'I'm sweating.'

'I am sweating too,' she pouted, patting her dry brow. I wouldn't normally fight a child over such a trifling object but in that unbearable heat, my fan was worth more to me than a million barrels of oil.

NEPA's erratic power supply had forced Helen and Loveday to buy a generator, which they used sparingly to keep down costs. In the evening, when the lights cut out, I followed Helen down the fire escape stairwell to the switch on the generator. She yanked its chord repeatedly to get the engine running, the movement straining her caesarean scars and making her wince. The neighbours all had generators too. The machines, four or five of them, rumbled from all sides of Helen's apartment. They vibrated through the windows and created a deafening roar that forced us to boost the TV volume; all conversation became a ridiculous bellowing exchange. Perhaps this is why Lagosians talk so loudly.

Late on a Sunday evening, the night before my flight back to

London, Loveday and Helen drove me through the dark, empty streets towards The Shrine, the club where the late musician and political activist Fela Kuti used to perform. Fela was the unanointed king of Nigeria, our highest-quality export, a near-deity who invented Afrobeat, a combination of jazz, funk and highlife rhythms that no normal person can resist dancing to. This marijuana-smoking maverick married twenty-seven women in one day, used his music to criticise military regimes, and once delivered his mother's coffin to the military barracks after the regime killed her during a raid on his commune. In the 1980s, Fela was jailed for nearly two years on currency smuggling charges.

Fela died of an Aids-related illness in 1997. Since then, his son, Femi, has carried on where his father left off, playing to the crowds every Sunday at The Shrine. As we approached, we could hear music saturating the night air even before we'd parked the car. Loveday was exhausted from work but, hypnotised by the Afrobeat rhythm, he bought tickets for himself and Helen too.

'What are you *doing*?' Helen exclaimed, surprised. 'We're not staying!' In his love for live music, Loveday had momentarily forgotten that they had two small children at home. Loveday relented, handing me my ticket before the pair of them said goodbye and returned to the car. I passed through the security and up the stairs to the mezzanine area. Although The Shrine has been subject to several police raids over the years, its posters, signs and graffiti still exuded a curious mix of moral rectitude, political sloganeering and hedonism. A signboard at the entrance listed several proverbs on wisdom and discipline, while another poster called for government corruption to stop. Wall-mounted signs warned against the smoking of marijuana, yet a defiant haze floated up towards the mezzanine from where I surveyed the audience below, sitting at tables and sipping their stout through straws.

Towards midnight, Femi entered the stage with his band and

sang 'One Day Africa Will Be Free'. His dancers, doubling as his backing singers, entered the stage with their backs to the audience. Like Fela's girls back in the day, these women shook their arses extremely seriously, staring down at their hips in their sequined mini-dresses, their faces betraying little expression, as if mesmerised by their own movement. All action took place below the waist. Having entered the stage with their backs to the audience, the dancers stayed in that position throughout most of the concert, waving their beautiful, sparkling booty at the crowd. Two more dancers were gyrating in cages on either side of the room.

Femi, like his father, often performs glistening and bare-chested, but on this night, he wore a long green shirt and matching trousers. He and his band played renditions of 'Summertime', 'I Want to Be Free' and the fast-paced 'One, Two, Three, Four'. Femi high-fived and bumped fists with fans crowding the front of the stage. During his sax solo, a woman in a gypsy dress spun around the tables; a leg-less man skidded excitedly near the stage on his skateboard, waving his baseball cap in the air; two Europeans boogied passionately, even during lulls in the music when everyone else sat still. I was hoping for a performance of the song 'Shotan', during which the fans go wild, hurling plastic chairs around the place, in an oddly punkish, un-Nigerian meltdown. But, disappointingly, Femi didn't perform the song.

It was 2 a.m. when the band finished. The crowd dissipated. I stayed behind at The Shrine with a few others until morning – Lagos isn't safe in the early hours, and there was no public transport anyway. While workers cleared the tables and swept the floor, we clustered around the chairs and tables beneath the ceiling fans to avoid getting mosquito bites. Fela's classics pumped out of the speakers. Fatigue and marijuana smoke stung my eyes, but I was happy, listening to the music in a sleepy daze. No one says it better than Fela. He's the embodiment of everything I love about Nigeria: intelligent, funny, passionate, exciting, raw, an 'Africa man original', not a 'gentleman'. He took the best elements of Nigerian music and mixed them with foreign genres to create something so fresh and superior, it gives listeners a swaggering pride in being Nigerian. But Fela was also incorrigible and untamed, railing against government immorality while grabbing his dancers' buttocks on stage; he had a messy family life and a distaste for upward mobility.

At The Shrine, I slouched opposite a mural depicting him making a clenched-fist power salute, a marijuana joint lodged between his knuckles. Next to me, people slept with their spines arched over the chair backs, their heads slumped on tables, mouths gaping open, bodies curled up. It was a shabby end to a fabulous night and a fabulous journey. But that's Nigeria for you: it can be stylish, sublime, beautiful, yet no matter how much it amazes or bedazzles you, it's always that little bit jagga jagga.

Acknowledgements

Firstly, I'd like to thank my agent Lizzie Kremer at David Higham Associates for believing in me. Immeasurable thanks go to Granta commissioning editor Bella Lacey, and my editors Sara Holloway and Amber Dowell for teaching me so much about writing and whipping me over the finishing line; I'm also grateful to Christine Lo, Benjamin Buchan, Jennie Condell and Kelly Pike at Granta. A non-repayable debt of gratitude goes to Rachel Wallman and Zilfa Al-Zaid for buoying up my morale and bearing the brunt of my writer's blocks. Special nods also for Owens Wiwa, Lizzie Williams, Ilka Schlockermann and Oliver Oguntade for their kind advice. And finally, I am forever indebted to my family, especially my mother Maria, brother Ken Jr, and sisters Zina and Singto.

Sources

Walter Ihejirika, 'Media and Fundamentalism in Nigeria', World Association for Christian Communication (WACC), 2005, http://archive.waccglobal.org/wacc/publications/media_development/2005_2/media_and_fundamentalism_in_nigeria

Chukwuma Okoye, 'Looking at Ourselves in our Mirror: Agency, Counter-Discourse, and the Nigerian Video Film', *Film International*, volume 5, issue 4, 2007